# The BLOCK SCHEDULING HANDBOOK

## Second Edition

*Again, I wish to dedicate this book (Second Edition) to my high school senior English teacher, Mary Shelton Drum at West Lincoln High School. Miss Shelton was a teacher different from many of my other teachers. She demanded respect, but gave it. She expected excellence, but demonstrated it. She searched for inspiration in her teaching, and inspired. Although unaware at the time, she inspired me. Twenty-three years later, I had the opportunity of working with Mary Shelton (as she prefers to be called) as a colleague sharing knowledge and belief in a new way of teaching. This new way was block scheduling. Now almost forty years later, I just want to simply say, Thank you, Miss Shelton (Mrs. Mary Shelton Drum) for being my teacher twice.*

—J. Allen Queen

# The BLOCK SCHEDULING HANDBOOK

## Second Edition

# J. Allen Queen

CORWIN PRESS
A SAGE Company

*For information:*

 Corwin Press
A SAGE Company
2455 Teller Road
Thousand Oaks, California 91320
www.corwinpress.com

SAGE Ltd.
1 Oliver's Yard
55 City Road
London, EC1Y 1SP
United Kingdom

SAGE India Pvt. Ltd.
B 1/I 1 Mohan Cooperative
    Industrial Area
Mathura Road, New Delhi 110 044
India

SAGE Asia-Pacific Pte. Ltd.
33 Pekin Street #02-01
Far East Square
Singapore 048763

Printed in the United States of America.

*Library of Congress Cataloging-in-Publication Data*

Queen, J. Allen
  The block scheduling handbook / J. Allen Queen.—2nd ed.
    p. cm.
  Includes bibliographical references and index.
  ISBN 978-1-4129-6300-8 (cloth)—ISBN 978-1-4129-6301-5 (pbk.)
  1. Block scheduling (Education).   2. Curriculum planning.   I. Title.

  LB3032.2.Q85 2009
  371.2'42—dc22                                        2008026493

This book is printed on acid-free paper.

09   10   11   12   13   10   9   8   7   6   5   4   3   2   1

| | |
|---|---|
| *Acquisitions Editor:* | Debra Stollenwerk |
| *Associate Editor:* | Julie McNall |
| *Production Editor:* | Appingo Publishing Services |
| *Cover Designer:* | Michael Dubowe |

# Contents

## Companion Web Site

Educators who have purchased this book will be able to visit Dr. Queen's Web site, www.blockscheduling.com, to download related classroom materials for staff development with teachers and instructional ideas for students. The Web site is updated on a monthly basis and a link allows you to contact Dr. Queen directly.

# Acknowledgments

I would like to thank, once again, the many graduate students, principals, and classroom teachers who assisted directly and indirectly with the development of the first edition and the new second edition of this book. Thousands of teachers have used my designs and materials, testing these with hundreds of thousands of students throughout the country. Thanks to all of the hundreds of teachers who continue to share instructional material with me (and more importantly) with their colleagues throughout the world. It has been wonderful seeing activities designed in one state work beautifully with students in another state across the country or in England, Spain, Germany, Holland, or China. Again, thanks to everyone for sharing materials, ideas, research notes, and creative activities, and especially to those mentioned here.

Special thanks go to some special current and former graduate students who provided much direct input into the book. These include Wendy Tomberlin, Kimberely Isenhour, Kim Mattox, Elaine Jenkins, Walter Hart, Rick Hinson, Thomas Fisher, Sherry Hoyle, Jim Watson, Christopher Lineberry, Kim Mattox, Ashlee Luff, Terry Smith, Phyllis Talent, and Jenny Burrell. All these individuals are educators who see the block schedule not only as a tool but also as a way of reforming education. Thank you.

Space does not permit the listing of all the educators nationally and internationally who have used many of these materials for teaching on the block, but I must list a few of the excellent teachers, principals, superintendents, and professors who have endorsed my work and encouraged the production of this book: These special individuals include Dr. Robert Algozzine, professor, UNC Charlotte; Dr. James Kracht, professor, Texas A&M; Bruce Smith, editor for *Phi Delta Kappan*; Dr. Martin Eaddy, former North Carolina Director of Standards of Quality; Dr. Karen Gerringer, former director of the North Carolina Principal Fellow Program; and to hundreds of superintendents, especially Dr. Jim Watson, and thousands of principals, especially Dr. Delores Lee, that I have worked with over the past 25 years throughout the United States and several foreign countries. I give to you my very special thanks and appreciation.

THE BLOCK SCHEDULING HANDBOOK

I would also like to thank all the professionals at Corwin Press. It has been an inspiration working with these folks, especially the editors. Thanks must go to Faye Zucker for her inspiration in making the first book a reality and to Debra Stollenwerk for seeing the need for a second edition . . . and thanks, Belinda Thresher at Appingo Publishing Services, for your guidance and patience.

# About the Author

 **J. Allen Queen** has served as a major consultant in block scheduling to school districts, public and private schools, and other interested groups throughout the United States, working with them to train teachers, collect data, and evaluate the effectiveness of block scheduling and the extended learning time. In the past 25 years he has worked with over 380 school districts in 48 states and 5 foreign countries. In 2005, Dr. Queen introduced block scheduling to China. In addition, he has authored or co-authored 38 books and more than 100 professional journal articles, and he regularly presents at international and national educational conferences on the topic of block scheduling and the closely related topics of classroom management for the block and effective time management for instruction.

He has been a classroom teacher, principal, curriculum specialist, and college administrator. He is professor and former chair of the Department of Educational Leadership at the University of North Carolina at Charlotte. His Web site can be accessed at www.blockscheduling.com.

# ONE

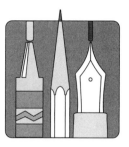

# The Current Status of Block Scheduling

**A**s the author works directly with educators in schools and school districts throughout the United States, the question about the number of schools on block scheduling is often asked. While this changes from year to year, the best estimate currently given is that about 72% of high schools use some form of block scheduling. This may range from the entire school on block to one grade or one subject.

The second question usually asked relates to the different block schedule designs being used. The author has counted at least 52 different designs. Most are similar and are variants of the two major designs, the $4 \times 4$, and the A/B, but include such names as modified, floating, rotating, progressive, etc. The design may not be as important as how the model is accepted and used.

## TEACHER AND STUDENT ■ PERCEPTIONS OF THE BLOCK SCHEDULE

Zepeda and Mayers (2006) reviewed several articles and numerous reports on block scheduling and found that a broad range of research has been conducted in a variety of settings and geographical areas with findings addressing perceptions and effects of organizing schools differently.

Teacher perceptions have been found to be basically positive despite some resistance to using block scheduling. For example, teachers have reported improved interactions with students (Adams & Salvaterra, 1998), more planning and preparation time and less stress (Davis-Wiley, George, & Cozart, 1995), and more opportunities to use varying instructional strategies under block scheduling (Queen, Algozzine, & Eaddy, 1996). Additionally, researchers have consistently reported teachers' perceptions of positive discipline under block scheduling (cf. Canady & Rettig, 1995a, 1997; Queen, 2000), while Staunton (1997) noted that teachers with more years of teaching experience with block scheduling had more positive perceptions. Years of experience teaching on the block schedule was not found to be an important predictor of opinions in another study (Wilson & Stokes, 1999a). Poor communication from administrators, a lack of justification for changing, and general satisfaction with the status quo were among the reasons Corley (1997) identified for teachers' resistance to using block scheduling. Davis-Wiley, George, and Cozart (1995) found that teachers viewed professional development as essential to success and reducing regression effects often observed when innovative approaches are implemented in schools. Queen and Algozzine (2007) agreed and found that sustaining professional development was imperative for success.

Studies on student perceptions about the benefits of block scheduling have revealed generally favorable opinions (Hurley, 1997b; Pisapia & Westfall, 1997c; Salvaterra, Lare, Gnall, & Adams, 1999; Wilson & Stokes, 1999b, 2000; Zepeda & Mayers, 2006; Queen, 2008). Reports from high-achieving students were better than those of their lower-achieving peers (Merchant & Paulson, 2001). The perceived benefits of block scheduling for students project into the preparation for college and higher education as well as in simply doing better in the academic content being offered in high schools (Salvaterra, Lare, Gnall, & Adams, 1999). Not all findings were positive. For example, Oxford and Letcher (1995) reported "inconclusive" support from students about the benefits of block scheduling after the first year of implementation. Queen, Algozzine, and Eaddy (1997) found that over 80% of high school students felt positive about block scheduling after the first year. Of course, while perceptions are often powerful predictors of behavior, the benefits of block scheduling are better measured by changes in instructional practices and improvements in learning outcomes.

## ■ THE EFFECTS OF BLOCK SCHEDULING ON STUDENT ATTENDANCE, BEHAVIOR, AND SUCCESS

Use of effective instructional practices to present the required curriculum and the changes that occur as a result of delivering instruction differently have also been studied. Some of the research has centered on what teachers do differently under block scheduling and other studies have focused on the difference changes in instructional practices have on attendance and student outcomes.

Teachers report having more time for different instructional objectives and increased opportunities to experiment under block scheduling options (Bryant & Claxton, 1996). In a study of more than 2,000 high school teachers in North Carolina, Jenkins, Queen, and Algozzine (2002) found that the opinions of block schedule teachers about the use and appropriateness of a wide variety of instructional strategies were basically no different than those of high school teachers teaching in traditional schedules. The work supported previous reports on the importance of continuing professional development in bringing about change as a result of implementing block scheduling (Davis-Wiley, George, & Cozart, 1995; Queen, 2000; Queen, Algozzine, & Eaddy, 1996, 1997, 1998; Zepeda & Mayers, 2006).

Results related to discipline have been consistently positive (Zepeda & Mayers, 2006). For example, Evans, Tokarczyk, Rice, and McCray (2000) found that office discipline referrals decreased with successful implementation of block scheduling and these findings were consistent with those of Queen, Algozzine, and Eaddy (1996, 1997, 1998) who found that teachers spent less time on discipline where block scheduling was being used.

Studies of the effects of block scheduling on student attendance have produced inconsistent findings (Zepeda & Mayers, 2006). Positive outcomes (Duel, 1999; Khazzaka, 1998; Queen, Algozzine, & Eaddy, 1996, 1997, 1998) were countered with reports of no effects or problems with attendance in other work (Lare, Jablonski, & Salvaterra, 2002; Matthews, 1997; Pisapia & Westfall, 1997b; Weller & McLeskey, 2000).

To no surprise, the difference block scheduling makes in terms of student outcomes remains inconclusive. For example, while Snyder (1997) reported general improvements in state-mandated test scores and slight decreases on advanced placement (AP) exams, others reported consistent improvements on similar measures (cf. Evans, Tokarczyk, Rice, and McCray, 2000; Payne & Jordan, 1999). No significant generalized achievement effects were evident in the work of Duel (1999), Knight, DeLeon, & Smith (1999), and Lare, Jablonski, and Salvaterra (2002). Queen, Algozzine, and Eaddy (1996, 1997, 1998) found that performance on state-mandated tests increased after implementation of block scheduling. Queen, Algozzine, and Watson (2008) found in a 15-year longitudinal study of a school system composed of four high schools, that with continuous staff development, and monitoring and steadily increasing teacher-student interaction within the instructional process, student achievement can increase dramatically. (This study will be discussed more later in the chapter.) Most of the research on student grades and grade point averages reflects positive outcomes for block scheduling (Duel, 1999; Knight, DeLeon, & Smith, 1999; Snyder, 1997; Zepeda & Mayers, 2006). Dexter, Tai, and Sadler (2006) found little relationship between college students' reports of block scheduling use in high school and their performance in undergraduate science courses. Similar results were reported by Maltese, Dexter, Tai, and Sadler (2007).

## PROMISES, PROVISIONS, AND PROVISOS FOR ■ BLOCK SCHEDULING IN THE HIGH SCHOOLS

Findings from the comprehensive review of literature of almost 60 studies and reports completed by Zepeda and Mayers (2006) indicate that knowledge about block scheduling is grounded in qualitative and quantitative methods using perceptions, ratings, or scores from schools, administrators, teachers, students, and parents. The work has been completed in rural, suburban, and urban settings and some broad generalizations provide support for organizing school schedules using blocks of instructional time. While not without limits, this body of knowledge provides a further foundation of fundamental conclusions about the use and value of block scheduling. Teachers believe that they have more time to plan and prepare for classes under a block schedule (Duel, 1999; Hurley, 1997a; Jenkins, Queen, & Algozzine, 2002; Pisapia & Westfall, 1997a; Weller & McLeskey, 2000; Wilson & Stokes, 1999b). Block scheduling also provides increased opportunities to be more effective by varying instructional strategies, thereby engaging students to a greater degree; also, due to the increased length of the classes, more in-depth study of subjects is possible (Queen, Algozzine, & Eaddy, 1998). However, some concern has been voiced by college professors, perhaps not directly related to block, that students come to college with a broad knowledge of content but with minimum depth. This may be more related to the volume of standards to be covered rather than any high school scheduling designs (Queen, 2008). Overwhelming evidence shows that in the past more than 70% of teachers reported going beyond the lecture approach and used interactive instruction (e.g., Queen, Algozzine, & Eaddy, 1997). Queen (2008) reported that this percentage may decrease at times due to the pressure of added state and local standards related to content to be covered in class. School administrators and teachers also reported that block scheduling has a positive effect on school and classroom climate and requires less time spent on procedures, routines, and management (Canady & Rettig, 1995a; Payne & Jordan, 1996; Queen and Gaskey, 1996; Queen, 2000; Wilson & Stokes, 1999a). This offers teachers more instructional time for extended laboratory periods, small group investigation, or classroom inquiry and experiments. Similarly, more guided practice and extra time are available for skill enhancement in music, art, and vocational classes. Field trips to locations close to the school may be taken during one period. Of the greatest importance, we have experienced in hundreds of classrooms that the longer class period allows more time for interactive instruction using varied instructional strategies such as cooperative learning, inquiry, case study, seminars, and simulations and games, all of which can increase student interest and performance (cf. Jenkins, Queen, and Algozzine, 2002). In addition, most block schedule designs allow students to receive more individual attention and, in some cases, personalized instruction (Queen, 2008). Overall, from a close analysis of numerous studies and direct school and classroom analysis, most school administrators, teachers, students, and parents believe that block scheduling is effective (Zepeda & Mayers, 2006; Queen, 2008).

Discipline remains an important consideration in schools and can often be improved under the block schedule (Canady & Rettig, 1995a; Gunter, Estes, & Schwab, 1990; Hottenstein, 1998; Siefert & Beck, 1994). Historically, teachers throughout the United States have stated overwhelmingly the positive discipline results of being on the block (Canady & Rettig, 1995a; Queen, 2000, 2008). Students' attendance in class improves, and they are less disruptive because of reduced time spent in changing classes. Additionally, students on the block are absent from class fewer times and usually have fewer classes to complete missed assignments. With block scheduling, students are usually able to take more classes, thereby broadening the scope of course selection. Students who were unable to take electives in a traditional schedule may be able to take the courses in the block model. In most states, credits required for graduation have increased (Queen, 2008). Despite its positive aura, or perhaps as a result of it, there are important cautions and lessons to be learned by studying the knowledge base on block scheduling. These caveats and directions also provide the groundwork for active and effective planning, implementing, and evaluating of block scheduling efforts. For example,

- Teachers were resistant to implementing block scheduling when there was poor communication provided by administrators (Corley, 1997).
- Teachers state that professional development is imperative but believe training has been insufficient for the successful implementation of block scheduling (Davis-Wiley, George, & Cozart, 1995); and for maximum success, teachers believe professional development must be of high quality and sustained over time (Queen and Algozzine, 2007).
- Few researchers report why schools move to a block schedule, the process undertaken to implement block scheduling, or the experiences of schools and school personnel in beginning or continuing a block schedule program (Zepeda & Mayers, 2006).

Creative and effective alternative scheduling practices emerge when parents, teachers, students, and administrators collaborate. Early in the transition, Hackmann (1995) suggested guidelines for implementing a block schedule, and Queen and Algozzine (2007) have modified and added to the list and clarified what we know about effective instruction.

1. Allow faculty, staff, parents, and students to have direct input in the decision process to move to the new model.

2. Develop a procedure for obtaining feedback from teachers, students, and parents on an ongoing and regular basis.

3. Develop, implement, sustain, and evaluate systemwide and schoolwide professional development opportunities for teachers in the areas of instructional pacing, instructional strategies, and instructional assessment.

4. Watch for teacher fatigue and stress, especially early and late in the semester.

5. Modify the scheduling process so that students take more challenging classes over the entire year, such as in an A/B or modified design.

6. Avoid starting with a negative effect for the second semester by eliminating the post-holiday down time of the exam period by

scheduling the fall semester so that either midterm or final exams can be completed before the holidays.

7. Continue to support and address the need for discipline with beginning teachers as an integral part of a block scheduling program.

8. Consider modifying selected courses to reduce risks inherent in certain content areas of instruction.
    a. Hire more language teachers so there is no great gap in time from the first to second levels of the subject; or
    b. Teach students in 90-minute periods of time for the entire year to create intensive courses that would meet requirements for advanced study.

9. School administrators need to monitor classrooms during the last thirty minutes of the periods to ensure that every possible minute is being used in an instructionally effective manner.

10. Review the skills that teachers identified as the most important for successful implementation of the block schedule. From interviews, surveys, direct observations, and working with educators from several school systems, the three most important skills or procedures to master are
    a. Develop pacing guides for each course for semester, weekly, and daily use.
    b. Incorporate or integrate standards/concepts within the pacing guides to gain a better sense of time management.
    c. Master several different instructional class designs and instructional strategies to vary ways in which materials are presented during the 90 minutes (or extended time), changing the classroom structure every 20 to 25 minutes (e.g., spend 10 minutes reviewing previous materials and setting the stage for what the students are going to learn. During the next 20 minutes, provide the background instruction/information that is needed to learn the content of the objective. In the next 30 minutes, have the students work in groups to experiment or gain an understanding of the content taught. Come back for large group discussion or group presentation for 20 minutes and then spend the last 10 minutes in review).

11. Share experiences with other schools that are using block scheduling on a regular basis, especially by content groups.

12. Adjust graduation requirements to accommodate additional and higher-level courses (e.g., increase requirements to 24 or 28 credits).

13. Obtain and maintain at least 80% support from every group involved and keep in mind that no group or organization gets 100% agreement, at least not all of the time.

14. Be aware that the high school has been resistant to change and remained fundamentally the same for the entire 20th century. Be sure of the reasons for any changes to be made and monitor closely for success.

15. Provide time for sustained professional development and monitor and evaluate for program and student success.

The extant knowledge base, then, illustrates the promises, provisions, and provisos in block scheduling but also points the way for additional research and ways to improve practices for block scheduling in the future.

# TWO

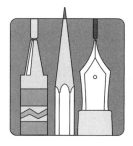

# Using Block Scheduling for the Senior High School

**N**aturally, in our never-ending quest to improve education, some experimentation has taken place with respect to high school scheduling. As early as 1959, Trump proposed eliminating the rigid traditional high school schedule and instituting classes of varying lengths based on the instructional needs of students. The Trump Plan allowed for a science class to meet for a 40-minute lecture, a 100-minute lab, and a 20-minute help session per week, whereas other classes could be short periods of 20 or 30 minutes. With limited success, Trump encouraged teachers to experiment with a variety of instructional strategies in an attempt to provide flexibility in the educational process (Trump, 1959).

Unfortunately, tradition rather than proven educational success has guided many principals in scheduling classes for students. Even today, in spite of the awareness of problems with the traditional schedule, some of us continue to resist a change in the schedule, choosing a return to the traditional format—claiming failure due to limited training, preparation, time, and resources. In addition, generations of Americans have graduated from high schools requiring the successful completion of a prescribed number of Carnegie units, which are based on accumulated seat time (Canady & Rettig, 1995a). This high school tradition appeared trite when, in 1983, *A Nation at Risk* reported that our students were academically behind their counterparts from a number of other industrialized nations. In response to the 1983 report, we began to examine alternatives that would result in higher student achievement and started a reform movement to restructure our schools. Block scheduling served as one avenue in this restructuring process.

While the various national education reports of the 1980s addressed the general condition of American education, including secondary schools, a few reports addressed high school exclusively. Ernest Boyer and Theodore Sizer wrote two of the most highly publicized proposals for high school reform.

*High School: A Report on Secondary Education in America,* written by Ernest Boyer (1983), was prepared for the Carnegie Foundation for the Advancement of Teaching. It was "based on a three-year study in which twenty-five educators collected data at fifteen diverse senior high schools" (Ornstein & Levine, 1989, p. 595). Boyer's proposals for improvement and reform included several themes. One of his main findings was "that high schools, lacking a 'clear and vital' vision of their mission, were unable to formulate 'widely shared common purposes' or 'educational priorities'" (Gutek, 1986, p. 347). Among Boyer's most important recommendations were those dealing with teacher's working conditions. "These recommendations included proposals that high-school teachers should have a daily load of only four regular classes and one small seminar, should have an hour a day for class preparation, and should be exempt from monitoring halls, lunchrooms, and recreation areas" (Ornstein & Levine, 1989, p. 595).

Theodore Sizer's (1984) major work, *Horace's Compromise: The Dilemma of the American High School,* was based partly on school visits he made to 80 high schools. "Sizer, former headmaster of Phillips Academy and former dean of Harvard's Graduate School of Education, created a synthesis that encompassed the liberating tendencies of the 1960s with the emphasis on academic competency of the early 1980s" (Gutek, 1986, p. 348). In his book, a teacher named Horace must choose between "covering" a multitude of low-level skills in the prescribed curriculum and in-depth teaching of important concepts and understandings. To develop in-depth learning, Sizer recommended that the curriculum be divided into four major areas: inquiry and expression, mathematics and science, literature and the arts, and philosophy and history. He also emphasized more active learning and reduced emphasis on what he considered mindless approaches to *minimal* competency testing. Sizer's particular concern was to eliminate the tacit understanding between students who say, "I will be orderly . . . if you don't push me very hard" and teachers who respond "You play along with my minimal requirements and I will keep them minimal" (Ornstein & Levine, 1989, p. 595). In addition, it is important to note that Sizer acknowledged the complexity of teaching high school. He pointed out that teachers could not effectively teach 150 to 180 students a day and recommended that a team of seven or eight teachers work with groups of about 100 students when teaching the four major curriculum areas he had prescribed (p. 595)

"Of all the reports of the 1980s, *Horace's Compromise* marked the greatest departure from the tendency to mandate more prescribed subjects in the curriculum. Sizer's recommendations were directed at raising expectations and achievement outcomes, but in a more flexible atmosphere" (Gutek, 1986, p. 349). As we move into the 21st century, Sizer's ideas for integrated learning are likely to remain significant since many schools in the United States are successfully teaming teachers to offer students a more interrelated curriculum.

In the 1980s, Mortimer J. Adler published his *Paideia Proposal* (Adler, 1982), which asserted that all students should have access to an intellectually-based curriculum. Adler argued that there exists a general learning that all human beings should possess. "Since American society is a democracy based on political and ethical equality, the same quality of schooling should be provided for all students" (Ornstein & Levine, 1989, p. 211). Adler and his Paideia associates considered the following subject matter as essential: language, literature, fine arts, mathematics, natural sciences, history, geography, and social studies. The subjects were viewed as a framework for developing a collection of intellectual skills necessary for all students. Some of the intellectual skills they wanted to focus on were reading, writing, speaking, listening, and problem solving. When the fundamental skills were coupled with the intellectual skills, a higher level of learning was reached. The *Paideia Proposal* allowed all students the opportunity to study the basics while achieving greater understanding of other ideas through Socratic teaching. In the late 1990s, the proposal reemerged in some schools as a means of teaching higher-order thinking skills and respect for others' opinions and views.

Perhaps the birth of the modern day block schedule began in 1984 when Goodlad argued in *A Place Called School* that the traditional high school did not allow enough time to individualize instruction, extend laboratory work, or provide much-needed remediation and enrichment to our students. He recognized then, as we do now, that an enormous amount of time and energy is wasted by changing classes from six to seven times a day. To be more effective, Goodlad encouraged schools to redesign their schedules into larger blocks of time. Six years later, Carroll (1994) suggested that we change to a format in which students concentrate on one or two subjects and encourage teachers to focus more on individual students. Block scheduling was beginning to take shape.

In 1994, Cawelti argued that by restructuring high schools, we, as teachers, could bring about fundamental changes in the expectations, content, and learning experiences provided to students. During the same year, we learned that 40% of schools in the United States were using some form of block scheduling. The number continues to grow nationally today with an estimated 72% of U.S. high schools using the block schedule in some form; for example, 9th-grade academy courses blocked (Queen, 2008).

In general, block scheduling is based on the idea of organizing a course around one semester in an extended class time of usually 90 minutes rather than the more typical 50 minutes, but many schools are experimenting with extended periods ranging from 60–150 minutes. Following are the three major formats of block scheduling still in use today:

- $4 \times 4$, four-block, compacted or accelerated model; the daily, four 90-minute periods per semester (very few schools have a pure $4 \times 4$ model today)

- *A/B,* eight-block, expanded model; the rotating daily, eight 90-minute periods per year (these can be rotating or fixed days and very few schools have a pure A/B design)

- *Modified periods* with an array of block-scheduled and traditional classes taught over varying periods of three months, semesters, or over the entire school year. Many of these designs have functionally sounding names such as the 8 day rotating block, the trimester, the 3 × 3, the split block, etc. By far, most of the schools today have a modified block with a 4 × 4 or A/B basic design for most of the classes (Queen, 2008).

The modified block classes can be scheduled in a variety of ways based on subject content or desired flexibility (Canady & Rettig, 1995a; DiBiase & Queen, 1999). Known as the modified block or the split block, this model is gaining popularity today in both middle and high school settings. While the modified model provides the most flexibility, it is the most difficult to schedule, and many teachers believe that some of the benefits provided by the 4 × 4 and A/B models are lost.

Teachers who instruct in block-scheduled schools have improved the academic environment for students by increasing the number of courses that can be completed in a four-year period. In the process, graduation rates have increased and discipline problems have declined. Since most students have been limited to four classes each day, lighter student loads can allow for greater immersion in the subject with less time spent changing from one class to another. An improved school climate can result in a more relaxed atmosphere with greater student-teacher rapport. In many cases, the schedule change has become a tool for curriculum improvement (Gerking, 1995). Teachers have learned quickly that both positive and negative results come with any change, and moving to a block schedule is a big adjustment. However, when weighing the advantages and disadvantages to the students, many schools have found that the change is worth the effort.

## ■ SPECIFIC SUPPORT AND CONCERNS FOR THE BLOCK

In the first chapter, a detailed discussion with respect to more general research on block scheduling was presented. What follows are more specific examples of early support and success in such areas such as content, specific designs, and so on, using block scheduling.

Previously, several educators have cited the advantages of the block scheduling in their studies. Day, Ivanov, and Binkley (1996) outline the benefits of a block schedule for science instruction. Day bases these benefits on her experience as the only science teacher at Center High School in Tennessee. The high school has an enrollment of 200 students and has used block scheduling for five years. The benefits she has found include increased student teacher interaction, smaller classes, long blocks of instructional time with fewer interruptions per class, time for more in-depth study, and uninterrupted experiments. Also, block scheduling allows students and teachers opportunities to get to know each other better, which helps to keep a positive classroom climate, leading to fewer discipline problems. In addition, the teacher has time to introduce a concept, do an activity to reinforce the concept, and have follow-up activities for closure all in the same period.

Edwards (1995), cites the advantages based on his research at Orange County High School in Virginia where they have been using the $4 \times 4$ plan since 1993. Advantages for the teachers include a more manageable schedule by having fewer students at a time, fewer classes for which to prepare, and increased planning time. Advantages for students include fewer classes a day, which gives them fewer subjects to focus on at one time; the opportunity to earn up to eight credits per year; and the chance to repeat any failed courses without falling behind. He also found that grades went up, students completed more courses, and more students enrolled in, and passed, advanced placement exams.

Huff (1995), reports the advantages of block scheduling as evidenced at Scotland County R-1 High School in Memphis, Missouri. These include the following: (a) teachers have enough time to develop key concepts, (b) there is a greater range of classes for students to select from, (c) students have two evenings to complete assignments, (d) there is an increase in teaching and learning creativity, (e) a variety of teaching techniques can be used in each class meeting, (f) activities are diverse, (g) study halls can be eliminated, (h) new concepts can be applied immediately, and (i) both teachers and students have only four classes to prepare for each day. Huff found that both students and teachers agreed that block scheduling should continue. Seventy-nine percent of the students believed instruction under this schedule was superior to instruction under the traditional schedule.

Shore (1995), the ex-vice principal at Huntington Beach High School in California, cites some of the benefits of block scheduling at her school. These include students receiving personal attention because teachers see fewer students, an allowance for the implementation of a tutorial period before school, smaller classes, and happier students and teachers. I have seen even greater attempts at personalization with many of the schools in California with the implementation of small learning communities with the block (Queen, 2008).

In late August of 2000, the author was fortunate to conduct an interview with Dr. Dennis Williams, the former principal of West Mecklenburg High School, and they discussed his experiences with the first $4 \times 4$ school in the system when he began the program in 1994. He stated the benefits of implementing the $4 \times 4$ block plan. The school has experienced an increase in the number of students on the A and B honor roll and a decrease in the number of failing grades. There was also a decrease in the number of suspensions, both in school and out of school. At the end of the first year, over 90% of theteachers and almost 90% of the students did not want to return to the traditional schedule.

Gerking (1995), a science teacher at Laramie High School in Wyoming, states that on a block schedule, there are not as many contact minutes with the students over the entire semester but that the learning is far more intense and there is time available for group work and cooperative learning. Although not as much material is covered, what is covered is in depth and the important concepts are emphasized with less wasted time. The teachers, students, and parents have indicated that they would not want to return to the traditional schedule.

Picciotto (1996), the revolutionary guru of the San Francisco Urban Plan, compares the traditional schedule and the new block schedule at the Urban School of San Francisco, an independent progressive high school, where he works. The advantages he found include the following: (a) Teachers usually teach three periods and have two different preparation times, (b) teachers see fewer students so they get to know them better, (c) students juggle fewer subjects and can concentrate better on the ones they are taking, (d) the half-day period makes it possible to take field trips and pursue major projects, and (e) the three 70-minute periods allow enough time to do something in depth or to do more than one activity. The disadvantages are fewer homework opportunities because the class meets for only one semester, students' taking four academic classes creates a great deal of intensity, and the longer planning periods can be challenging for novice teachers.

In a study of 4 × 4 block scheduling at Wasson High School in Colorado Springs, O'Neil (1995) identifies the following advantages: a lower student-to-teacher ratio, a decline in discipline problems, and the creation of a less stressful climate. He concludes that the weaknesses are the teachers' failing to use scheduling effectively, inappropriate instructional strategies for the longer period of time, and the possibility of not as much curriculum being covered.

Wilson (1995), a teacher at Hope High School in Arkansas, states the advantages and concerns experienced with the 4 × 4-block schedule since its implementation during the 1994–1995 school year. The advantages were that students could earn more credits, the schedule was more flexible, homework was limited to four classes, and more work occurred in the classroom, with the teacher having the time to completely cover a concept before class is over. The concerns included students who transfer in and out of schools.

It is interesting to note most of these schools continued to make improvement by either providing greater staff development, modifying the block schedule, and in at least one instance, moving off the block schedule. While the author is a great supporter of block scheduling when maximized for success, he has encouraged several schools to either abandon the block or return to a more traditional schedule. The major reason for these recommendations was for lack of preparation, or no or limited sustained professional development several years after starting off quite successfully.

While the promises for success have been numerous, many pitfalls have been identified. Block scheduling has been criticized for the loss of content retention from one level of a subject to the next and the extensive time required for independent study outside of class. Transfer students from schools different schedules, the limited number of new electives offered, and the increased overuse of lecture in the classrooms can be problems as well.

The first year on block scheduling remains the most challenging for teachers and principals. Many teachers are anxious about the uncertainties associated with teaching in longer blocks of time. Many veteran teachers complain that the first year of block scheduling is much like being a beginning teacher again. As a result, careful planning is required for teachers to adapt successfully to the block schedule. Block scheduling requires teachers to prepare lessons that engage students during longer periods of instructional time. Depending on the subject taught, teachers have varying views and suggestions related to the block schedule.

Foreign language teachers continue to stress the importance of providing course sequencing in the block. These teachers believe that a long period of time between the first and second courses of a sequenced subject can be problematic and could hinder retention and seriously affect achievement. Principals may need to schedule students to take two sequenced courses in one subject area during the year in the block schedule format. Careful planning during the scheduling process will limit the time gap between the first and second courses of specific subjects.

Teachers of performing arts, particularly band instructors, complain that limiting instruction to one semester could hurt the quality of performance. However, many band teachers note improved quality when students with serious musical interests sign up in the program for the entire year. These teachers find increased student participation in music as additional elective opportunities become available.

Advanced placement courses that allow students to earn college credit while in high school can present challenges to some blocked schools. Problems specifically emerge in the 4 × 4 design when these courses are offered during the fall semester, but the examination for awarding college credit is not administered until the end of spring semester. Schools using block scheduling have developed unique approaches to assist students in their exam preparation. For example, many schools conduct afterschool and Saturday review sessions prior to administering the test. In some schools, students are allowed to take a related elective course during the semester preceding or following the advanced placement course to enhance their knowledge in that area. Advanced placement testing should become available on a semester basis, but it appears that ETS is not waning on one admission of the test per year.

The author's recommendation is to do as several schools have done in some states; encourage students to take the honors and/or AP class and take available CLEP exams that are much more flexible and appear to work just as well. One school district in Minnesota pushes the CLEP exam over the AP exam. School districts can check with their state department of public instruction for guidance. With an increase of online courses offered by colleges or college classes brought directly on the high school campus, the AP Exam may be one of many options available to educators and students in the near future. Many scheduling concerns involve students who transfer schools during the school year. In the beginning of block scheduling when most schools were on the traditional model, transfers were a major concern for some teachers. This is now becoming less of a problem because so many schools are on the block. The problem may arise more in the future with so many different block and flexible models being used as part of the continued reform process.

Block scheduling has been attacked because of the reduction of total instructional time per class. However, since blocked classes meet a little more than one-half as many times as traditional classes, the total amount of time lost for routine administrative tasks such as taking class attendance, improving time loss with in-class transitions, and moving more to student directed instruction, can greatly lower the time loss. Teachers find that the total time lost is negligible and that coverage of course content is not greatly reduced.

Students in a traditional course meet in 50-minute classes for 180 days, which is a total of 9,000 minutes of instructional time. Students in a block schedule meet in 90-minute classes for 90 days for a total of 8,100 minutes of instructional time. If 10 minutes are lost for administrative functions at the beginning and end of classes, then 1,800 minutes are lost under the traditional schedule (180 days [10 minutes] and 900 minutes are lost under the block (90 days [10 minutes]). Using these numbers, a teacher has 7,200 minutes of instruction under either format: $9,000 - 1,800 = 7,200$ minutes under traditional scheduling, and $8,100 - 900 = 7,200$ under block scheduling (Hackmann, 1995; Rettig & Canady, 1996; Shortt & Thayer, 1998). Wasted instructional time becomes a key concern for schools using block scheduling. Instructional time is wasted when teachers fail to use a variety of learning activities and teaching strategies. As presented in the research section in Chapter 1, the lecture method is overused in at least of 30% of blocked classes, but the author has seen an increase in the overuse of lecture since the implementation of No Child Left Behind and the related increase in content standards. This problem can lead to parent and student complaints about the longer class periods becoming boring. Many teachers consider the overuse of lecturing the single most damaging factor to success of the block schedule. This issue will be covered in greater detail later in this section.

It is important to restate that the mere changing of the amount of time students spend in class through block scheduling does not guarantee school success. Unfortunately, it is possible for a school to change scheduling patterns without making appropriate changes in instruction practices. In some cases, modifications in classroom practices appear not to parallel the restructuring initiatives. Appropriate changes in instructional practices and the effective use of class time are the essential keys to the success of block scheduling. One may conclude that the major problem in block scheduling remains either the teacher's use of excessive lecture or the inability to employ more effective, engaging instructional methods in the classroom (Hart, 2000; Queen, Burrell, & McManus, 2000; Queen & Isenhour, 1998b; Schroth & Dixon, 1996; Skrobarcek et al., 1997; Queen & Algozzine, 2007).

## THE LECTURE ■

As previously stated, the continued problem in block scheduling today is the overuse of lecture. The lecture has become an "institution" in the American public high school, perhaps even to a greater degree than is found at the university level. When lecture is the major instructional strategy for teaching students, the time for using more appropriate instructional strategies is severely limited. Much of the research on the block schedule shows that teachers are better able to employ a variety of instructional strategies that address the learning needs of students in extended class periods. Some of these instructional strategies are more difficult to complete in a traditional class of 50 to 60 minutes. Unfortunately, the lecture method remains the most used instructional strategy in high school today. With public pressure to increase test scores, it is hard to eliminate the lecture method, because it is used to facilitate coverage of the curriculum. Educators complain that they have to lecture more because there is limited time to use interactive methods with students given the amount of content to cover in preparation for state-mandated tests. Unfortunately, these teachers have missed a wonderful opportunity not only to have students gain a better understanding of the course content through student-engaging activities but also to have them retain more subject content and consequently perform more effectively on these very same mandated tests. Simply zipping through course content using lecture with passive learners is easier for teachers and students. However, the low retention and application of what is learned is alarming. Again, the block can provide more time for a variety of learning activities. With more time in class and an emphasis on action-oriented strategies, teachers have an opportunity to engage students in activities that allow them to apply content knowledge to real problems, to work together in teams, and to employ modern technology.

A 1997 study by Corley found that veteran classroom teachers (those having 15–20 years of classroom experience) were complacent about their teaching strategies in schools that had positive reputations for preparing students for college. These teachers saw no need to change their instructional approach because they were effective. Conversely, in the same year, Adams and Salvaterra (1997) found that some teachers in specific subjects discovered most instructional strategies were easier to implement in a block schedule. The teachers surveyed stated that they used a variety of instructional methods, changing strategies as often as four times per class. Of no surprise was the fact that teachers who used a variety of instructional strategies during longer class periods also did so during shorter periods. In this study, the researchers found that teachers from some school districts used significantly more instructional strategies than teachers in others. This phenomenon was related directly to the amount and quality of staff development prior to the change to the block schedule and the continued training opportunities that were provided by the school districts.

In that same year, Queen, Algozzine, and Eaddy (1997) found that when appropriate staff development was provided, there was an increase in the variety of teaching strategies used in block scheduling. More specifically, it was discovered that, once prepared, two-thirds of teachers consistently used a variety of interactive instructional strategies. Comparatively, Khazzaka (1997) found that 77% of high school teachers surveyed agreed that they had received adequate staff development and implemented a variety of teaching strategies in the block schedule.

Obviously, if one-third of teachers in block-scheduled schools rely heavily on lecture and do not experiment with different instructional strategies, blocked schools will have greater barriers to success. In addition, many of these same teachers not using interactive methods also waste instructional time in the classroom by not instructing during the last 30 minutes of class. The success of block scheduling will be determined by the degree to which teachers adopt instructional techniques that take advantage of the extended time blocks to create improved learning opportunities for students (Queen, 2000, 2008).

In the next section you will read about the sustained 10-year study of a school system that the author and research colleague, Dr. Robert Algozzine (Queen & Algozzine, 2007), worked with to become the longest longitudinal study ever conducted on the block schedule. It is presented in a case model format for easier reading and, perhaps, duplication by other school systems.

## A Case Model

While data from research on block scheduling are favorable, it is interesting to note that few reports have indicated "why the schools . . . went to a block schedule" or ". . . the process used to lead a school toward its implementation" (Zepeda & Mayers, 2006, p. 141). There is also a need for large scale, longitudinal evaluations of the effects of block scheduling with descriptions of the context for implementing alternative schedules and the details of the program that was implemented, including steps taken to prepare and support teachers. Further, these studies should provide "a sufficient amount of data, collected over time, to enable [stakeholders to draw] informed conclusions" (Zepeda & Mayers, 2006, p. 163).

Again, from the author's vast experience with block scheduling, there have been three main approaches that schools chose to move to the block. In the early 1990s, the first approach was often a decision made in principal meetings or more directly from mandates sent down from the superintendents office. This was not the case in many schools that were "unionized" that required a majority or greater of teacher approval. In these schools, it often took six to seven years to get a positive vote to move. A second approach was more of a "grass roots" movement among a select group of teachers building support for change. On occasion, some of these teachers were voted down by teachers, the superintendent, or the school board. The third major approach, especially in the past five years, has been a combined, usually focused effort among most stakeholders to change to a block schedule.

Educators still experience situations where the first approach is used, often complete with "scripted" pacing guides for teachers, removing creativity, and usually, greater student interaction in these classes. Two problems still exist with schools moving to the block. The first problem is limited to no preparation for teaching in the block. So, in the case where there is effective staff development initially, it greatly affects the first year. In this regard, the work in the Lincoln County schools in North Carolina provides a baseline for drawing implications for future efforts to structure schedules differently based on the development, implementation, and evaluation of block scheduling practices.

### Context

Two years prior to the implementation of the block scheduling model, central office personnel, school administrators and teacher representatives from the four local high schools spent time during the school year visiting a few sites that were in their first or second year of experimenting with alternative scheduling. At the conclusion of the exploratory period, each School Improvement Committee was asked to review the initial findings of the site visits. Representatives of these committees also conducted follow-up visits to schools. These early *assessments of readiness* made it clear that the educators in the school district were interested in moving to block scheduling, but a few administrators were concerned that teachers at the sites visited had expressed frustration at the lack of preparation they had in their transition to the block. In this regard, it became apparent that a *strong professional development program* was needed prior to, and during, implementation to prepare administrators and teachers for the conversion from a traditional format of scheduling instruction to an innovative block scheduling design.

After the two years of investigating the pros and cons of converting to a block schedule, the system decided to make the change. Once the decision was made, the author, serving as the major consultant, designed and directed an intensive professional development program implemented during the spring and summer prior to the first full year (1994–1995) of block scheduling. The effort focused on preparing teachers in developing instructional pacing guides, which were aligned with the North Carolina Standard Course of Study in each discipline, and developing skills in interactive instructional strategies to be used with students. From the teacher evaluations of the initial training, interviews with participating teachers, and direct observations, the planned inservice was an effective and positive experience; and as a result, administrators and teachers were highly motivated about the new program.

After completing the summer professional development sessions, the superintendent, a representative committee of teachers and principals, and the author serving as the consultant from the local university, determined that ongoing support and follow-up activities were needed to assist teachers in the delivery of instruction in the new block scheduling format. A detailed plan was developed for periodic refresher sessions, along with regular classroom visits to sustain the effort and provide continuous information about the implementation process. That process was continued consistently since the first planning sessions.

### Setting and Participants

Lincoln County, located in the southwestern Piedmont area forty miles northwest of Charlotte, was named for a hero of the American Revolution, General Benjamin Lincoln. The high schools in Lincoln County (North, Lincolnton, East, and West) are modern in design. Each school has a principal and at least two assistant principals on the administrative staff. The population in each site ranged from 350–700 students who share similar demographics across the schools. For example, when we surveyed over 2100 students from East Lincoln High School (34%), Lincoln High School (30.7), North Lincoln High School (16.3%), and West Lincoln High School (19.0), representation was similar across grades and gender as well as advanced and technical classes (see Table 2.1). (Note: Student populations composing North were taken from Lincolnton and East High Schools and percentages readjusted after the completion of North High School.)

Administrators and teachers in Lincoln County decided to adopt the $4 \times 4$ block scheduling alternative. In this program model, students no longer would take six subjects during the academic year in 50-minute periods, but rather four courses during a semester in 90-minute blocks.

**Table 2.1**  Student Demographics

**The Schools**

|  | East | Lincolnton | North | West |
|---|---|---|---|---|
| Number and Percentage of Students | 715 (34.0%) | 646 (30.7%) | 342 (16.3%) | 400 (19.0%) |
| Students by Class in the School | Freshman | Sophomore | Junior | Senior |
| $n = 2,102$ (99.8%) | 29% | 27% | 26% | 18% |

**The District**

| Students by Gender in the District | Male | Female |
|---|---|---|
| $n = 2,104$ (99.9%) | 52% | 48% |
| Students Enrolled in Advanced Classes in the District | Yes | No |
| $n = 2,093$ (99.3%) | 49% | 51% |
| Students Enrolled in Technical Classes in the District | Yes | No |
| $n = 2,075$ (98.5%) | 43% | 57% |

*Research Design and Data Analysis*

The major purpose of this research was to evaluate overall effects of implementing a $4 \times 4$ plan in the four different high schools. Data were gathered prior to and during the multi-year implementation. These continuous monitoring efforts were designed to identify what it takes to be effective and to provide evidence of implementation fidelity and program outcomes from administrators, teachers, parents, and students.

Data were collected through the use of questionnaires in which participants could remain anonymous, formal and informal observations, teacher and student focus groups, and personal interviews. Surveys were designed for teachers, students, and parents. Each contained similar items which focused on the perceptions of individuals with respect to the effectiveness of the $4 \times 4$ model. Specifically, questions concerning use of time, ability to complete the expected course of study, academic achievement of students, and classroom management were included.

Data were also collected using the state teacher performance instrument. The documentation from these formal observations was used to develop individual/group professional development sessions in specific instructional strategies for use in block scheduling. Teachers who were identified as marginally-performing were required to develop a professional improvement plan to improve their classroom teaching performance. State yearly performance assessment data (known as end-of-course tests) were also compared. Formal and informal training sessions for school administrators were conducted to assist them in improving their role as instructional leaders throughout the entire period.

*Outcomes*

From observations, interviews, and surveys with parents, teachers, and students, and detailed analysis of test data, the researchers attempted to classify the instructional practices of highly successful teachers working in the block design. Perceptions of the overall success of the $4 \times 4$ model were analyzed and compared for several years of using the block schedule.

## Findings From the First Year Using the $4 \times 4$ Model

The primary consultant to the school system was a university professor with expertise in block scheduling. He met with representative groups of teachers in each school to inform them that he would be observing classroom instruction in a "non-threatening format." Teachers were observed on a weekly basis as they instructed students in their classrooms. Constructive criticism and suggestions for instructional improvement were given.

During the first year, administrators, teachers, parents, and students were interviewed to gather perceptions of the effectiveness of the new program. In the last month of the school year, data were collected through the use of three questionnaires (i.e., teachers, students, and parents) on which respondents could remain anonymous. State assessments (in NC, known as End-of-Course tests) were compared with the previous year's test data. Outcomes documented after the first year of using the 4 × 4 design were as follows:

1. The program had the strong support of school administrators, central office staff, and superintendent.

2. Seventy to 80% of teachers, students, and parents believed the program was successful, indicating a strong desire for block scheduling to continue in the future.

3. Although teachers were using a variety of instructional strategies, in general, there was an identified overuse of lecture in at least 30% of the classes.

## Findings From the Second Year Using the 4 × 4 Model

During the second year of the project, the block scheduling expert continued to serve as a consultant to the schools on a weekly basis. Teachers were evaluated using the state teacher performance instrument. Documentation from the formal observations was used to develop individual/group training sessions in specific instructional strategies for use in block scheduling. Teachers who were identified as marginally-performing teachers were required to develop a professional improvement plan to improve their classroom teaching performance. From observations, interviews, and surveys with parents, teachers, administrators, and students, and detailed analysis of test data, the researchers classified the instructional practices of highly successful teachers working in the block design. Perceptions of the overall success of the 4 × 4 model were analyzed and compared with the major findings from the first year using the block.

Teachers at all of the high schools rated the overall effectiveness of the block design as high. Similarly, the teachers indicated that the block model affected student achievement at a high average level. Teacher use of instructional time and pacing was rated at a slightly higher level. The effectiveness of block scheduling with respect to the teacher's ability to complete a course was somewhat different in the schools. At one high school, teachers expressed the highest degree of confidence in their ability to complete the courses in the 4 × 4 model. Teachers at the other schools showed slightly less confidence in their ability to complete course work; in these schools the teachers rated this item as high average to high. At one school, teachers indicated only average ability.

With respect to percentage of time used in interactive instruction with students, teachers expressed that they were spending 70% of their instructional time engaging students interactively. In the area of discipline problems, slight differences were expressed by the teachers in different high schools. On the whole, teachers expressed using less than 15% of class time managing discipline problems.

Teachers strongly supported the concept of continuing with the block scheduling model, but some believed modifications were necessary. The range of desire to modify the plan ranged from low in three of the schools with one school stating a greater need for modification.

## Most Effective Teaching Behaviors for the 4 × 4 Model

From survey data, observations, and interviews of teachers during the two years, four behaviors were obvious in relationship to effective instruction. Teachers identified instructional pacing as the major teaching skill for success in the block. Following closely was the ability to use a wide variety of instructional strategies. These two skills were rated far more important than any other teaching skill identified. Teachers also viewed having a high level of competency in the discipline in which they taught as being of great importance. Instructional leadership at the school and department levels was considered as extremely important, if block scheduling is to succeed as an instructional design. Other skills that were highly valued included creativity, flexibility, and classroom management.

## The Pros and Cons of the 4 × 4 Model

In the area of student achievement, teachers, students, and parents overwhelmingly supported the block as the best design for student learning. From direct observations and interviews with teachers, we identified the top five positive and negative components of the 4 × 4 model. Positive features included

- Greater flexibility in classroom instruction.
- Longer planning periods for teachers.
- Greater course offering for students.
- One or two class preparations per semester.
- More time each day for in-depth study.

Teacher comments that further illustrate their positive attitudes include

- Block scheduling is a positive approach to education.
  I can now do away with the overhead projector.
- Positive change . . . it revitalized my teaching.
- I love it.

In the negative areas, the list is as follows:

- Loss of retention from one level of a course to next; for example, Spanish I taken first semester of the freshman year and Spanish II taken first or second semester of the sophomore year. (No longer a problem in well-planned schedules.)
- Too much independent study needed outside of class.
- Student transfers from schools not using the 4 × 4 model.
- Limited number of new electives being offered.
- Too much lecture is being used in the classrooms.

Teacher comments included such statements as, "You need the wisdom of Solomon, the strength of Samson and the patience of Job." "We should not assume this is the major solution." "Three preps a semester is too much." "It takes a master in time management." In a more balanced statement, one teacher summed up our observations and opinions about the block when she said, "The advantages of block scheduling far outweigh the disadvantages from my perspective."

## Students' Assessment of the 4 × 4 Model

Slightly more than 80% of students indicated that the success of block scheduling was good to excellent; in fact, a majority of students (54%) indicated that the success of block scheduling was excellent. Only 7% of students rated the system poorly. A large majority of students (73%) affirmed that block scheduling should be continued, whereas only 10% indicated otherwise. The remaining students (17%) were undecided.

Students were asked to indicate the type of instruction that teachers used in the classroom. Lecture was identified by students as the dominant type of teaching format used by teachers, accounting for 38% of classroom time. Classroom discussion followed closely, accounting for 36% of teaching time. Students indicated that student group work was used by teachers 22% of the time. Drill and experimentation were used, according to students, only 5% of the time.

To verify this information, students were asked to indicate the approximate percentage of time teachers lectured to them in the classroom. (32%) of students perceived that 60% to 100% of the time teachers lectured; (30%) of students indicated that 40% to 60% of instructional time was used to lecture. Only 38% of students indicated that teachers lectured less than 40% of the time. To further clarify this important issue, students were asked to indicate how teachers spent the last 20 minutes of classroom time. Interestingly, only 18% of students indicated that teachers lectured during this period. Another 18% of students indicated that they were permitted to work in small discussion groups. Thirty percent (30%) of students indicated that they reviewed what they had learned during the previous 70 minutes. Another 30% indicated that teachers directed them to complete homework assignments. And 6% of students indicated they were permitted to do whatever they wanted to do. There were few differences in the distribution of approaches to instruction used during the final 20 minutes of class; however, one important issue is apparent in that students reported that teachers were having them complete homework assignments during this final 20-minute period at relatively high percentages.

Teaching instructional materials at a rapid pace has been shown to be important to student achievement. Students indicated that 48% of their teachers maintained a fast to very fast pace of instruction. (46%) indicated that the pace was normal, and only 7% indicated that the pace was slow to very slow. Discipline is another important factor related to student achievement. Students were asked to rate student discipline in the 4 × 4 block. (41%) of students indicated that school discipline had improved over the previous year; in fact, 11% indicated that behavior had improved very substantially.

No change in behavior was observed by 42% of students, and only 18% indicated that there was a decrease in the quality of student behavior.

Another important issue related to student learning and achievement was teacher creativity. Accordingly, 64% of students indicated that the block system permitted teachers to use more creative methods to teach than they had previously. Of the respondents, 22% indicated no change in approach, and 14% registered a negative impact on teacher creativity. Further substantiating student perception that the block system is successful, a substantial majority (64%) of students indicated that teachers were more creative using the 4 × 4 model than they had been under the more traditional model.

To verify student perceptions of the effectiveness of the block system, they were asked to indicate whether they had learned more effectively under the new 90-minute schedule or the old 50-minute model. A substantial majority of students (66%) indicated that the block model had improved their learning. Of these, 28% indicated that the block system had a very positive impact on their learning. Only 14% of students indicated that the model affected their learning negatively. The remaining students registered no substantial change. In evaluating the data, a substantial majority of students (66%) indicated that they were actually learning better under the new system of scheduling.

## Parents' Assessment of the Second Year

Parent survey responses and data collected by the researchers indicated that a large percentage of the respondents strongly support the block scheduling design. With a return rate of approximately 30%, parents rated the overall effectiveness of block scheduling as very good and the majority agreed that the block should continue in the future. Many of the parents viewed the block as giving their children a greater opportunity to choose course electives and extra academic experiences during the four years of high school. A few parents were concerned there were some teachers still teaching under the old design and had not made the transition to the new 4 × 4 design. Some parents stated their concern that the last part of the class period was wasted time. They also believed and reported that some teachers did not use the extra time effectively.

## Students' Academic Performance in the Block

When comparing the test scores of students for the year before the block, to the first year of the program and the second year of the program, a definite pattern in achievement appeared. Student scores improved for the first semester and then decreased in most academic areas for the second semester. Although the yearly averages showed improvement for the two years since beginning use of the model, there would be greater increases if teachers and students could sustain the same level of achievement for the second semester as in the first semester (see Table 2.2). The trend was consistent across content areas of instruction. This pattern of performance may be reflective of two important factors. One may be the excitement of a new semester after a summer break when everyone was more rested and energized. Fatigue, a possible second factor, may have developed near the end of the second semester. Another factor is that more of the lower performing students may be taking the state measured EOC (End-of-Course tests) courses during the second semester. Standard deviations are included under each individual score. Percentage of students passing the Social Studies areas increased from the year before block was 60.45% and showed a statistically significant improvement for the next three semesters, but dropped the fourth semester after starting the block. Fatigue appeared to be the biggest problem. The following year, the school system moved to starting school earlier in August and finishing exams before the winter holidays. We begin to see an increase that has continued and has improved for the past 12 years in all tested areas. (See Table 2.2.)

**Table 2.2**   Average Goal Performance Across All Schools (NC End-of-Course Tests)

| Area | Control | 1st Fall | 1st Spring | 2nd Fall | 2nd Spring |
|---|---|---|---|---|---|
| Math | 68.24 | 68.80 | 58.05 | 62.01 | 55.39 |
| Science | 62.10 | 64.43 | 62.71 | 58.30 | 55.74 |
| Social Studies | 60.45 | 67.09 | 67.20 | 66.01 | 56.11 |

## Block Scheduling Revisited

Data from surveys of 230 teachers with teaching experience ranging from 1 to more than 20 years, 2,100 students from 9th through 12th grade, and 1,000 parents of high school students in Lincoln County were used to explore the multi-year strengths and weaknesses of block schedule, its effects on discipline, instructional strategies used with block scheduling, and recommendation for improving block scheduling.

A majority of students, parents, and teachers regarded block scheduling in Lincoln County as a success (see Figures 2.1, 2.2, and 2.3). When asked if they would rate block scheduling as a success, 82.1% of the students surveyed agreed. Similarly, 84.5% of the teachers surveyed agreed that the overall effectiveness of block scheduling was good. Based on their children's performance on block scheduling, 89.8% of the parents surveyed also agreed that the success of block scheduling was good. An average of 85.5% of all participants in the study agreed that block scheduling was a success. These findings regarding the success of block scheduling are consistent with later studies published nationally (Queen & Algozzine, 2007; Zepeda & Mayers, 2006).

Strong feelings regarding the success led many of the participants to suggest continuing block scheduling. Of those surveyed, 86.6% of the students, 86.4% of the teachers, and 74.0% of the parents agreed that block scheduling should remain in Lincoln County. The reason for the strong support of block scheduling was due to its benefits, including: (a) more time for instruction, (b) differentiation of instruction, and (c) fewer classes during the school day.

Many benefits of block scheduling positively affect students' opinions regarding their learning. For example, when questioned whether they learned better on block or traditional schedule, 78.6% of the students agreed that they learn better in the block schedule. These students' perceptions about their learning experience in the block schedule support other results from the student-related benefits of block scheduling (Queen, 2000; Queen, Algozzine, & Eaddy, 1996, 1997, 1998; Queen, Algozzine, & Isenhour, 1999; Pisapia & Westfall, 1997a, 1997b, 1997c; Zepeda & Mayers, 2006).

- Students have less homework, which leads to reduced anxiety over workload.
- Students have fewer classes per day, which reduces the amount of time wasted between classes and allows the students to spend more time interacting with teachers and classmates.

**Figure 2.1**   Perceptions of Success of Block Scheduling

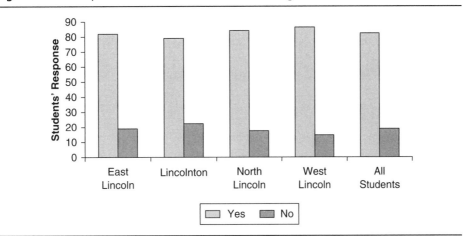

**Figure 2.2**   Perceptions of Success of Block Scheduling

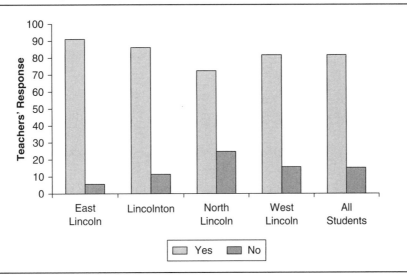

**Figure 2.3**   Perceptions of Success of Block Scheduling

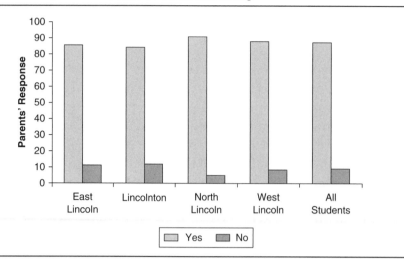

Semester-long classes provide opportunities for students to retake courses. Knowing this also reduces anxiety related to grade retention or summer school.

Other studies have also identified how block scheduling supports student learning and offers opportunities for the differentiation of instruction (Zepeda & Mayers, 2006).

The additional instructional time provided by the block scheduling, allows teachers to address the different learning styles of their students. The 90-minute periods commonly available in the block schedule allows teachers to use a variety of instructional strategies such as lecture, Socratic seminar (student controlled class discussion), cooperative learning, structured and unstructured inquiry, and guided or independent practice.

Sixty-three percent of the students in the study agreed that blocked periods allowed teachers to use more creative and effective teaching methods. Teachers recognize a shift in the instructional approaches used most often. Initially, lecture was the primary method of instruction; however, 87% of the teachers in the survey reported that approximately 40% or more of the class period involved interactive instruction with students.

Researchers propose that differentiation of instruction allows all types of learners (i.e., auditory, visual, and kinesthetic) to learn the material.

Lecture remains one of the continued methods for instruction among teachers, especially those new to block scheduling. Sixty-two percent of the students in the study reported that more than 40% of class time was spent lecturing. Although lecture is still used, the data indicate that the most effective teachers use various instructional strategies. Of the students surveyed, 56% commented that the best teachers use a variety of teaching approaches. Similarly, research shows that teachers who differentiate instruction are more successful in the block schedule. In addition to differentiated instruction, effective teachers in the block utilize the entire class period.

- The first 10 to 20 minutes, teachers engage students with cooperative learning activities, homework reviews, and synopsis of previous material.

- The majority (87%) of teachers use more than 40% of the period to engage students in lecture, class discussion, group activities, and experiments and lab activities.

- The last 10 to 20 minutes, teachers engage students with summary of lesson, guided and independent practice, and authentic assessment activities.

- It is important that teachers maximize the instructional time available because it is a major strength of the block schedule.

- The researchers in this study found that classroom management and school discipline improved under the block schedule. When questioned about school discipline, 71.1% of the students stated that discipline had improved. Teachers agreed that classroom discipline was less of a problem on the block schedule:

- Fifty percent of the teachers surveyed stated that less than 20% of instructional time was spent handling classroom problems.

- Twenty-six percent of the teachers stated that less than 40% of the instructional time was spent handling discipline.

When questioned about their teacher's skills, 68% of the students surveyed stated that the best teachers "use class time for teaching." Of these students, 12% commented that the teachers "care about me, but do not allow me to get away with anything." This supports the argument that block scheduling allows teachers to develop positive relationships with students. These relationships allow teachers to provide a more caring learning environment void of major discipline issues. These findings are consistent with those of other studies.

- The previously mentioned benefits of block scheduling are consistent with research findings. Yet, the real question is whether block scheduling is effective. We addressed these questions in three areas: (a) student achievement, (b) completeness of the course, and (c) use of instructional time and pacing. Similar to the responses of the students, 77.9% of the teachers reported that the "effectiveness of the block scheduling with respect to achievement is good." Teacher satisfaction with the students' academic performance on the block schedule was consistent with earlier research.

- The teachers' responses regarding the use of instructional time were also positive. Eighty-six percent of the teachers reported that on block scheduling, the use of instructional time was effective.

- The students' comments regarding their grades provided additional support to the effectiveness of block scheduling. More than 90% of the students in the study reported that their average grades in most subjects were C or better. Sixty-eight percent of the students reported average grades of As and Bs.

- The ability of teachers to cover all of the required material is still an issue of concern. Some research suggests teachers often fail in the area of completeness of the course. In the study, some teachers commented that they do not have enough time in the semester to complete the entire course. Nonetheless, 68% of the teachers still agreed that effectiveness with respect to completeness of the course was good.

## Ten-Year Comparison

During the first year on the block (1994–1995), we conducted an initial study to establish a baseline regarding the students' opinions of block scheduling. The results of the study indicated a majority of the participants believed block scheduling was better than the traditional schedule. Eighty-one percent of the students rated the success of block scheduling as good. Over the ten-year period in Lincoln County, block scheduling has continued to gain support among students, parents, and teachers. In the 2004–2005 study, 83% of students, 85% of teachers, and 90% of parents surveyed rated the success of block scheduling as good. Districtwide support for the continued use of block scheduling increased from 74% in 1995 to 87% in 2005.

In addition to increased support, the comparison of data from 1995 to 2005 indicates block scheduling is effective in maintaining school and classroom discipline, promoting differentiation of instruction, and instructional pacing. Results of the two studies show the following:

The belief among students that school discipline has improved on block scheduling, increasing by 30% over the past ten years. In 2005, 71% of the students agreed that school discipline had improved, as opposed to only 41% in 1995.

The teaching methods used during the block has shifted from lecture to interactive instruction such as class discussion, cooperative learning, and structured inquiry. In 1995, 38% of the students reported that teachers used lecture most often to teach, while 36% reported the use of other instructional methods (e.g., class discussion, group work, experiments). In 2005, only 35% of the students reported that teachers used lecture most often, while 44% reported the use of other instructional methods.

Teachers have improved the pace of the lessons on block scheduling. In 1995, 48% of the students stated that the pace of the lessons on block scheduling compared to the traditional schedule was fast; however, in 2005, only 30% of the students made similar comments.

## The Three Most Important Changes Over the 10 Years

1. These findings indicate that, over time, teachers adjusted to block scheduling and learned to maximize the strengths and minimum the weaknesses.

2. Sustained staff development over the time period was essential to the overall and continued success and improvement.

3. Students improved dramatically on End-of-Course state tests. The system experienced a significant increase from a pre-block 63.6% passage rate to an 81.1% passage rate. I must add that there were no socio-economic or other population factors that could have influenced the increase. In fact, a greater percentage of the students live in poverty now than the students before the block started. There was minimum teacher turn-over. (See Table 2.3.)

## What We Know About Block Scheduling From Many Years of Practice

Teachers, students, and parents in the participating school district felt that the block was effective. There was even greater support for the block to be continued in the future. Observed behaviors of teachers and students in and out of the classroom, along with specific focus groups that I conducted at each school, further verifies these perceptions into beliefs by actions observed. Some areas of academic achievement have improved as measured by end-of-course testing either as a direct result of the block and/or better pacing of instruction and the use of a variety of instructional strategies. This was especially true in the social science areas.

There was an increase in the variety of teaching strategies that teachers used in their instruction over previous years. However, there was evidence that 30% of teachers were still relying on the lecture method, and strong evidence that the last 20 to 30 minutes of instructional time was sometimes either wasted or used for homework time. Some modification made in the scheduling structure for such courses, semester lab courses, and AP courses require some review, and perhaps, adjustments.

Data from this analysis of a school district implementation of $4 \times 4$ block scheduling program are favorable. They provide a baseline for drawing implications for future efforts to structure school schedules differently.

## Years 11 and 12

With the increase of technology in the instructional process, and with continued staff development in methodology and even more focus on instructional pacing, we found that student achievement scores based on North Carolina End-of-Course Tests continued to increase on average the last two years as can be seen in Table 2.3 (Queen, Algozzine, & Watson, 2008).

**Table 2.3**  Composite Average End-of-Course Tests

| The Year Before Block | After First Year on Block | Year 10 | Year 11 | Year 12 |
|---|---|---|---|---|
| 63.6 | 64.7 | 81.1 | 81.6 | 82.1 |

## ■ SUMMARY

To be a successful teacher in a blocked class it is important that teachers have direct influence in the decision process of going to the block schedule. Teachers must demonstrate an ability to develop well-developed curriculum alignment and pacing guides (preferably within the school environment and by content area). Teachers must master at least four instructional strategies, choose a design for teaching, and adjust instructional activities basically every 20 minutes in most cases. Beginning teachers need special assistance from mentors and principals, and staff development must be provided and sustained annually. The more effective the training, the better for the teacher and the student; this was especially true if the training is viewed as positive and practical by the teachers.

At the district or school level, principals and/or staff development personnel must provide initial and continuous training for teachers to master instructional strategies. Cooperative learning, synectics, Socratic seminars, concept attainment, case methods, inquiry methods, simulations, games, and role-playing strategies are excellent methods for teachers to use in blocked classes. Queen, Burrell, and McManus (2000) identified and reviewed several strategies in *Planning for Instruction: A Year Long Guide.* However, just as a 90-minute lecture is inappropriate, a 90–minute discussion session may be too long. After years of observing in hundreds of classrooms, the author is highly convinced that teachers must change the grouping pattern and specific activities at least every 20 minutes (Queen, 2008). This prevents student boredom, elicits class interaction, and encourages teachers to meet the needs of diverse learners. Instruction in these extended periods should always begin with a review, include various activities of a direct and indirect approach, and conclude with an adequate summary.

In the Chapter 5, the author will present three class designs that teachers can use for improvement. The first lesson design can be used for teachers just starting in the block or for teachers still struggling (Traditional Block Lesson Model). The second design is for very successful teachers ready to move to more student involvement and who believe that teaching is not just being a giver of knowledge, but rather an architect for designing and using an environment for student learning (Transitional Block Lesson Model). For the true master teacher, the author will introduce the transformational model that is for the teacher that is ready for personalized instruction. In addition, suggested instructional approaches for teaching in the block with the models are presented in detail later in this book and by using my Web site at www.blockscheduling.com, especially redesigned for readers of this book. But before we focus on class design and instructional strategies, it is important to review some basic information on growth and development.

# THREE

# Developmental Aspects of Growth and Behavior

**R**egardless of scheduling, teachers should understand the fundamental principles of child growth and development so that they can effectively instruct students. Children move from an immature and less complex and skilled dependent state to a mature and more complex and skilled independent condition. This process involves a series of invariant stages of physical, intellectual, and personal development. By understanding the stages of development that children invariably move through, teachers know what to expect of children, what and how to instruct, and how to communicate with children based on their stage of development.

Although part of the education and training to become a teacher focuses on these stages of development, it is imperative to keep these stages in mind when designing instruction. Without this knowledge, effective instruction is difficult. The goal of this chapter is to refresh understanding and give an overview of the various developmental stages.

## PHYSICAL DEVELOPMENT FROM EARLY CHILDHOOD THROUGH ADOLESCENCE

We only need to watch young children for a short time to see that they tend to be unsteady. This instability is caused by several factors in their physical development. Children in the early childhood stage have a high center of gravity because their heads are out of proportion to their bodies, and their abdomens protrude, which makes balancing difficult. Gaining control over their motor activities is their biggest achievement, during which they also begin to favor the right or left side of the body. As their dexterity improves, children learn to perform fine motor activities, such as tying shoelaces and printing letters of the alphabet. Their ability to jump, run, and walk also improves significantly by the end of the preschool period.

By the time most children reach school age, they have already learned many skills such as buttoning and zipping pants and jackets, buckling belts, cutting with scissors, and coloring within borders. In addition, children print letters and words with greater accuracy. After the 7th year, most children continuously improve the quality of their fine and gross motor skills, but learn few completely new basic capabilities.

Through the primary years, children experience comparatively small alterations in their weight and height. Until children reach age nine, boys are generally only slightly heavier and taller than girls. During the early elementary years, children need frequent exercise to accommodate skeletal growth and muscular development and to improve their physical skills. By the age of nine, children begin to participate in complex activities, such as playing musical instruments or constructing models.

From their 8th through 10th years, both sexes are similar in size. Although boys and girls are similar in size at the beginning of 4th grade, by the end of the year, many girls have begun to gain height and weight over boys. The rapid growth of their arms and legs, combined with the slower development of their torsos, causes girls to temporarily appear ungainly and lose a degree of strength and coordination. Most early maturing females rapidly regain lost ground. By the end of 5th grade or the beginning of 6th grade, they are generally taller and heavier than most boys of the same age. By this point, many girls have reached the size that they remain until puberty.

With the onset of female menstruation at approximately age 13 and male ejaculation between 13 and 16 years, girls and boys enter puberty, a time of particularly significant and substantial changes. The order in which these changes occur is basically the same for each person, but the rate at which females and males mature can vary widely. Some adolescents may fully mature in as little as 18 months from onset, while others may require five or six years. During this period, almost every organ and system in the body are subject to change and stress.

Puberty is a particularly difficult time for children for many reasons. Their bodies change drastically in relatively short periods of time, making them quite self-conscious; size, muscular development, amount and location of hair, and body proportions are all changed during this period. Since they are experiencing this stage at different rates, additional stress is placed on these adolescents. For those who experience puberty early, the notoriety caused by their advanced development is confusing and generally unwelcome. But as they successfully work through these changes, awkward self-consciousness diminishes and confidence improves. Those who undergo puberty "late" may experience even greater stress. An apparent lack of physical maturity can cause self-doubt, loss of self esteem, and withdrawal from involvement with others. These problems can carry over into adulthood.

## Cognitive Growth

Arnold Gesell notably achieved insight into the progressive nature of child development. Gesell (1971) established a center for research into child development at Yale University, where he worked on the premise that children's growth and development occur in an unvarying sequence within strict boundaries of time. Although his ideas were later found to be inadequate in explaining the true nature of development, his fundamental principle—that children move through several phases of reorganization during which they develop new ways of understanding the world—has been generally accepted.

While Gesell worked at Yale, psychologist and epistemologist Jean Piaget (1954) quietly explored the intellectual development of his children in Switzerland. His discoveries and the work that followed have become the basis of cognitive science in the fields of psychology and education. Piaget concluded that cognitive growth occurs in specific developmental stages, during which significant differences in the nature and substance of intelligence are developed over time. Piaget saw these differences as real transformations of consciousness.

Based on extensive observations, Piaget (1954) defined several stages of cognitive development. He described from three to six stages of development with several substages (see Table 3.1).

## Characteristics of Piaget's Stages of Cognitive Development

Piaget (1954) established a general time frame for the onset of the stages of cognitive development. From birth to two years of age, a child is in the sensori-motor stage of development. The period of preoperational thought is active from the second year until approximately the seventh year. This is followed by the stage of concrete operations, which generally appears by the age of seven and continues through the 11th year. The onset of formal operations, the fourth stage, occurs sometime between the 11th and 16th birthdays.

Piaget (1954) determined that the onset of each stage is signaled by a major shift in intellectual activity from the preceding stage of development.

Although the beginning of each stage varies for each individual, the sequence of the stages does not change. A child must navigate through the succession of stages; he or she cannot intentionally avoid or miss a stage through superior cognitive attributes. Piaget noted that although definable intellectual activities describe each period, mixing of capabilities from other stages, especially those from stages just experienced, would occur. In addition, as children age, there is an increasing variation in the age at which children begin a stage, with the onset of formal operations in adolescents subject to the greatest age variation. But before examining the four stages of development further, let us look at the ideas that describe the cognitive processes responsible for the changes within those stages.

**Table 3.1**   Piaget's Cognitive Stages

| Cognitive Stages | Ages | Characteristics |
| --- | --- | --- |
| Formal Operations | 11 to Adult | • Cognitive structures mature to the adult level<br>• Capacity to engage all categories and classes of problems: the verbal abstraction, the hypothetical, and consideration of past and future conditions<br>• Ability to evaluate a logical argument separate from its content |
| Concrete Operations | 7 to 11 years | • Logical examination of the observable relationships between events, objects, and people<br>• Involves the development of the cognitive structures of seriation and classification<br>• Expression of a strong tendency to organize and apply strict rules to activities undertaken |
| Preoperational | 2 to 7 years | • Not restricted to immediate environment<br>• Expansion of use of mental images<br>• Application and understanding of vocabulary expands<br>• Intuitive thought defines preoperational thought |
| Sensori-motor | 0 to 2 years | • Period of simple reflexes<br>• Restricted to immediate experience<br>• Events are uninhibited by sight and feeling<br>• Children build first cognitive structures |

## Schemata and the Process of Assimilation, Accommodation, and Equilibration

In Piaget's (1969b) scheme of cognitive development, assimilation and accommodation are the ways children integrate new experiences into cognitive structures called schemata or schemes. According to Piaget, "A scheme is the structure or organization of actions as they are transferred or generalized by repetition in similar or analogous circumstances" (p. 4). These structures develop from birth, at which time they are simple and undifferentiating. As a child develops and is more able to differentiate among stimuli, the number of schemata grows by absorbing additional relevant material that resulted from encounters with the environment. At major periods of transformation, schemata undergo significant changes that allow a child to deal competently with more complex problems.

The process of assimilation and accommodation is unending, and it reflects people's continuous interaction with an infinite number of stimuli. The process is "a constant filtering of input and modification of internal schemes to fit reality" (Piaget, 1969b, p. 6). Schemata expand as they encounter stimuli that fit into recognizable patterns. A change in the schemata may occur, however, when a child cannot assimilate an experience into the established structure. If the experience cannot be assimilated, then two alternatives are available to the child: (a) The insufficient schemata can be adjusted to accommodate the new material, or (b) a completely new structure can be established to accommodate the material.

The process of assimilation and accommodation (Piaget, 1969b) is the basis for cognitive growth and development that occurs during the life of the individual. Yet the process would be unworkable if the comparative quantities of assimilation and accommodation were not balanced. A person who assimilates everything would have too few schemata and be unable to differentiate experiences. Conversely, a person who accommodates experiences excessively would have too many schemata and would find too few commonalties to generalize to the broader world of experience. This balancing process is called *equilibration*. It is a process to which the engaging intellect is constantly drawn. Equilibrium must be sustained if the intellect is to develop effectively.

## The Sensori-Motor Period

From birth through two years of age, children move through what Piaget (1969b) has called the sensori-motor period, which consists of six substages. During this period, children move from a period of simple reflexes to a period in which representation of unseen objects readily occurs. Within these first two years, children are restricted to immediate experience. Without any previous experience, children of this age group have no basis on which to build categories for organizing reality; rather, they experience events uninhibited through sight and feeling.

One of the most important events that a Stage 1 child experiences during the early months of life is the constant appearance and disappearance of familiar objects. From this activity, the child builds cognitive structures, such as object permanence, which are essential to continued mental development. Piaget (1969b) says that during the sensori-motor period,

> The system of sensori-motor schemes of assimilation culminates in a kind of logic of action involving the establishment of relationships and correspondences and classification of schemes; in short, structures of ordering and assembling that constitute a substructure for the future operations of thought. But sensori-motor intelligence has an equally important result as regards the structuring of the subject's universe, however limited it may be at this practical level. It organizes reality by constructing the broad categories of action that are the schemes of the permanent object, space, time, and causality, substructures of the notions that will later correspond to them. (p. 13)

Adults who restrict or deny a child strong visual experiences during this period can cause deficits in the development of important cognitive structures. An environment filled with a variety of visual and reacting stimuli provides the most supportive conditions for developing a child's intellectual capabilities. An environment without appropriate stimuli can result in serious delays in a child's cognitive development that may not be easily corrected.

## The Period of Preoperational Thought

The second stage of a child's development is called the period of pre-operational thought (Piaget, 1969b). To enter this stage, a child undergoes a major intellectual transformation. No longer restricted to their immediate environment, children expand on the use of the mental images that they began to develop during the previous stage. They quickly expand their capacity to store information, such as words and the implicit rules of language. During this period, children's application and understanding of vocabulary increase substantially. At two years of age, the average child can use a few hundred words, but by the age of five, that same child may be using over 2,000 words. This major advance in language capability is a distinguishing characteristic of intellectual development. Piaget (1969b) says the following about the acquisition of language:

> This has three consequences essential to mental development: (1) the possibility of verbal exchange with other persons, which heralds the onset of the socialization of action; (2) the internalization of words, i.e., the appearance of thought itself, supported by internal language and a system of signs; last and most important, (3) the internalization of action of such, which from now on, rather than being purely perceptual and motor as it has been, heretofore, can represent itself intuitively by means of pictures and "mental experiments". (p. 17)

The underlying mode of thought during Stage 2 is intuitive. During this period, children are experimenters, explorers, and imitators. They are unconcerned about the exactness of their pronouncements. Their use of sounds and language is often inventive and unique. Another aspect of speech during this period is that it is self-centered; children seem to be talking "at" rather than "with" others. To stimulate their language growth, children need a verbally rich environment. Denying children the use of their language faculty can result in developmental delays that may be very difficult to correct.

Piaget (1969b) has observed that preoperational children's use of intuitive thinking often causes them to misinterpret reality. A child at this stage is generally unable to determine which container holds more water—a tall, narrow beaker or a short, wide one. Often a child's response to this problem is that the taller container holds more water simply because it appears so. According to Piaget, it would do no good to explain to a child at this stage why each container holds the same amount since the child is intellectually unable to process this information. Piaget also indicates that Stage 2 children have difficulties with reversible relationships. For example, Jennifer may understand that Matt is her brother, but she may not understand that she is Matt's sister. Regardless of its apparent lack of logic, the intuitive approach is powerful because it provides a way to learn language quickly and solve problems in imaginative ways.

## The Period of Concrete Operations

The third stage of Piaget's (1969b) theory of child development is the period of concrete operations. Once again, children experience an intellectual revolution, progressing from the free-form thinking of the preoperational stage, they now logically examine the operative relationships among events, objects and people. Of operations during this period, Piaget says,

> The operations, such as the union of two classes or the addition of two numbers, are actions characterized by their very great generality since the acts of uniting, arranging in order, etc., enter into all coordinations of particular actions. They are also reversible (the opposite of uniting is separating, the opposite of adding is subtracting, etc.). Furthermore, they are never isolated but always capable of being coordinated into overall systems (a classification, the sequence of numbers, etc.). Finally they are not peculiar to a given individual; they are common to all individuals on the same mental level. (pp. 96–97)

Unlike children in the intuitive state, Stage 3 children are not limited to understanding through perception. Children in concrete operations are able to focus their perceptions and to understand concrete transformations that events or objects undergo. They can now reverse operations. Communications also become less egocentric; children begin to talk with rather than at others. Language becomes functional and purposeful and begins to reflect the child's basic social nature. Piaget (1969b) also found that children in the concrete operations stage develop the cognitive abilities of seriation and classification. With this improvement, children's concepts of space, time, speed, and causality improve dramatically.

The development of logical operations and the associated capabilities of reversibility and classification allow children to solve problems more effectively and with more confidence than during the previous period. But the logic requires real and observable objects. Children at this stage still have great difficulty with verbal or hypothetical objects. Therefore, Stage 3 children are very literal-minded; they interpret situations concretely, failing to understand abstractions. Children presented with an abstract idea will convert the abstraction into a concrete event relevant to their experiences. A child will have a difficult time solving a problem presented in abstract verbal terms but will be able to apply logic to the same problem if it is presented in the form of real, observable objects.

During this period, children express a strong tendency to organize and apply strict rules to activities they undertake. The concrete operational child is often more concerned with establishing rules for an activity than with the activity itself. Working out the functional relationship among various elements in an activity is a focal point during the third stage of development. Once children establish relationships and rules for action, they have a particularly difficult time modifying their ideas during this period. They see things distinctly—things are or they are not; subtleties or shades of gray are not acceptable. Altering the rules of a game is a difficult undertaking for children in this category of intellectual development.

Unless children who are operating concretely are offered direct experiences, preferably hands-on, their learning will be inefficient. To support cognitive growth during this time, practical skills such as such as organizing, constructing, classifying, sorting, counting, and arranging should be taught.

## The Period of Formal Operations

According to Piaget (1969b), formal operations is the fourth and final stage of intellectual development. During this period, the adolescent's cognitive structures mature to the adult level. Piaget predicts that no additional structural improvements will occur beyond the period of formal operations, although the efficiency and reach of those structures can be expected to improve during the course of adulthood.

The great novelty of this stage is that by means of a differentiation of form and content, the subject becomes capable of reasoning correctly about propositions he does not believe, or at least not yet; that is propositions that he considers pure hypotheses. He becomes capable of drawing the necessary conclusions from truths that are merely possible, which constitutes the beginning of hypothetical-deductive or formal thought (p. 132).

Logical operations, the onset of which began during the concrete operational period, are brought to their full development during Stage 4. This final period of cognitive development allows a considerably broader range of logical applications to problem solving than the previous period did. During the period of concrete operations, a child was limited to applying logic to the solution of tangible problems as they occurred; he or she did not permit projection into the future or consideration of hypothetical situations. The child who has achieved formal operations, however, has the capacity to engage all categories and classes of problems. The verbal abstraction, the hypothetical, and consideration of past and future conditions are all subject to the power of the logic of formal operations.

The adolescent operating in formal operations can employ several strategies simultaneously in solving problems. Understanding the concept of causation, using scientific reasoning to approach a problem, and building and testing hypotheses are all hallmarks of the fourth stage of Piaget's theory. In addition, adolescents are able to consider problems involving a combination of several variables rather than focusing on one aspect of a problem as they did during the concrete period. They are also able to undertake complex verbal problems. Problems involving proportion and conservation of movement can also be solved with their advanced logic.

For the first time, a child can separate personal perception from objective reality. The result is the ability to evaluate a logical argument separate from its content. The child in concrete operations was restricted to dealing with the world according to personal perception; thus, a child would be unable to consider a problem involving yellow snow, for example. The more advanced child, however, is able to deal with such a hypothetical condition and, in fact, derive a logical and valid argument not dependent on the observable reality of white snow. As in the previous stages of development, formal operations evolve as a direct result of those intellectual abilities developed in preceding stages. With the transformations that occur from one stage to another, cognitive structures are continuously subject to structural changes. The assimilation, accommodation, and equilibration processes are constantly at work from the sensori-motor period through the period of formal operations.

## Cognitive Theory and Block Instruction

According to cognitive theory, children's development is marked by periods when they are particularly sensitive and responsive to outside influences. However, children are not blank slates on which teachers compose whatever they desire. Children, who have inherent dispositions and tendencies and are subject to their external environments, develop and grow intellectually in an invariable sequence form birth through adolescence and beyond. To teach effectively, teachers should be aware of the materials and approaches most appropriate for a child's readiness to learn. Cognitive theory provides insights and guidance into these issues.

Piaget (1969b) suggested that children's cognitive structures should be carefully considered when presenting instructional materials. According to Piaget, intellectual capabilities are not set at birth; they are ultimately dependent on the appropriateness of the activities and the environment in which a child develops. In preparing their lessons, teachers should pay close attention to the children's intellectual stages so that they can develop activities that stimulate cognitive development. If teachers do not consider the children's cognitive structure, the classroom experience will be less effective than it could be. A carefully tailored classroom experience produces cognitive growth and a successful child.

We tend to think that accelerating intellectual growth is always a positive step and one that teachers should pursue. However, attempting to push children beyond the level they are currently experiencing may serve only to frustrate a child. Children's intellectual accomplishments can be strengthened within each period of development. This improves a child's intellectual capacity and broadens the foundation for future growth. Expanding on learning opportunities that are relevant to each child's cognitive level improves learning conditions in the classroom by minimizing frustrating conditions for children.

## ■ PERSONALITY DEVELOPMENT

The development of personality coincides with physical and intellectual developments. Discussing the personal-psychological character of development helps us achieve greater depth in our understanding of the total child. The development of personality follows a sequence of interdependent periods that generally correspond to the stages of cognitive development. Satisfaction of needs during one stage determines the child's ability to progress to the next stage. When needs are not met, children have difficulty making the transition to the following stage and may be delayed or even prevented from continuing their personal advance to more mature stages of development.

As Jean Piaget's theories describe the area of cognitive development, Erik Erikson's (1980) ideas have become the basis for much of our understanding of personality development in children and adolescents. (See Table 3.2 for a comparison of Piaget's cognitive stages and Erikson's personality stages.) Erikson's (1980) ideas about human development arose out of his work in Freudian psychology. Sigmund Freud, originator of the concepts of the id, the ego, and the superego, believed that to understand adult personality and behavior, the experiences and relationships the adult had as a child must be analyzed. Within these experiences and relationships, Freud saw the basis for later emotional development. As the psychiatrist investigated child and adult behavior, he recognized that children and adults move through a series of emotional stages from birth to adulthood. Freud described five such stages: (a) the oral stage, from birth to 18 months; (b) the anal stage, from 18 months to three years; (c) the phallic stage, from three to seven years; (d) the period of latency, from seven to 12 years; and (e) the genital period, from age 12 through adulthood.

**Table 3.2**  A Comparison of Piaget and Erikson

| Piaget's Cognitive Stages | Age and Erikson's Personality Stages | |
| --- | --- | --- |
| Concrete Operations | Ages 13–18 | Identity vs. Diffusion |
| | Age 12 | Industry vs. Inferiority |
| Preoperational | Ages 8–11 | Industry vs. Inferiority |
| | Age 7 | Industry vs. Inferiority |
| | Ages 4–6 | Inferiority vs. Guilt |
| | Age 3 | Autonomy vs. Shame |
| Sensori-motor | Age 2 | Autonomy vs. Shamey |
| | Ages 8–11 | Formal Operations |
| | Birth–18 months | Trust vs. Mistrust |

Freud found that as children undergo this sequence of emotional transformation, their experiences have a profound effect on the formation of adult personality. Specific areas of personality that are particularly vulnerable to alteration define these transformative periods. Based on these periods of change, Erikson (1980) developed eight stages that further define the contents and mechanisms operating in the maturing human being. In this section, the first five stages, from birth through adolescence, will be examined (see Table 3.3). For a comparison with Piaget's stages of cognitive development and Freud's stages of emotional development see Table 3.4.

**Table 3.3**  Birth Through Adolescence According to Erikson

| Stage of Development | Approximate Age | Characteristics |
|---|---|---|
| V. Identity vs. Identity Diffusion | 12 to 18 | • Uses logic to solve hypothetical problems<br>• Undergoes significant body system alterations, resulting in reproductive capability<br>• Decisions made on objective evidence<br>• Ideas of others considered less egocentrically<br>• Capable of empathy<br>• Needs to improve things<br>• Requires responsibility for growth |
| IV. Industry vs. Inferiority | 6 to 12 | • Focus turns to friends and school<br>• Forms social alliances reflecting growing interest in other people and in things outside family<br>  ○ Important to encourage children to actively explore the world, to test themselves, and to work hard to achieve goals |
| III. Initiative vs. Guilt | 3 to 6 | • Begins to explore sexual identity and identify with appropriate male and female models<br>• Important to reinforce identity at this point, to establish a sense of self |
| II. Autonomy vs. Shame | 18 months to 3 years | • Conflicted by attempts to gain a degree of independence and competence<br>• Begins to express a strong sense of self<br>• Intensely investigates environment<br>• Should be encouraged to express themselves verbally |
| I. Trust vs. Mistrust | Birth to 18 months | • Develops varying degrees of trust and mistrust<br>• Parents must provide supportive and nurturing environment<br>• Quality of care has profound effect on the degree to which the maturing child expresses trust and dependability |

**Table 3.4**  A Comparison of Freud and Erikson

| Ages | Freud | Erikson |
|---|---|---|
| 12 to 18 years | Genital | Identity-Identity Diffusion |
| 7 to 12 years | Latency | Industry-Inferiority |
| 3 to 7 years | Phallic | Initiative-Guilt |
| 18 months to 3 years | Anal | Autonomy-Shame |
| Birth to 18 months | Oral | Trust-Mistrust |

## Erikson's Stages of Personality Development

The first of Erikson's (1980) stages is concerned with the development of trust and mistrust. Erikson has defined trust as "what is commonly implied in reasonable trustfulness as far as others are concerned." He defines mistrust as characterizing "individuals who withdraw into themselves in particular ways when they are at odds with themselves or with others" (pp. 57–58). The stage of *trust versus mistrust* occurs during the infant stage, from birth to 18 months. Erikson has determined that during this time children develop varying degrees of trust and mistrust. To successfully establish a solid foundation on which to build a balanced personality, he believes that parents must provide a highly supportive and nurturing environment. The quality of attention and degree to which a parent attends to a child during this period will have a profound effect on the degree to which the maturing child expresses trust and dependability. When parents provide consistent care and affection during interactive periods, a child will be prepared to begin the next level of personal development successfully.

During the second stage of Erikson's (1980) theory, which he called the period of *autonomy versus shame and doubt*, children continue their emotional development. Between the age of 18 months and three years, children experience the conflict created by their attempts to gain a degree of competence and independence from their parents. Erikson describes the significance of this period:

> The overall significance of this stage lies in the maturation of the muscle system, the consequent ability (and doubly felt inability) to coordinate a number of highly conflicting action patterns such as "holding on" and "letting go," and the enormous value with which the still highly dependent child begins to endow his autonomous will. (p. 68)

While seeking independence, children begin to express a strong sense of self and engage in a period of intense investigation of their environment. At this stage, adults who prevent a child from fully developing personal autonomy can easily frustrate him or her. Therefore, adults at this stage should support a child's attempts to explore the world. Also at this time, children will begin to express themselves verbally. As noted in the discussion on cognitive development, vocabulary increases dramatically during this period; much practice is required to accomplish this. To increase the probability of success during this stage of development, children should be encouraged to express themselves verbally. Constantly correcting word pronunciations and grammatical forms will often hinder a child's development. Rather than inhibiting a child at this time by overcorrection, Erikson (1980) suggests that adults model the speech desired. Accordingly, adults should avoid speaking in unnatural ways, such as baby talk, which will only confuse a child's efforts.

There is a clear relationship between the way parents behave during this period and a child's self-confidence and sense of autonomy. The most productive patterns are those in which parents provide an imaginative environment that stimulates speech and exploration. Supportive parents constantly involve their children in stimulating activities during which they question and elicit a child's ideas. This indirect form of teaching, in combination with the experience of self-initiative, establishes the basis for a child's feeling of competence. As children learn independence and begin to see themselves as active and effective participants in the management of their environment, they establish a strong foundation on which to build a healthy and maturing personality.

Unfortunately, a child will not always successfully navigate through the demands of this period. Sometimes children develop a sense of shame because of their failure to develop independence effectively. When parents or other adults fail to provide stimulating experiences, restrict activity too narrowly, ignore the need for attention and love, and deny or harshly criticize expression, children will not advance and may be prevented from developing a productive and well-balanced personality. Their sense of shame will limit their ability to engage life directly and confidently.

The third stage of Erikson's (1980) theory is concerned with *initiative versus guilt*. Children develop these personal characteristics during the third through sixth years. This period especially affects a child's gender identity. While in the previous stage of development children generally began to explore sexual identity, they now begin to identify with appropriate male and female models and behave in accordance with what they see. It is especially important to reinforce their sexual identity at this point so that they will establish the sense of self needed to successfully advance to the next stage of development.

Children naturally possess feelings of inferiority at this time. To avoid establishing a sense of guilt about their desires and inabilities, they should be assured that they will eventually be able to do what they see adults doing. Taking personal initiative is inherently connected to children's personal identity and overcoming this sense of inferiority. According to Erikson (1980), a child possesses the capacity to overcome the difficulties of this stage as the child

> (1) learns to move around more freely and more violently and therefore establishes a wider and, so it seems to him, an unlimited radius of goal; [as] (2) his sense of language becomes perfected to the point where he understands and can ask about many things just enough to misunderstand them thoroughly; and (3)[as] both language and locomotion permit him to expand his imagination over so many things that he cannot avoid frightening himself with what he himself dreamed and thought up. (p. 78)

When children have been successfully weaned of their sole reliance on adults for meeting their needs, adults will have been successful in supporting them in the development of their personal identities. As children express independence by effectively meeting the demands of various situations, they develop greater confidence in their own competence and enhance their growing sense of self.

During Erikson's (1980) fourth stage, industry versus inferiority are the primary issues. From approximately six until 12 years of age, children turn away from their focus on parents to a more generalized focus on the world in which they find themselves, most notably with friends and at school. During this period, children learn to communicate with others in an increasingly less ego-centered approach. By behaving in this manner, children free themselves from the isolation and control related to their total dependence on parents. They become more socially oriented, forming social alliances that reflect their growing interests in other people and in things outside their family and home. During this time, they exert enormous amounts of energy trying to perfect their skills in dealing with the demands of the world. Erikson describes the focus of this period:

> While all children need their hours and days of make-believe in games, they all, sooner or later, become dissatisfied and disgruntled without a sense of being useful, without a sense of being able to make things and make them well and even perfectly: this is what I call a sense of industry. Without this, the best-entertained child soon acts exploited. It is as if he knows, and his society knows, that now that he is psychologically a parent, he must begin to be somewhat of a worker and potential provider before becoming a biological parent. . . . As he once untiringly strove to walk well and to throw things away well, he now wants to make things well. He develops the pleasure of work completion by steady attention and preserving diligence. (p. 91)

During this period of developing greater self-sufficiency and independence, children are particularly stable emotionally. Also during this period, children experience the concrete operational period, when the world is seen as stable and predictable and shades of gray are unwelcome intrusions into their ideas about the world. As children learn new social, practical, and academic skills, they enhance their sense of industry. When they fail to do so, they develop a sense of inferiority that further limits their ability to develop personal competence. At this time, it is important to encourage children to actively engage the world, to explore and test themselves, and to work hard to achieve goals. With success comes the knowledge that their efforts have results. Children who fail to develop a sense of industry based on their skills in achieving goals will not achieve independence. Their sense of inferiority will diminish their capacity to meet the demands of the world.

Development of industry during this period occurs to a large extent where children spend most of their active time—in school and among friends. The experience in school is particularly important to children's development of self-confidence and skill mastery. Within the classroom, children can be given the opportunity to learn many new skills that will result in a growing ability to solve problems competently. With this accomplishment, the promise of adulthood made in an earlier age comes closer to reality.

The final period of personal development relevant to this topic occurs between the ages of 12 and 18 years. According to Erikson (1980), the formation of *identity,* or the failure of that formation, which he calls *identity diffusion,* is the main issue of the adolescent age. During this period, children undergo their most tumultuous changes, often causing them to behave in aggressive, confused, and unpredictable ways. It is a time of significant body system alterations that result in physically mature individuals capable of reproduction. But it is also a time when they begin to see the contradictions of the world more clearly, further increasing their emotional instability.

> But in puberty and adolescence all sameness and continuities relied on earlier are questioned again because of a rapidity of body growth, which equals that of early childhood, and because of the entirely new addition of physical genital maturity. The growing and developing young people, faced with the psychological revolution within them, are now primarily concerned with attempts at consolidating their social roles. . . . In their search for a new sense of continuity and sameness, some adolescents have to re-fight many of the crises of earlier years, and they are never ready to install lasting idols and ideals as guardians of a final identity. (p. 94)

Cognitively, adolescents leave the world of predictability where right and wrong are certain and where their skills have an immediate and direct effect on the environment in which they operate. As adolescents they begin to evaluate conditions, comparing what they see with what might be. They begin to separate the world around them from their own desires and perceptions. Objective reality begins to assert itself in the adolescent mind. They begin to understand and use metaphorical descriptions. The advancing adolescent considers the ideas and positions of others less egocentrically. They sometimes are able to put themselves in another's position, developing empathy and a need to change things.

Alternatively, with greater uncertainty and a heightened sense of self, children become particularly self-conscious as they advance into adolescence. In this state, they try to fit in by conforming to peer groups. They can be excessively egotistic, demand attention, and look for as many ways to conform as is possible. Their world becomes relativistic, where behavior is tested against rationalizations of their own and of their peers. Where they previously conformed to authorities' wishes, they may now rebel.

The effect of this change and uncertainty leads to an adolescent identity crisis. The successful evolution of personality during this period depends on the adolescent's ability to meet the demands of this stage of personal development successfully. If an adolescent overcomes the difficulties associated with this period, it is likely that he or she will have established a strong foundation for advancement into adulthood. If, on the other hand, a person has succumbed to these conflicts, the personality will not solidify. Instead, it will remain uncertain, diffuse, and alienated with little sense of purpose or satisfaction. To avoid this failure, Erikson (1980) strongly suggests that adolescents be given every opportunity to develop a sense of responsibility for themselves and others. Real, self-directed experience, working to meet the needs of others, and satisfying the demands of society will help an adolescent to develop purpose and a strong identity on which to build a mature adulthood.

## Implications of Erikson's Theory for Block Instruction

It is important to stress that a knowledge of the theories presented in this chapter is necessary for all teachers, regardless of the schedule their school uses. However, we now focus on these theories as applied specifically to block instruction. The scope of Erikson's theory permits us to see the needs and potential problems experienced by all children in their development toward adulthood. Each stage of development requires that adults provide the necessary environment and tools for children to succeed in overcoming the obstacles of the period in which they are operating. Children's behaviors and abilities expressed at each stage of development depend on the degree to which they successfully managed the issues of the preceding stage. If children fail to overcome difficulties or to learn the skills necessary to fulfill their growing responsibilities at any stage, problems will be compounded in each successive stage. It is important to make certain our instructional effort is effective and our knowledge and sensitivity to the transformations of childhood are substantial.

When Erikson's ideas about personality development are considered in conjunction with Piaget's theories about intellectual transformation, teachers have at their disposal a powerful perspective from which to view the conditions of childhood and adolescence. Teachers should evaluate their students from this theoretical perspective to determine children's readiness to learn. Teachers will have success in the classroom when they apply these ideas effectively. Dealing with a child's intellectual capacity as if it exists in isolation, separate from a child's personality, will not lead to effective instruction. This means that block teachers must consider the entire child, the cognitive and affective domains, and how to best use time when delivering instruction. All this must be kept in consideration if the faculty is going to build an effective culture for block scheduling. While blocking can positively affect the teacher, and that is important, we must keep our focus on the student.

# FOUR

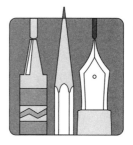

# Building the Block Culture in the School

Increasingly, as more schools have moved to the block, a distinct culture has developed. For schools to be successful on the block today, the faculty must accept a change in the culture of the school. This cultural transformation is more than a simple change in when the bells ring. The block culture allows for a school environment in which teachers and students have greater freedom in the instructional process. This means that in addition to faculty members, students and parents have to be willing to accept change. But although student and parent input and concerns should receive great attention, those of us involved with the block for 10 years or more know that the ultimate key to a successful conversion is the classroom teacher; teachers make or break this transformation.

For schools on a traditional schedule that are planning to look at block models, principals can start by conducting a survey during a faculty meeting. Along with the survey, a simple discussion of present school needs can elicit the level of interest needed to change perceptions about the block. Many teachers have misconceptions about the block, so it is imperative to begin research on scheduling methods and have solid answers for any inquiries. The top five perceptions that traditional teachers state as advantages and disadvantages about the block include are these:

### Advantages

1. Time to complete activities in one period

2. Fewer subjects for students at any one time

3. Increased planning time for faculty on a daily basis

4. Greater opportunity to practice effective teaching strategies

5. Time for review, teaching, and practice

### Disadvantages

1. Limited staff development during the initial stages of implementation

2. Motivating students and keeping their attention for an extended period of time

3. Teachers being unwilling or unable to change instructional strategies

4. Possible larger gaps of time between sequential courses

5. Fear of not enough time to cover the complete course content

Once the decision is made to move to the block, it is imperative that the block culture in the school maintain faculty confidence. School leaders must assure faculty members that the change process will be deliberate and will progress cautiously. The school should not move hastily into a block schedule without proper training of faculty and staff. Collecting research, visiting schools, and completing appropriate training takes one to two years. During these planning years, various opportunities for training should include mastering a minimum of FOUR major instructional strategies. Some strategies include synectics, cooperative learning, case method, inquiry, and concept attainment. (See Chapter 10 of this text for more in-depth coverage of instructional strategies.) In addition, the planning years should be spent realigning curriculum and developing instructional pacing guides.

Communication is essential. Positive communication among teachers helps to build confidence in block scheduling. Experienced teachers can help newer teachers work in teams in harmony. In addition, committees can be a vital tool in maintaining effective communication and monitoring success. They can also serve to keep the administration aware of developing activities and concerns. Maintaining effective communication should include frequent classroom visits and encouragement by the principal. Each faculty meeting should include a period of time allocated for talk on block scheduling success stories and problem issues.

When monitoring the implemented block schedule, lead teachers and school administrators should search for improved instructional techniques and successful classroom experiences. They should also monitor the degree to which test scores are affected and the extent to which students are adjusting. It is important to keep students involved and to know their feelings about the block and their classes. A survey of the students, as well as the parents, is a good way to learn about their feelings concerning the block schedule.

In the unfortunate event that the administration requires a unilateral move to the block or fails to seek faculty support, teachers may feel undervalued, angry, and adversarial. Resenting the change, teachers will not benefit from the philosophy of block scheduling as a reform tool. Reassuring teachers that the cultural change to the block will be completed in an appropriately paced and orderly fashion can help eliminate their insecurity. Many teachers retain a degree of wariness of the unknown. This is usually mild and will subside with periods of success. In more severe cases, teachers who have major reservations, but who have agreed to make the change, must be given special attention and greater reassurance.

### International and National Experience on Building Block Culture and How to Teach on the Block Schedule

In working with over 380 school systems in 48 states and five foreign countries, the author has found that there are three important factors for schools going to or remaining on block scheduling, or any extended learning periods beyond the traditional 50–55 minute schedule in maintaining and maximizing success. Listed below are factors for building culture related to instructional success, classified under the major concept of Instructional Insurance.

## INSTRUCTIONAL INSURANCE    ■

Within instructional insurance the author has found the embedded skills within this factor to be a clearly defined readiness among educators for continuous exploration and acceptance of change for refinement, multiple levels of staff development, masterful skills of with-in school team building, a focus on student achievement over teaching, and recognition of a hierarchy of instructional delivery systems.

As educators, we tend to think of readiness as the process at the beginning. In our comparison of numerous schools, the most effective schools as measured by student achievement and teacher, parent, and student positive attitudes were the *individuals* that implemented Continuous Exploration and Acceptance of Change for Refinement.

### Continuous Exploration and Acceptance of Change for Refinement

While there remains a high number of teachers in schools instructing on the block that had not received any formal staff development before using block scheduling, perhaps one of the biggest problems remaining is the lack of continuous staff development after the first year on the block.

Schools that experienced the most success are the schools that continue to have staff development such as the following:

- Planned activities for teachers throughout the year (school and/or district levels)
- Principals and Assistant Principals and Central Office Staff are involved in the staff development
- Creating and sustaining a teaching environment where teachers worked for refining teaching skills
- Modeling or sharing of a lesson or technique by a school faculty member who had been successful with the new idea
- Special staff development for using effective strategies for block scheduling with new or first-year teachers

## Focus on Student Learning Over Teaching

In addition to continuous exploration for improvement in the classroom, the most successful teachers are the ones who significantly changed the way they looked at instruction. Most educators, when beginning to teach, check the standard and related objectives, select the content and then determine *how best to teach* these facts, concepts, etc., *to* students. The most effective teachers on block are the teachers who have changed their entire paradigm from *being givers of knowledge to students* for academic achievement to the much more participatory approach of *being facilitators for learning to students* for academic achievement. Teachers using learning over teaching:

- showed a fundamental change in attitude that students learn better by participating directly into the learning process;
- used a variety of instructional strategies on a daily and weekly basis;
- were unafraid to take instructional risks;
- believed that true learning was more important than just test scores;
- allowed the students to have much control of the environment of the classroom as opposed to being rigid or totally teacher directed; and
- believed and knew that high schools are teaching content an ocean wide, but only an inch deep.

*Block Scheduling will be far more successful when teachers embrace and use a student-focused approach for students.*

## Awareness of the Relationship Between Teaching and Learning

Another set of findings are closely related to the above. The author classified effective teachers using what he has labeled as the "third tool" as a heightened awareness of the relationship that clearly exists between the teaching and learning process. As one of his former professors, R. L. Canady, is fond of saying, "It is not just seat time," and effective teachers learn this early in the process of moving to block scheduling. When asked in seminars throughout the country, "Does block scheduling improve academic achievement?" the author's answer is a quick "no," rather it is what the teacher *and* students do within the extended period. If students sleep for 50 minutes, these same students just sleep 90 minutes without a change in the relationship. The research that the author has done with Robert Algozzine and others shows that the block schedule, when maximized, allows for the greatest possible gain in student achievement and authentic learning. Effective teachers continually demonstrate the following:

- Seat time is mostly interactive and highly student focused.
- The degree of teacher and student interaction is based upon the *acceptable relationship* the teacher has with the student.

  1. Teacher respect is *earned* and not just expected (this is not the 1950s).

  2. Teachers have learned that to earn respect they have to give respect.

  3. Effective teachers knew student names, usually by the first day.

  4. Students are greeted positively by name, and not with a question about homework or an accusation.

Teachers focus more on student levels of learning

  1. Teachers believe and practice the fact that there are several levels and types of learning, regardless of the theory practiced.

  2. Teachers move quickly from lower level recall and comprehensive facts and concepts to embedding these into higher level activities requiring application, evaluation, etc.

  3. While academic achievement remains the major goal, the most effective teachers value creativity, individuality, and the entire range of what is often referred to as multiple intelligences.

  4. By far, the most effective teachers are the ones who ask questions over giving answers, and they know the importance of going *deeper in content*.

Operationally, teachers who continually prepared and focused on the above Tools for Success were the most successful. Within the framework, the most effective teachers, regardless of subject area within the school, and regardless of the model (4 × 4, A/B or Modified), were those who began the process of converting to block scheduling by preparing with In-School Teams.

In the early days of preparing for block scheduling, trainers, teachers, and principals collected pacing guides from any and all sources to help teachers in the transition. After many years of failure or hit-and-miss success, effective educators learned that the best method to prepare for transitioning to block scheduling is to do it within subject or content teams at the school level.

## Using With-IN-School Teams for Instructional Preparation

There are four extremely important elements effective teams follow in starting and/or sustaining instructional preparation into instructional practice:

- Curriculum Alignment
- Instructional Pacing
- Instructional Strategies
- Student Assessment

Curriculum alignment is an essential element in the total success of implementing the block. The first elements in curriculum alignment include scoping out and sequencing the units or content to be taught. In sequencing, educators examine the order of information or skills that must be taught to achieve the desired outcomes. For example, in the language arts program, teachers instruct readiness skills in reading at kindergarten to basic skills in elementary and middle schools to English in the high school. Teachers strive to put content in a meaningful order. Some courses, such as mathematics and science, are sequential and require a step-by-step approach. In processing skills such as observing, comparing, and inferring, there can be a definite order in which higher-order processing skills are developed. In the sequencing, evident patterns emerge at various levels in the middle schools and high schools. While often more flexible in the middle schools, in the high schools, course sequencing becomes extremely important to ensure the inclusion of all required content to be tested. Unfortunately, the practice of "scripted lessons" is becoming more common in urban high schools and, in some cases, the middle and elementary schools. Most subject content has been prescribed by various state departments of public instruction with some additions by local boards of education. For example, in most states, teachers will find biology being taught in the 10th grade; however, in other places, it may be taught in 11th or 9th grade. However, the scope of the content is similar. To be educationally sound, the material is taught in a sequence; the basic biology class is taught before advanced biology and usually before chemistry and physics courses. Before courses are to be scoped out for content, it is important that teachers know the courses to be taught for the semester and/or year. Curriculum Alignment, Instructional Pacing, Instructional Strategies, and Student Assessment will be presented in later chapters.

# FIVE

# Selecting the Best Fit

**C**urrently, there are several organizational methods of block scheduling. These methods are divided into three types: the 4 × 4 block schedule, the A/B block schedule, and the modified block schedule. The modified block combines *all* combinations. The author has seen over 50 different types of models, including 8-day rotating, the 3 × 3, the FAN (which is described in the next chapter on Middle Schools), and many others with different names. For a complete description of these and other models, please see the forthcoming book with Corwin Press, *Flexible Scheduling for America's Schools* by Watson, Queen, and White (2009). Please keep in mind that most modified block models have as the base either the 4 × 4 or the A/B model.

## THE 4 × 4 BLOCK SCHEDULE MODEL ■

Classes in the 4 × 4 model of block scheduling are taught in longer periods of approximately 90 minutes and meet for only a part of the school year, usually one semester (see Table 5.1). The 4 × 4 model is also known as the semester, or accelerated schedule, because only four courses are taught per semester. Students have the opportunity to take eight different classes in one academic year. Teachers teach three classes per semester and use the fourth period of their day for planning, which is an advantage for teachers. "Educators have always been concerned about having enough time to complete the course content. Because of that, they found themselves looking for ways to change the traditional six- or seven-period day." (Queen, Algozzine, & Eaddy, 1997, p. 251).

**Table 5.1**   The 4 × 4 Block Schedule

| Class Period (90 minutes) | First Semester | Second Semester |
|---|---|---|
| 1st period | Biology | Algebra 1 |
| 2nd period | Chorus | Health/Physical Education |
| LUNCH | LUNCH | LUNCH |
| 3rd period | ELP | English 1 |
| 4th period | Freshman Seminar | French 2 |

Unlike the A/B schedule, the 4 × 4 model further limits the focus of students to four classes per semester so that there are fewer homework assignments, quizzes, and tests. This allows for concentration on new topics and time for mastery. Students also have the opportunity to repeat failed classes within the same year and still graduate on time, which is an incentive to remain in school. Where applicable, many students opt for advanced study on and off campus since greater freedom is possible within the 4 × 4 block. For teachers, the 4 × 4 block reduces the preparation to three classes, having a total of between 50 to 90 students, depending on the size of the school. Planning must involve more than preparing the usual lecture. Various instructional strategies that meet individual learning styles, alternative assessments, and integration of content should be planned for students. Lunch periods in smaller schools have sometimes been reduced to a single 45-minute period that serves for club meetings, teachers' office hours, detention, transfer student remediation, and general remediation.

The 4 × 4 scheduling model does, however, raise questions about the ability of students to retain information over the long periods of time that may occur between courses. It is possible for a student to finish Algebra I in the fall of his or her 9th-grade year and then take the next math class in the spring of the 10th-grade year. Although it is advisable to take sequential building courses as closely together as possible, teachers on the 4 × 4 block have not noticed any great difference between students who had recently finished a prerequisite course and students who finished the same course some time earlier.

## THE A/B BLOCK SCHEDULE MODEL    ■

Alternative day schedules or A/B block schedules alternate periods within the day or week. The classes usually meet every other day for extended blocks of time or a combination of alternating blocks and shortened classes taught every day for the entire year. Other modifications may be made to the A/B model by doubling a blocked class so that "A" days are Monday and Tuesday, followed by "B" days on Wednesday and Thursday. Fridays are rotated each week between "A" and "B" courses (see Table 5.2). Problems may arise with the A/B schedule; because the course load for students is not focused on four courses at a time; the students are enrolled in eight courses for an entire year. Many students have also expressed confusion as to keeping up with whether a day is "A" or "B."

**Table 5.2**   The A/B Block Design

| "A" Day | "B" Day | "A" Day | "B" Day | "A" Day | "B" Day |
|---|---|---|---|---|---|
| MONDAY | TUESDAY | WEDNESDAY | THURSDAY | FRIDAY | MONDAY |
| Course 1 | Course 5 | Course 1 | Course 5 | Course 1 | Course 5 |
| Language Arts | Spanish 1 | Language Arts | Spanish 1 | Language Arts | Spanish 1 |
| Course 2 | Course 6 | Course 2 | Course 6 | Course 2 | Course 6 |
| Introduction to Computers | Math | Introduction to Computers | Math | Introduction to Computers | Math |
| Lunch | Lunch | Lunch | Lunch | Lunch | Lunch |
| Course 3 | Course 7 | Course 3 | Course 7 | Course 3 | Course 7 |
| Science | Social Studies | Science | Social Studies | Science | Social Studies |
| Course 4 | Course 8 | Course 4 | Course 8 | Course 4 | Course 8 |
| Health/P.E. | Band | Health/P.E. | Band | Health/P.E. | Band |

## THE MODIFIED BLOCK    ■

In the modified block, classes are arranged in differing lengths of time during a quarter, semester, or year; it might be found in many schools throughout the country. The modified block offers students the opportunity to take a variety of classes, ranging in periods of 30 to 180 minutes in length. For example, if classes are typically 90 minutes in length on a particular block schedule, one period of the day may be modified by dividing it into two 45-minute sections, allowing students to take an additional course (see

Table 5.3). Carroll (1990) asserted that every high school in the nation could increase course offerings and reduce the total number of students with whom a teacher works each day by more than half. Seminars dealing with complex issues can be offered with greater flexibility for a more productive instructional environment. This flexibility is the strength of the modified block schedule. From the author's experience of working with schools throughout the United States, he has found that there really are few pure 4 × 4 or A/B models used. Most schools have modified a grade level, subject area, or both to accommodate their students and provide the best fit for their schools. In fact, he has seen 56 different modified models, with descriptions such as floating, rotating, revolving, expanded, etc in the schedule title.

**Table 5.3** The Most Typical Modified Block Schedule

| Class Period (90 minutes) | First Semester | Second Semester |
|---|---|---|
| 1st period | Biology | Algebra 1 |
| 2nd period | Chorus | U.S. History |
| LUNCH | LUNCH | LUNCH |
| 3rd period | English 1 | English 2 |
| 4th period | Band (45 minutes) | Band (45 minutes) |
| | P.E. (45 minutes) | Art (45 minutes) |

In 1994, Carroll reported his findings from a study of eight high schools that used a type of modern, block plan known as the Copernican Plan. His findings included improved student attendance, a decrease in suspensions, reductions in dropout rates, greater content mastery seen in higher grades and credits earned, and a favorable rating for the Copernican Plan compared with the traditional schedule. With these approaches becoming more widely used, educators began pushing for and rushing to the block. After high school teachers learned the value and benefits of the block, middle school educators raised the banner for block scheduling in their schools.

## New Lesson Designs

Listed below are three different classroom designs that have been used with great success, regardless whether the design is a 4 × 4, or A/B or modified. The designs are used to show how teachers used instruction in the 90–minute periods (Queen & Algozzine, 2007). In consulting with schools and districts today, the author teaches these models as more advanced models for designing and delivering instruction, especially the last three designs.

### Traditional Instructional System

30/30/30 Minutes Class Structure

- First 30 Minutes
  Detailed Review
  Instructional Objective
  Teacher Input (Lecture/Demonstration/Discussion)

- Second 30 Minutes
  Student Small Groups
  Investigate, Discover, or Complete Tasks
  Students Practice or Experiment

- Last 30 Minutes
  Usually Return to Large Group
  Debriefing with Students and Teacher
  Teacher Closure of the Lesson
  Student Assessment

### Transitional Instructional System

20/40/30 Minutes Class Structure

- First 20 Minutes
  Detailed Review
  Instructional Objective or Inquiry Question
  Limited Teacher Input/Student Presentation
  Cooperative Groups, Case Study, Inquiry

- Second 40 Minutes
  Student Organization/Focus
  Individual or Group Investigation
  Experiments, Model Building, Projects
  Researching New Information

- Last 30 Minutes
  Individual Presentation OR Sharing
  Group Presentation or Comparisons
  Individual, Group, Class Assessment
  Teacher-Student Closure
  Preparation for Next Meeting Time

### Personalized Instructional System

90 Minutes Class Structure
　　Transformational Focus
　　Individual or Same Need Group
　　Individual or Group Contract
　　Use of Any and All Strategies

Observations, surveys, and interviews over the past five years have concluded that in successful classrooms (where students achieve in the top 25% academically and have a positive attitude about learning), about 72% of the teachers use the Traditional Instructional System on an almost daily basis. This was the purpose of designing block scheduling for teachers. In about 28% of the classes, cutting across all subject areas (including math), teachers are using a more advanced method of teaching on the block: The Transitional Block Instructional System.

In the traditional block, successful teachers have expanded the planned block into three phases where students receive content through usually one or two methods and then move to the second phase to work in groups testing out hypotheses, completing tasks, or conducting inquiry activities. Once the groups, teams, or pairs get back into the whole class for the third phase of the lesson, they share their findings, results, or models, etc., with the class. Again, this was the intention for changing to a block model. Students are more involved in the learning process and that has been a great step forward. Today, though, it is estimated that a large percentage of teachers (32–36%) throughout the high schools in the nation, are not using this model effectively. Many still cling to the 55–minute period lecturing and then allow students to spend the remaining amount of time completing homework assignments, involved in play, or doing nothing.

In the transitional model, teachers have moved to a higher level of teaching by incorporating more student-engaged activities in the instructional process. Again, across all subject areas, there are teachers who have made the transition to thinking bigger and operating with a more personalized approach to teaching. In this model, content is usually given in larger chunks such as the entire unit or integrated concepts that are taught from a student-centered approach, usually over a three-day period of time. Teachers using the Transitional Approach focus more on moving deeper into the content as opposed to spreading so wide. Many university professors have been heard complaining that students come from the high school with knowledge that is perceived as "a mile wide and an inch deep." Teachers are often required to teach so many standards that it becomes easy to become focused on just "getting through the material" and with this there becomes an imbalance of content width and depth. It becomes too easy to fall into the trap of covering material as opposed to really enabling student learning to occur.

Transitional teachers use themes, topics, or even book chapters for content, but instead of giving the content to the student directly, these teachers set up a system for indirect teaching. Contracts, modules, web activities, a variety of inquiry methods, and ever-changing grouping patterns from shared pairs to small groups to individual investigation were used. As can be seen from the model, students meet usually for about 20 minutes (once they have received or selected their assignments) sharing with the teacher and other student groups what was learned or completed on the previous day. The time limit varies from 10 to 25 minutes according to topics and class size.

**Table 5.4**  Advanced Lesson Designs for Use With Block Scheduling

| Type | Design | | Components/Responsibility/Grouping | | Time Focus | Direction |
|---|---|---|---|---|---|---|
| I | Traditional Pattern in Minutes 10 20 40 10 10 | 10 | Review/Objective (T) | LG | Single Period for One Day | Teacher Directed |
| | | 20 | Instructional Input (T) | Large Group | | |
| | | | Lecture | | | |
| | | | Demonstration | | | |
| | | | Directed Discussions | | | |
| | | 40 | Student Activity (S) | SG, Pairs, Triads | | |
| | | | Workbook | | | |
| | | | Experiment | | | |
| | | | Problem Solving | | | |
| | | | Simulation | | | |
| | | 10 | Debriefing/Assessment (T/S) | LG | | |
| | | 10 | Closure (T) | LG | | |
| II | Transitional Pattern in Minutes 10 20 45 15 | 10 | Review/Objective | SG | Multiple Periods for 3–5 Days | Teacher-Student Shared |
| | | 20 | Instructional Input (T/S) | Large Group | | |
| | | | Inquiry | | | |
| | | | Discovery | | | |
| | | | Case Method | | | |
| | | | Cooperative Learning | | | |
| | | 45 | Student Activity (S) | SG, Pairs, Triads | | |
| | | | Research (Days 1–3) | | | |
| | | | Presentations (Days 4–5) | | | |
| | | 15 | Assessment/Closure (T/S) | LG | | |
| III | Personalized Pattern in Minutes 30 50 10 | 30 | Focus/Checkpoint (S/T) | Individual | Extended Periods Two or Three Weeks OR Complete Semester | Student Focused |
| | | | Seminars | | | |
| | | | Tutorials | | | |
| | | | Case Studies | | | |
| | | | Mini Socratic Seminars | | | |
| | | 50 | Student Activity (S) | Shared Pairs Individual | | |
| | | | Research/Projects/Products | | | |
| | | | Individual Contracts | | | |
| | | 10 | Debriefing/Assessment/ | SG/ Teams | | |
| | | | Closure (S/T) | | | |

Students spend most of the class time, usually from 35 to 45 minutes, working in their teams or pairs, investigating content, collecting and analyzing data, solving problems, completing a simulation, etc., and preparing to do a major individual presentation or provide a major work product for class. The options and combinations are only limited by the teacher. Students return back to the large group for the remaining part of the class period to share findings, report data, or make informal or formal presentations. Here true learning takes place.

It is exciting to see a master teacher work the groups, often pulling individuals or groups together for additional assistance or sharing new content, or even adding or modifying situations to make learning more challenging.

In the remaining percentage of extremely successful classrooms, teachers are going beyond expectations and setting up what is labeled as the Personalized Instructional System. In this approach, the methods varied as greatly as did the teachers. Again, these teachers were representative of all disciplines. While some classes may appear chaotic, the teachers were extremely organized and knew where each student was academically in the class. Most of these teachers used informal or formal diagnostic instruments to determine the abilities of each child or modified the class structure every few days as some students advanced and others needed more time or assistance. Individual contracts (or assignments that were individualized for periods ranging from one to ten days) were used either to help students to manage writing projects or to build models, conduct experiments, etc. Some assignments covered weeks, while others covered as little as one class period. More technology is used in most classes, but one geometry teacher did each class based on paper and board work, and reassessed each student daily for progress. Interestingly, she teaches in an urban school where students are involved in gangs and learning is not the major goal of the students, but her students score among the highest performing students on state tests. In addition, of the 45 to 50 match teachers in her school system, she has the largest number of students attend and complete a four-year college program.

While most teachers are unable to give the time that Ms. M. does to her classes, with careful preparation and ample time to plan instruction, all can personalize their classes much better than usual. For more detail on personalizing instruction on the block schedule please visit the Web site www.blockscheduling.com.

# SIX

# Block Scheduling in the Middle School

## THE MIDDLE SCHOOL DEFINED ■

There is really no established or set definition for the middle school. Typically, school systems place Grades 6, 7, and 8 in the middle schools. Nevertheless, the main purpose behind the middle school movement is to recognize that early adolescence is a distinct stage in development. The task for middle schools is to protect, nurture, counsel, and teach the individuals at this unique stage of life (Farmer, Gould, Herring, Linn, & Theobold, 1995). Many educators believe there are five to seven program characteristics that make the middle school unique. The more characteristics or concepts that are present, the greater the chance that the purpose of the middle school can be achieved.

The characteristics of the middle school are usually described in programmatic terms such as

Team teaching/interdisciplinary teaching
Block classes or periods
Advisor program/advisor/teacher or student mentor
Exploratory studies/electives
Interactive instructional strategies
Basic subjects or core curriculum
Effective transitions

**63**

While all of these characteristics are important in their various forms, the author is focusing on the first three in this chapter. Instructional strategies will be discussed in detail in later chapters. (Queen, 2002; Rettig & Canady, 2000; DiBiase & Queen, 1999; Russell, 1997; Farmer et al., 1995; George & Alexander, 1993).

## ■ CHARACTERISTICS OF THE MIDDLE SCHOOL TEAM

### Team Teaching/Interdisciplinary Teaming

The grouping of students and teachers is an important characteristic of the middle school concept. One of the most important grouping concepts is interdisciplinary teaming. Students are organized into heterogeneous teams of 70 to 150 students (Farmer et al., 1995). It is important to note that they are not grouped by ability, race, sex, or any other specific characteristic. The teams can be established by grade level or they can be multiage. Multiage grouping allows students to stay on the same team with the same teachers throughout their middle school years (McClure, 1998). The teaming approach allows teachers to meet the individual student's needs by providing a variety of groupings within their teams.

Two to five teachers are usually organized in areas of math, science, social studies, and language arts. In this professional collaboration, teachers are involved in an interactive process that brings staff members together to make decisions (Gable & Manning, 1997). The teaming approach allows for better communication and understanding among the disciplines. There are also nonacademic benefits to interdisciplinary teaming. For example, teachers can better deal with discipline issues when they work together on a regular basis. Students tend to be more comfortable discussing problems or asking for advice because they interact with fewer teachers. Consequently, teachers are better able to serve the needs of those students.

### Block Classes or Periods

One of the most important concepts in middle school is the schedule. The schedule serves many functions. According to Rettig and Canady (2000), the schedule

> provides a more reasonable workload for teachers and students. . . . determines the number of student/grades/records for which a teacher must be responsible . . . can reduce how frequently students and teacher teams change classes . . . determines how many teachers a student must interact with on any given day/term/year. . . . [and] can fundamentally affect the relationship among staff and between staff and students. (pp. 6–7)

Although the schedule is a critical component for middle school, it must not be allowed to dominate and must still be flexible enough to meet the students' needs.

Interdisciplinary teams cannot use the traditional schedule if they truly want to meet the needs of the adolescent student. With a block scheduling approach, the academic courses are scheduled within a large block of time, and other subjects, such as art, music, drama, physical education, and foreign language, are scheduled during shorter time periods. These other subjects are designed to be, and should remain, exploratory in nature. The focus of the schedule should be on the core academics.

Block scheduling in the middle school setting offers many advantages. For example, teachers have a common planning time for team collaboration and conferencing. The interdisciplinary teams have the flexibility to schedule classes to meet student needs. Other advantages to consider are that teachers can team teach in any given subject area, can more easily integrate the disciplines, and can more easily schedule field trips, speakers, and community projects (Farmer et al., 1995).

There are many block scheduling models for the middle school. Some use variations of the $4 \times 4$ or A/B designs used by the high schools. Rettig and Canady (2000) recommend a simple procedure that allows each interdisciplinary team to create its own schedule for the school year. First, the specific number of time modules needs to be determined. The schedule of events that occur outside "team time" must be plugged in. These events include lunch and exploratory time slots for specific teams (Rettig & Canady, 2000). It has also been recommended that once the core subjects are plugged in, the academic courses rotate. This prevents a course from meeting exclusively in the early morning or late afternoon (Rettig & Canady, 2000).

## Advisory Programs

One of the most important characteristics of the middle school concept is the adviser/advisee program. The program developed from a commitment to meet the needs of the adolescent student. One teacher works with a small group of students—typically, between 20 and 30. All teachers, including art, physical education, and life skills teachers have a group of students as advisees. Every student needs to have a positive relationship with at least one adult in the school. This is such an important concept that time is provided for advisement daily. Students are provided with an "adult advocate" who knows each one personally and can help in making responsible choices.

Student academic progress is monitored on a regular basis, and parents are contacted to provide information about the student's progress. When teachers take this responsibility seriously, students have someone in the school with whom they can talk and who can arrange help for them, both of which help to prevent student problems (Farmer et al., 1995).

## ■ BENEFITS OF THE BLOCK SCHEDULE IN THE MIDDLE SCHOOL

DiBiase and Queen (1999) believe that the middle school is prime for gaining the benefits of the block. In the middle school model, block scheduled classes involve blocking math/science and language arts/social studies with the expectation that instructional time within the blocks be adjusted as needed. However, any additional time provided to one of the paired subjects is at the expense of the other.

Many reform documents recommend lengthening the amount of time that middle grades students spend in a learning environment. In its report *Turning Points: Preparing American Youth for the 21st Century,* the Carnegie Council on Adolescent Development (1989) cautioned against limiting classes to 40 or 50 minutes and emphasized the need for concentrated time blocks of learning: "Students need time to learn and teachers should be able to create blocks of time for instruction that best meets the needs of students, responds to curriculum priorities, and capitalizes on learning opportunities such as current events" (p. 52). Furthermore, the report asserts that for most adolescents, the shift from elementary to junior high or middle school means moving from a small neighborhood school and the stability of one primary classroom to a much larger, more impersonal institution. In this new setting, teachers and classmates will change as many as six or seven times a day. This constant shifting creates formidable barriers to the formation of stable peer groups and close, supporting relationships with caring adults. The chances that young people will feel lost are enormous (Hackmann, 1995).

Time management is usually perceived as the most important tool that administrators use in scheduling the school day. Time management, however, is not the only concern that educators have in developing a successful schedule. A continual search for the best way to meet the needs of all students remains a primary focus. Block scheduling makes time more than just a tool. As such, block scheduling provides choices and various alternative means to address key factors in middle schools today. In addition, block or flexible schedules can be configured to meet any middle school's physical plant, student management, accountability, assessment, instructional, and fiscal needs. As such, block scheduling plays an integral role in helping define the school's climate.

## ■ SHORTFALLS OF THE TRADITIONAL SCHEDULE

Traditionally scheduled middle schools are generally organized around six to eight daily periods of instruction. The length of these periods ranges anywhere from 40 to 55 minutes, with three to five minutes for changing classes. In these short instructional periods, course content rather than the students' learning needs becomes the teachers' focus. Middle grade students find themselves overwhelmed by six to eight different teachers, a disjointed curriculum, several sets of class rules, multiple homework assignments, and stacks of books. The typical day for a middle school student with this type of schedule consists of several different classes, an advisory period, and lunch—all in different locations—in a six-and-a-half hour day. Students are expected to accumulate fragments of information and are tested on how well they can memorize details and facts. This is not a schedule that fosters reflection (Carroll, 1990).

Not only do the students languish in the 40- to 55-minute period, teachers are limited in the types of instructional strategies they are able to use. Just as in the high school, lecture is the most efficient way to expose students to a large amount of information in a short time frame. Highly effective teaching strategies such as cooperative learning, exploration, concept attainment, inquiry, role-playing, and simulations are difficult to implement in a span of 20 to 35 minutes (Canady & Rettig, 1995a). In addition, a six- to eight-period day promotes isolation of teachers and works against teaming, a practice that is integral for effective middle school instruction. Also, short periods favor the compartmentalization of knowledge rather than an integration of the curriculum. Teachers are unable to get to know their students as individuals because a great deal of their daily energy is spent monitoring student movement through the halls up to eight or nine times a day, recording attendance in as many as eight classes, and recording grades for as many as 150 or more students (Miller, 1997). As the student population increases in diversity, teachers must struggle to meet the emotional and academic needs of heterogeneous classes in which they may not have time for either effective instruction or authentic assessment.

## THE FLEXIBLE/ALTERNATE/NAVIGATE (FAN) MODELS ■

Queen's flexible/alternate/navigate (FAN) block models, particularly the 3 × 2 FAN, are the most effective block schedules to implement at the middle school level. The 4 × 4 and the A/B block are better suited to meet the teaching and learning needs at the high school level. The 3 × 2 and related modified models of block schedules meet the needs of middle grades learners. In the FAN models, classes meet either every day or every other day. The master schedule includes an advisory and a combination of core and elective classes. Classes meet for either extended or shortened blocks of time. Classes are taught on a yearly or semester basis. Teachers teach four or five periods per day and use the remaining period(s) for both individual and/or team planning. Students carry anywhere from five to six classes. Table 6.1 depicts the basic framework of the 3 × 2 model. By way of example, the scheduling of science and social studies is highlighted.

In the basic 3 × 2 schedule, three classes meet in 90-minute blocks (Blocks A, B, and C) and two classes meet for 45 minutes a day (Block D).

**Table 6.1**   The 3 × 2 Model

| The Basic Schedule | | | | | |
|---|---|---|---|---|---|
| | *Monday* | *Tuesday* | *Wednesday* | *Thursday* | *Friday* |
| 90 min. | Block A | Block A | Block A | Block A | Block A |
| | Language Arts | | | | |
| 90 min. | Block B | Block B | Block B | Block B | Block B |
| | Mathematics | | | | |
| 90 min. | Block C | Block C | Block C | Block C | Block C |
| | Science/Social Studies | | | | |
| (90 min.) | Block D | Block D | Block D | Block D | Block D |
| 45 min. | Elective | | | | |
| 45 min. | Elective | | | | |
| | Advisory | Advisory | Advisory | Advisory | Advisory |
| *Science/Social Studies: Alternate Days* | | | | | |
| Block D | Social Studies | Science | Social Studies | Science | Social Studies |
| Week 1 | | | | | |
| Block D | Social Studies | Science | Science | Social Studies | Social Studies |
| Week 2 | | | | | |
| *Science/Social Studies: Semester* | | | | | |
| Block D | Social Studies | Social Studies | Social Studies | Social Studies | Social Studies |
| Semester 1 | | | | | |
| Block D | Science | Science | Science | Science | Science |
| Semester 2 | | | | | |

Classes can meet every day or alternate on an A/B schedule. In the A/B configuration, Monday and Wednesday are "A" days and Tuesday and Thursday are designated "B" days. Fridays can rotate each week between "A" and "B" courses or contain a shortened schedule during which all classes meet. Blocks A through C meet for the whole year, whereas the classes in Block D can meet on either a yearlong or semester basis. Science and social studies are offered during Block D. In addition, Fridays can be used to implement special exploratory and research courses, electives, seminars, clubs, or assemblies.

Queen (2009) has developed eight major FAN block scheduling models. Tables 6.2 and 6.3 demonstrate two such examples.

**Table 6.2** The Eight-Period Queen Model

| The Basic Schedule | | |
|---|---|---|
| Period | Time Allotment | Description |
| 1 & 2 | 90 minutes | Language Arts: Block A—This class meets daily or on alternating days for a 90–minute block of time. |
| | 90 minutes | Mathematics: Block B—This class meets daily or on alternating days for a 90–minute block of time. |
| 3 & 4 | 45 minutes Science/Social Studies | Mini-Block C, or if combined with Mini-Block D below, it will become a full 90-minute period or Block C |
| | 45 minutes Science/Social Studies | Mini-Block D |
| 5 & 6 | 45 minutes Elective | Mini-Block E |
| | 45 minutes Elective | Mini-Block F |
| 7 & 8 | Advisory or Club Period or 45-minute elective | Mini-Block G, or if combined with Mini-Block F for designed times, daily or weekly, it can become a full period |

| EXAMPLE Science/Social Studies: Alternate Days (Weeks 1, 2, 3, or Alternate Semesters 1 & 2) | | | | |
|---|---|---|---|---|
| | Monday | Tuesday | Wednesday | Thursday | Friday |
| Per. 3 Week 1 | Social Studies | Science | Social Studies | Science | Social Studies |
| Per. 4 Week 2 | Science | Social Studies | Science | Social Studies | Science |
| Per. 3 & 4 Semester 1 | Social Studies | Social Studies | Social Studies | Social Studies | Social Studies |
| Per. 3 & 4 Semester 2 | Science | Science | Science | Science | Science |

The FAN block model provides the middle school with an almost lim-itless number of scheduling options. Classes can be offered in combina-tions of 90-, 45-, and 30-minute blocks of time. This allows for core and elective classes to be configured in the format that best serves the needs of the students. Table 6.2 shows how the FAN model can be embedded into an eight-period day. In this model, the school day is divided into two 90-minute and four 45-minute blocks of time.

- Classes in Blocks A and B meet daily for 90 minutes.
- Classes in Mini-Blocks C through G meet either daily or on alternat-ing days for combinations of 45- and/or 90-minute blocks of time.
- Mini-blocked classes are either yearlong or semester length in dura-tion. In this model, science and social studies are scheduled during Periods 3 and 4 using either Science and Social Studies every day, all year long, for 45 minutes each; or alternate days with Science taught for 90 minutes one day and Social Studies taught for 90 minutes the next day; or teaching the alternate semester model with Science taught during both mini-periods for the first semester and Social Studies the second semester.

Table 6.3 depicts a FAN block schedule configured around a seven period day.

- The class in Block A meets daily or on alternating days for a 90-minute block of time.
- The classes in Mini-Blocks B through D meet daily and/or on alternat-ing days for combinations of 30- and/or 60-minute blocks of time.
- The classes in Mini-Blocks E and F meet daily and/or on alternat-ing days for either two 45-minute or one 90-minute block of time.

The model in Table 6.3 provides a great amount of flexibility when scheduling classes. This model allows for the scheduling of core and elec-tive courses, an advisory, one or more exploratory classes, and club meet-ings, as well as seminar classes. In this model, science and social studies can be offered either during Periods 3 and 4 or during Period 6.

## ■ ADVANTAGES OF MODIFIED SCHEDULES IN THE MIDDLE SCHOOL

There are many advantages to moving to a modified block schedule, a number of which are presented below. The list was gleaned from com-ments made by middle school teachers who are teaching in schools that have adopted block scheduling (Queen, 2009). The 3 × 2 block schedule achieves the following:

- Relieves the fast-paced, pressurized atmosphere found in many middle schools.

**Table 6.3**   The Seven-Period Queen Modified Model

| *The Basic Schedule* | | | | | |
|---|---|---|---|---|---|
| *Period* | *Time Allotment* | *Description* | | | |
| 1 | 45 minutes | Block A—Language Arts | | | |
| 2 | 45 minutes | | | | |
| 3 | 30 minutes | Mini-Block B | | | |
| 4 | 30 minutes | Mini-Block C | | | |
| 5 | 30 minutes | Mini-Block D | | | |
| 6 | 45 minutes | Mini-Block E | | | |
| 7 | 45 minutes | Mini-Block F | | | |

**Block A:** Meets daily or alternating days for a 90-minute block of time (Language Arts)

**Mini-Blocks B–D:** Meet daily and/or on alternating days for combinations of 30– and/ or 60– minute blocks of time (electives, math, science, social studies)

**Mini-Blocks E & F:** Meet daily and/or on alternating days for combinations of 45– and/or 90–minute blocks of time (electives, math, science, social studies)

*Science/Social Studies: Alternate Days*

| | *Monday* | *Tuesday* | *Wednesday* | *Thursday* | *Friday* |
|---|---|---|---|---|---|
| Per. 3 & 4 or Per. 6 Week 1 | Social Studies | Science | Social Studies | Science | Social Studies |
| Per. 3 & 4 or Per. 6 Week 2 | Science | Social Studies | Science | Social Studies | Science |

*Science/Social Studies: Semester*

| | *Monday* | *Tuesday* | *Wednesday* | *Thursday* | *Friday* |
|---|---|---|---|---|---|
| Per. 3 & 4 or Per. 6 Semester 1 | Social Studies | Social Studies | Social Studies | Social Studies | Social Studies |
| Per. 3 & 4 or Per. 6 Semester 2 | Science | Science | Science | Science | Science |

- Offers teachers and students innovative ways to interact with one another and accomplish their objectives.
- Provides opportunities for creativity in classroom instruction designed to promote in-depth learning (inquiry, research, cooperative learning groups, thematic units, computers and other learning technologies, and hands-on learning experiences).
- Supports teaming by providing time for individual and/or team planning.
- Facilitates integration of the curriculum.
- Cuts the number of class changes and movements that large groups of students make in one day.
- Reduces the number of administrative tasks performed in one day by teachers and students.
- Improves the student-teacher ratio so that teachers can know more about each student's individual learning and social needs.
- Helps teachers make effective use of planning time by reducing the number of courses taught in one day.
- Matches learning time to the learner and to the course content.
- Results in fewer discipline problems.
- Provides time for one-to-one interaction between students and teacher.
- Provides time for teachers to get to know their students and develop better rapport.
- Establishes a classroom environment that is more amenable to students.

The major advantage of the FAN model is that it allows for the schedule to be configured so that it meets the individual and collective needs of middle grades learners. FAN block scheduling gives individual students the opportunity to experience a wide variety of innovations, and this can bring about a positive change in the school's climate.

The positive change in school climate is a result of the reduction in class size, the ability of students to engage in open-ended learning experiences, and the ability to flex schedules to meet the needs of an increasingly diverse middle grades student population. The change in the school and classroom is also positive when teachers move away from the "introduction-lecture-review" format and vary the presentation of content. If the class structure changes every 20 to 30 minutes, interest can be maintained. An experiential-based curriculum encompassing reflection, cooperative learning, critical thinking, process writing, and active learning experiences will keep the pace brisk and the students engaged. Teachers and students are often surprised by the positive change in the classroom climate; the atmosphere is charged with energy and bustling with activity.

Evidence of improved school climate can best be seen in the decrease of reported discipline problems and in the cleanliness reports of the custodial staff. Students move around the school fewer times throughout the day, and that produces a safe and less frenzied atmosphere, which can be significant for student motivation and management. The pace of the school day is slowed, while active learning and interaction among teachers and students is increased (Queen & Gaskey, 1997).

By varying instruction, teachers are able to reach students from diverse backgrounds and learning styles. Methods such as cooperative learning increase positive social attitudes, increase self-confidence and self-efficacy, and foster open-mindedness and appreciation of others. Class projects require interdependence, individual responsibilities, and specified goals. Along with varied teaching methodologies, block scheduling provides students with the time to demonstrate what they know.

## TEACHING IN THE BLOCK IN THE MIDDLE SCHOOL ■

Planning in block scheduling involves more than preparing a traditional classroom lecture. Instead, teachers need creative ways to actively engage students in learning. Various strategies that meet individual learning styles, authentic assessments, and integration of content can now be planned and implemented. Lunch periods can be reduced to 45 or 30 minutes, with the remaining time used for advisory time, club meetings, detention, and remediation.

One of the biggest concerns among teachers of block-scheduled classes is effective organization of instructional time. It is almost impossible to keep students' attention for a full 90 minutes. Passive sitting is especially inappropriate for the physical needs of middle school students (Hackmann, 1995). As such, teaching strategies in blocked classes must include more than the traditional chalk and talk. Cooperative learning, group problem solving, learning centers, and discovery learning are methods consistent with what is known about the social and emotional nature of middle grades learners. Following is a list of strategies designed to improve the quality of instruction in blocked classes:

- Make certain that all learning experiences are developmentally appropriate for middle grades students.
- Include topics of interest for the students. Make the content real and relevant.
- Have the students work alone and in collaborative groups.
- Incorporate the use of computers and other learning technologies.
- Use pacing guides for long-term planning.
- Structure learning experiences in a learning cycle format of preassessment, exploration, concept development, and concept application. This method of instruction incorporates the use of discovery and open-ended inquiry. This will allow the students to discover personal meanings and understandings and construct their own knowledge.
- Do not let the adopted text drive the curriculum.
- Use a variety of resource materials, including, but not limited to, texts, trade books, magazines (such as *Cable in the Classroom),* newspapers, and the Internet.

- Use assessment alternatives, including journals, portfolios, traditional pencil-and-paper tests, and performance-based tasks. This will provide students with more than one way to demonstrate what they know, what they can do, and what they have learned.
- Use higher-level questions.
- Engage the students in a variety of student-directed activities.
- Let students do the work. Teachers become assistants to the learning process. "Do not do anything that students can do!"(Bohince, 1996, p. 21).
- Make students take responsibility for a variety of tasks.

## ■ SUMMARY

With more schools adopting block scheduling to restructure the school day so that time is used more effectively, the author proposed the following question for research: What is the effectiveness of block scheduling when compared with traditional scheduling? After reviewing the work of several researchers, the author found the following advantages most often: increased instructional time, smaller classes, fewer classes to prepare for, more in-depth study of concepts, a decrease in the number of discipline problems, increased student-teacher interaction, students and teachers getting to know each other better, students earning more credits per year, increased planning time for teachers, better grades earned by students, and an opportunity for students to take more electives. The disadvantages found most often included: less content within the curriculum being covered, a decrease in the number of contact minutes with students in each class, difficulty in placing transfer students, and problems with the succession of courses. When asked, most students and teachers believe the block schedule to be successful and would not want to return to the traditional schedule. With so many schools finding success with the block schedule, its adoption is becoming increasingly popular. It has proven to be an effective means of restructuring the school day to use time more effectively. With more changes being made every day to increase its effectiveness, more schools will adopt the schedule, possibly making the traditional schedule obsolete. But before all this can happen, there is a need for further research on the long-term effects of block scheduling.

Middle schools exist to meet the educational and social needs of young adolescents. As such, middle school programming concepts need to be aligned with the social, biological, and cognitive development and achievement needs of middle grades learners. The programming concepts that middle schools have adopted to meet these needs include interdisciplinary teaming/blocked classes, advisory, exploratory, developmentally appropriate teaching strategies, and a core curriculum. There is a growing ethnic, racial, linguistic, and socioeconomic diversity within the middle school population. As such, there is a growing consensus that collaboration, student grouping, and scheduling options are essential if the needs of all middle grades learners are to be met.

Before the implementation of blocked classes, middle school schedules were generally organized around six to eight daily periods. In these short instructional periods, the teacher's focus is on course content and not on the student's learning needs. In addition, teachers are limited to the types of instructional strategies they are able to use. Block scheduling provides choices and alternative means to address these issues as well as other key factors in middle schools today.

The modified models are the most effective block schedules to implement at the middle school level. These models meet the needs of all middle grades learners by supporting each of the five middle school programming concepts. In addition, FAN block models provide middle schools with an almost limitless number of scheduling options. This allows for core and elective classes to be configured so that the individual and collective needs of middle grades learners are met. Adoption of either a $3 \times 2$ or some variant model will bring about a positive change in a middle school's climate.

Visit the special middle school link on the author's Web site and check out additional suggestions and ideas for teaching block at the middle school level.

# SEVEN

# The Elementary School on the Block

## A Note to Alice and Dorothy

*"If you don't know where you are going, then any road will get you there; and if you know and then get lost, just follow the yellow brick road. In either case, hold on to the shoes, Dorothy!"*

These words, adapted from two childhood classics, may best parallel the latest reform efforts of the past twenty-five years and the sense of hopeless frustration that has grown toward America's system of public education. Following the infamous report *A Nation at Risk: The Imperatives of Education Reform* in April of 1983, numerous governmental and educational agencies at the national, state, and local levels produced goals, standards, programs, and incentives to solve the problems of America's ailing system of public instruction. The general public blamed the schools and teachers. Teachers blamed parents. Apathy rose. Attempts to fix the schools were evident as presidents and governors pledged to make educational reform central in their administrations. Superintendents, principals, and parents focused on higher test scores. Every concerned citizen was aware that American children were behind academically when compared to children from other industrialized countries. Yet the needed route had no clear map. In fact, there was little agreement about where Americans wanted or needed the educational system to go.

In the recent past teachers were prepared to teach subject matter or specific skills such as reading and writing. They were expected to teach basic processing skills such as observing and classifying. Attempts at values clarification and citizenship development were included within the curriculum. For prospective teachers preparing to enter the teaching profession in the

21st century, these teaching skills will remain important, but additional skills will be needed. One teaching skill that will be needed by teachers is the skill to challenge a growing number of apathetic children and youth. Apathetic for a multitude of reasons, teachers of tomorrow will have to promote or create within these children and youth the desire to learn. This will be a most challenging task, but it must be achieved if the American system of public education is to survive. Designing curricula and instructional environments that revive the desire to learn and achieve must be an integral part of any road map to better education for which Americans keep searching.

What is educational reform? Reform can be viewed as a panacea to assure a concerned populace that change is being made to improve the condition of the nation's system of public education. It can be compared to a Band-Aid that is used to cover a festering wound to conceal the injury without treatment of the wound to promote a cure. The latest buzz words and educatnese deflect attention from the malaise. Assessment and research data are often interpreted to provide the results people *want* to hear. The educational system is ill; however, the Third Annual International Mathematics and Science Study (1997) found improvement in math and science for U.S. 4th-grade students at international levels among 26 nations included in the study. These results are positive but must be considered as small first steps. True reform is much more than covering the wound and allowing nature to take its course. It is the process of bringing about sustained change that goes beyond treating an ailing system of education.

## ■ NATIONAL CONCERNS: *A NATION AT RISK*

In recent American history two educational occurrences have brought great fear to the American people. The first was the launching of the spaceship Sputnik in 1959 and the scare that Russia was beating America in the space race and in science technology. The second was the publishing of *A Nation at Risk*. In 1980 when Ronald Reagan was elected President of the United States, he appointed Terrell Bell as Secretary of Education. Terrell Bell formed the National Commission on Excellence in Education in August of 1981. Secretary Bell wanted the commission to examine the U.S. educational system, report the quality of education, and make any suggestions for improvement. The results of this examination were written in *A Nation at Risk* (1983).

The authors of *A Nation at Risk* reported that the educational gap between America and other industrialized nations was slowly closing. The American educational system was being bombarded by social, political, and personal problems that were flowing into the classroom and interfering with the quality of education. Foreign students were gaining on American children academically, and in some areas foreign students were surpassing the children in the United States. Children in American schools had lost most of the gains made since wake of Sputnik. Political leaders wanted action to lessen the widening gap.

The authors of *A Nation at Risk* listed several indicators that America was at risk. Some of these indicators follow:

- When comparing American school children internationally, the United States was never first or second and was last seven times
- Many American adults were functionally illiterate, as were almost 40% of the teenage population
- Achievement was lower than 26 years ago when Sputnik was launched
- Declining test scores were reported on high school and college measures
- A decline in science achievement was observed
- Costly remedial education was on the increase (*A Nation at Risk*, 1983)

These declines in achievement occurred at a time when achievement needed to be higher than ever. Technology was booming and the need for highly skilled workers was increasing. Computers were becoming as common as televisions, and many lower skill jobs were being eliminated. Practically every profession across the country was being invaded by technology.

The authors of *A Nation at Risk* addressed many of the tools Americans already possessed to remodel the educational system, including voluntary efforts, traditions, natural abilities, commitment, dreams, dedication, understanding, ingenuity, and beliefs. The problem with these qualities was that they had been buried deep inside most people for the preceding thirty years and would only work if Americans found a way to bring them to the surface by creating a burning passion in society to revamp education (*A Nation at Risk*, 1983).

Bell (1993) described his appointment of the Commission after President Reagan declined a presidentially appointed commission. Reagan had campaigned on the issue of a lesser role of the federal government in education and had vowed to dismantle the Department of Education and the cabinet post, Secretary of Education. Included in the eighteen-member Commission group were scholars, corporate executives, and prominent educators. In a 1993 *Phi Delta Kappan* article, Secretary Bell stated his purpose in establishing the National Commission on Excellence in Education as to conduct a study of the nation's schools and evaluate the quality of American education. He wrote:

> *A Nation at Risk* was front-page news in virtually every daily newspaper across the country and was a feature story on all the network television news shows. . . . The commission's findings were much more negative than I had anticipated. (Bell, p. 593)

In the study researchers concluded that the fabric of the American public school system had deteriorated so much that the United States had lost much of its international status in the education of its youth. In conclusion, the National Commission on Excellence in Education (1983) found that the nation was at risk due to a "rising tide of mediocrity" which had permeated America's schools and society at large. The authors of the report warned that the status of the schools threatened the nation's future. Government and business leaders, educators, and the general public reacted with alarm to the Commission's report. They were unpleasantly surprised by the extensive negative findings.

American educators and the general public were in for a major shock. The Commission's (1983) findings about indicators which put Americans at risk educationally will be quoted, debated, and analyzed for decades to come. Many of these have been included in this chapter. Some of the major indicators of risk outlined by the Commission follow:

1. International comparisons of student achievement completed a decade before revealed that on 19 academic tests American students were never first or second and, in comparison with other industrialized nations, were last seven times.

2. Some 23 million American adults were functionally illiterate by the simplest tests of everyday reading, writing, and comprehension.

3. About 13% of all 17-year-olds in the United States could be considered functionally illiterate. Functional illiteracy among minority youth ran as high as 40%.

4. Average achievement of high school students on most standardized tests was now lower than 26 years earlier when Sputnik was launched.

5. Over half the population of gifted students did not match their tested ability with comparable achievement in school.

6. The College Board's Scholastic Aptitude Tests (SAT) demonstrated a virtually unbroken decline from 1963 to 1980. Average verbal scores fell over 50 points and average mathematics scores dropped nearly 40 points.

7. College Board achievement tests revealed consistent declines in recent years in such subjects as physics and English.

8. Both the number and proportion of students demonstrating superior achievement on the SAT (i.e., those with scores of 650 or higher) had dramatically declined.

When the curriculum of the sixties was compared to the curriculum of the late seventies a decline in quality was noticed. Students were taking more general courses and were allowed to choose up to 50% of their high school courses required to graduate. The authors of *A Nation at Risk* suggested establishing the five new basics; 4 years of English, 3 years of Math, 3 years of Social Studies, and one-half year of computer science in high school. These new basics would increase standards and give American high schools a starting place in redesigning education.

Another area of recommendation was standards and expectations. It was suggested that colleges and universities create more challenging standards. Grades, in addition to standardized test results, should be used to assess student achievement. Textbooks should be reevaluated to see if more challenging books were necessary. Any new materials should include the latest in technology or the latest research in a content area (*A Nation at Risk*, 1983).

Further findings of the Commission focused on time students spent in school and how effectively that time was used for instruction. Compared to students in other industrialized countries, the findings indicated that American students spent less time per day and fewer days per year in school. An average of 22 hours was used for instruction per week, significantly less time than the norm in many other industrial nations.

> In many elementary schools where time was used inappropriately, students received less than one-fifth of the instruction in reading comprehension than was received by students in classrooms where time was used more effectively.

The Commission (1983) also examined the role of teaching. It found that too many teachers came from the bottom quartile of college graduating classes. Teacher preparation programs were composed largely of courses in educational methods. Teacher salaries were low, causing many teachers to supplement their income with additional jobs after school and during summer break. Teacher shortages existed in the fields of science, mathematics, foreign languages, and special education.

Given these revelations, it was not surprising that the members of the Commission concluded that the findings indicated a threat so great that had the conditions which existed been imposed by an aggressive foreign power, our nation would have considered it an act of war.

Based upon these findings, the Commission (1983) provided recommendations for school improvement in five major areas: Content, Standards and Expectations, Time, Teaching, and Leadership and Fiscal Support.

1. *Recommendation A: Content* suggested that State and local high school graduation requirements be strengthened and that, at a minimum, all students seeking a diploma be required to meet increased minimum course requirements in the Five New Basics—English, mathematics, science, social studies, and computer science; with students planning continued study to also include two years of a foreign language.

2. *Recommendation B: Standards and Expectations* called for schools, colleges, and universities to adopt more rigorous and measurable standards and higher expectations for academic performance and student conduct, with an additional requirement for higher admission standards at four-year colleges and universities.

3. *Recommendation C: Time* acknowledged the necessity of restructuring the existing school day and/or establishing a longer school day or school year to provide more time for learning the New Basics.

4. *Recommendation D: Teaching* consisted of seven distinct and separate parts, each intended to improve the preparation of teachers or to make teaching a more rewarding and respected profession.

5. *Recommendation E: Leadership and Fiscal Support* challenged citizens to hold educators and elected officials accountable for providing the leadership and fiscal support and stability needed to bring about the proposed reforms.

Although the majority of the Commission's findings and recommendations focused on secondary schools, implications were strong that elementary schools had failed to prepare children for successful study in secondary education. The impact was felt at all academic levels and brought much reaction and debate.

## Reactions to *A Nation at Risk*

Reaction to *A Nation at Risk* was immediate. States established their own commissions to examine the problems of education statewide. Professional organizations in almost every academic discipline began to rethink standards and required content. Emeral Crosby (1993), a member of the National Commission on Excellence in Education, termed the decade of the 1980's the "At-Risk Decade." Crosby stated that while advancements in technology and commerce had improved at a steady pace, American education was still at great risk. He concluded that the concept of universal education found only in the United States and critical to its continuing national prominence was in such a state of disrepair that in spite of tremendous technological advances, the nation's social ills in the areas of family, health care, guidance, housing, child care, and compassion were overwhelming the education system's ability to cope.

The 1980s was the decade of being at-risk in education. Even with several reform efforts in process, the unclearly defined term "at-risk children" became a major focus for educators. A lack of civility appeared to govern the discussions about improving education in general. Without a clear national direction, effective schools, and an engaged system of parent support for schools, academic gains by these students were limited.

Theodore Sizer (1989) presented almost a comical reaction to what had been accomplished in the reform efforts after *A Nation at Risk*. He compared the reform effort to entering a war without weaponry, suggesting the nation's current course which required teachers to decrease the risk to the nation's future without the appropriate tools and the training to effectively use these tools was silly.

The literature was divided as to the impact of *A Nation at Risk*. According to Crosby (1993) and Goldberg and Renton (1993), gains had been made in several of the recommended areas. High school graduation requirements and college admission requirements were strengthened. The previously required one year of Math was increased to three years in ten states, four states increased Science requirements to three years, 37 states increased English to four or more years, and 28 states required three or more years of Social Studies (Goldberg and Renton, 1993). The content area of computer science boomed after *A Nation at Risk*. The number of schools owning computers increased from 18% in 1981 to 98% in 1991 (Crosby, 1993). Standards for athletes were raised, and the graduation rate of these athletes increased from 48.1% in 1984/85 to 56.5% in 1986/87 (Crosby, 1993). The school calendar was lengthened by 3–5 days in many systems. Although the cap of the school year remained 180 days, many of the schools that had shorter school years increased the length of the year. The recommendations on teaching received a lot of attention. Many districts began administering competency tests to practicing teachers. In 1990, thirty-nine states required passing of such competencies to become a teacher (Goldberg and Renton, 1993). College admission standards for education programs increased and the courses themselves were changed. Teacher salaries increased (Crosby, 1993).

The opposite end of the spectrum included those who thought *A Nation at Risk* was only a spark to the system which, without direction and support, would not go very far. Assays (1993) stated, "It made a scapegoat out of education when the problems reflected in our schools are a symptom of profound shifts in American life that need to be addressed in a broader societal context" (p. 9). Some agreed that the focus of *A Nation at Risk* was wrongly placed. It was good because it alerted the nation that there was a problem; however, the prime focus was on schools rather than the ever-changing community. Many acknowledged that a redesigning of communities as well as the school systems needed to occur. The focus could not be national in the beginning because not all communities and schools were starting at the same level for redesign. The focus needed to be school to school and community to community. An evaluation of what needed to be done in each school and each community regarding textbooks, attendance, teachers, administrators; quality of the buildings, poverty, etc. would be different for each school. Some would need slight changes and others would need extensive repair. Only when all schools were on the same playing field, might it possible to set standards across the board. However, the first challenge was to educate the players.

Edwards and Allred (1993) had some ideas as to why *A Nation at Risk* did not have a big impact on education. First, there was no financial support for changes that were too large anyway. *A Nation at Risk* met with a natural resistance to change which was increased by the fact that the changes were not created at the local level and, therefore, were not their own ideas. Given that educators and government officials could never agree on school improvement, one might think there was not agreement on the recommendations of *A Nation at Risk*. Finally, there was no strong leadership and time constraints limited the amount that could be accomplished.

Goodlad (1990) stated that there were two basic reform movements following *A Nation at Risk*. The first movement was "politically driven." In this movement national, state, and business organizations tried to cement an ill-defined reform effort. The second movement was "diffuse, sporadic, and local." This effort restructured or modified prior practices such as nongrading, teacher empowerment, and cooperative learning to improve test scores.

A decade after the infamous report, Terrell Bell (1993) gave his personal reaction to *A Nation at Risk* and reform efforts that had occurred since 1983. In his evaluation of the Commission's report and the present reform efforts, Dr. Bell stated that as a nation "we are still struggling ten years afterward with the problem of American Education" and challenged the leadership to provide the support for learning that is needed to educate students from all backgrounds.

Confirming these findings, the Department of Education (1993) released the results of the five year study, Adult Literacy in America, which measured the literacy of 26,000 randomly selected individuals. Irwin Kirsch, project director for the study, found that many of the respondents had basic word attack skills in decoding words for reading; however, respondents lacked skills in using the information for practical application or problem solving. Estimates from the study projected that half of American adults were illiterate in translating information to solve daily problems. Major findings of the study concluded that white Americans outscored all other ethnic groups. Black Americans had the lowest scores. Individuals with more formal education and those with higher salaries usually scored higher on the survey, although a low percentage of college graduates scored at the lowest levels.

In an alarming interview written for *Newsweek* (Kaplan, 1993), Kirsch stated that employers were concerned that new workers would lack the basic skills required to complete tasks in the changing workplace in the move away from a manufacturing society to an information society.

He further stated that many businesses had invested large sums of money to train employees in the basic skills they had not learned in school. In reaction to the findings of the study, former Secretary of Education William Bennett remarked, "Yeah, we're dumber than we thought we were."

On a more positive side Crosby (1993) reported that many of the Commission's recommendations had been implemented. Most apparent were the increased high school graduation requirements as colleges and universities raised their admission standards. Techniques and technologies in teaching science and mathematics had improved significantly. The number of computers in schools and classrooms had increased dramatically.

At the beginning of the last decade of the century, a major reform effort in response to *A Nation at Risk* was initiated at the national level. President Bush presented his ideas to the nation's governors.

## ■ *AMERICA 2000*

In April 1991, eight years after the release of *A Nation at Risk*, President George Bush and the nation's governors held an educational summit in

Charlottesville, Virginia and produced a document which was titled *America 2000: An Education Strategy* (1991). The six major goals detailed within the document were designed to direct national efforts in regaining status as a leader of nations. The six goals follow.

By the year 2000,

1. All children in America will start school ready to learn.

2. The high school graduation rate will increase to at least 90%.

3. American students will leave Grades 4, 8, and 12 having demonstrated competency in challenging subject matter including English, mathematics, science, history, and geography; and every school in America will ensure that all students learn to use their minds well, so they may be prepared for responsible citizenship, further learning, and productive employment in our modern economy.

4. Students will be first in the world in science and mathematics achievement.

5. Every adult American will be literate and will possess the knowledge and skills necessary to compete in a global economy and exercise the rights and responsibilities of citizenship.

6. Every school in America will be free of drugs and violence and will offer a disciplined environment conducive to learning.

The intentions of the authors of *America 2000* exceeded a listing of national goals and establishment of a timeline for reaching these goals. *America 2000* was intended to be a strategy for restructuring the public schools.

## Reactions to *America 2000*

In the 1992 Gallup/Phi Delta Kappa Education Poll (Elam, Rose, & Gallup, 1992), the public was asked to indicate their level of awareness of the six national goals. Of the population sampled, 28% or less of the respondents was aware of the six national goals. The percentages were slightly less when the data were analyzed with respect to respondents with no children in school.

Thirty three percent of public school parents were aware of Goal 1, "By the year 2000, all children in America will start school ready to learn." The public school parents also exceeded the general population and the population with no children in school in awareness of all goals, scoring near or slightly above the 30% level with the following exception. Awareness of the Goal 4, "By the year 2000, American students will be first in the world in mathematics and science achievement," was lowest for public school parents with 22% of those respondents aware of this goal. Surprisingly, the final group in the study, the nonpublic school parents, indicated greatest awareness of Goal 4 with a total score of 32%. This group also scored the highest on the awareness scale of all groups with Goal 3, "By the year 2000, American students will leave Grades 4, 8, and 12 having demonstrated competency in challenging subject matter, including English, mathematics, science, history, and geography," with a total awareness of 36% aware of this goal. In the remaining areas (Goals 1, 2, 5, and 6) public school parents scored higher than nonpublic school parents.

In the same Gallup Poll, these groups were asked to rate the progress being made toward achieving each goal. An overwhelmingly negative perception of the progress of *America 2000* was given by the respondents. In fact, more than more than half of the responders felt that there had been little or not progress in achieving individual goals and almost one-fourth either held no opinion or did not answer. These findings were consistent among all groups regardless of ethnic group, sex, and age.

During the election campaign of 1992 President Bush focused upon *America 2000* while his opponents criticized the education initiative. Opponents asserted that the schools and school districts which were showing great gains in the six areas had, in fact, been performing well prior to the development of *America 2000*.

At several low points in recent history, the federal government has stated national goals. Goals were set in the late 1950s after Sputnik and during the War on Poverty in the 1960s. Presidents were often quick to get involved. President Eisenhower established the Commission on National Goals in the 1950s, and President Reagan developed four goals in response to *A Nation at Risk* in the 1980's. Little if any noticeable improvement resulted from any of these reform attempts. The nation continued to remain in a state of jeopardy (Brown, 1992).

Sewall (1991) observed that one of the problems of *America 2000* was that no educators or parents had participated in the design process; yet these were the people most intimately engaged in the process of fulfilling the goals. He compared it to establishing goals for medicine without involving doctors. Would Americans stand for that? Would educators?

Howe (1991) noted that several items were left out of the design of *America 2000*. These items included school finance, an increase in the number of children living in poverty, and the growing cultural and racial diversity of American society. *America 2000* was doomed to failure without any financial support at the national and state levels.

When President George Bush and Secretary of State Lamar Alexander released *America 2000* in April of 1991, four main support elements were recommended for the educational system: national assessment of achievement, new schools to act as models of American schools, a challenge to increase the skills of adults, and *America 2000* communities which would work in conjunction with the new American schools (Lewis, 1991).

*America 2000* had several major omissions. Three were finances, poverty, and diversity. A possible explanation for the elimination of these issues may have been the misplaced idea that all schools were starting with enough resources to adopt *America 2000*. These issues were at the heart of the American educational problems and need to be addressed. *America 2000* did not offer any real assistance to American schools.

*America 2000* was supported by many in the beginning. Five hundred thirty five new American schools, one in each congressional district, would receive funding to begin a program to redesign the school and break the mold. These new schools would reevaluate everything—teaching, time, space, staffing, technology, administration, tools for education, even assessment (Howe, 1991). Schools would be required to apply for acceptance into the program in order to receive the grant money. They would be required to be within *America 2000* communities. To become an *America 2000* community, the community was required to accept the national education goals of *America 2000* as its own, develop a plan to achieve the goals, develop a form of assessment, and demonstrate that it was ready and willing to support the new school (Doyle, 1991).

National assessment was also proposed in *America 2000*. The goal of the testing was to measure the achievement of all students, not just those who were college-bound. Local educators would have to raise their educational standards in order to ensure that all the students in their schools were achieving at a high enough level to pass national tests. These tests were proposed to be administered in 4th, 8th, and 12th grades. The fact that the tests would be voluntary threw a wrench in the whole situation. Because of the tests' voluntary status, potentially only the highest achieving students would take them. Therefore, accurate assessment of the level of achievement would be nearly impossible (Sewall, 1991).

*America 2000* met with opposition when people began to question the federal government's role in education. Although the disclaimers of the document acknowledged state control over education, which was not what the specific ideas of *America 2000* seemed to support. The national standards, national testing, and requirement of communities to adopt goals as their own in order to be funded foreshadowed significant involvement of the federal government (Howe, 1991).

## GOALS 2000 ∎

In 1993, newly elected President Bill Clinton appointed former governor of South Carolina Richard W. Riley as the new Secretary of Education to lead the national reform efforts in education. Secretary Riley lost no time in organizing a legislative package for submission to Congress. Riley had been extremely successful as an education governor in South Carolina, leading his state in improving test scores, increasing teacher salaries, developing business and school partnerships, and achieving a "bottom-up approach" to restructuring schools (Riley, 1993). The legislation developed under the leadership of Riley in the Clinton Administration expanded the elements of *America 2000*. Termed by President Clinton as "reinventing education," the new legislation became law in March of 1994 and became known as *GOALS 2000: Educate America Act*. This legislation included the original six goals of *America 2000* and two additional goals. By the year 2000,

1. All children in America will start school ready to learn. (School Readiness Goal)

2. The high school graduation rate will increase to at least 90%. (School Completion Goal)

3. All students will leave Grades 4, 8, and 12 having demonstrated competency over challenging subject matter including English, mathematics, science, foreign languages, civics and government, economics, the arts, history, and geography, and every school in America will ensure that all students learn to use their minds well, so they may be prepared for responsible citizenship, further learning, and productive employment in our Nation's modern economy. (Student Achievement and Citizenship Goal)

4. U.S. students will be first in the world in mathematics and science achievement. (Mathematics and Science Goal)

5. Every American adult will be literate and will possess the knowledge and skills necessary to compete in a global economy and exercise the rights and responsibilities of citizenship. (Adult Literacy Lifelong Learning Goals)

6. Every school in the United States will be free of drugs, violence, and the unauthorized presence of firearms and alcohol and will offer a disciplined environment conducive to learning. (Safe, Disciplined, and Alcohol-and-Drug-Free School Goal)

7. The Nation's teaching force will have access to programs for the continued improvement of the professional skills and the opportunity to acquire the knowledge and skills needed to instruct and prepare all American students for the next century. (Teacher Education and Professional Development Goal)

8. Every school will promote partnerships that will increase parental involvement and participation in promoting the social, emotional, and academic growth of children. (Parental Participation Goal)

*GOALS 2000* was a major focus of the Clinton administration. It authorized $647 million for school reform, including $400 million in state and local grants. The bill also established a National Educational Standards and Improvement Council to oversee the adoption of state standards and plans for full implementation (Brisco, 1994).

The Department of Education under the leadership of Secretary Riley sought to keep educators, state law makers, and the public in general informed and involved in restructuring education. As part of *GOALS 2000* (1994), the Department of Education established a 19-member board, known as The National Education Standards and Improvement Council for Voluntary National Standards. NESIC was the independent agency responsible for certifying criteria, content, and standards for national and state agencies.

The NESIC was designed to certify state standards and assessment procedures to be appropriately aligned with the Educate America Act. The Council members were appointed by the President from nominations received by Congressional leaders and the Secretary of Education. Appointed members included professional educators, business and industry representatives, and members from the public.

Directly overseeing *GOALS 2000*, also known as the National Education Goals, was the National Goals Panel. Its function and major responsibility were to monitor the progress of *GOALS 2000* and to build a "nationwide, bipartisan consensus for the reforms" for implementing a national direction to ensure the success of the national goals. The Goals Panel could disapprove any national standards or state standards certified by the National Education Standards and Improvement Council for Voluntary National Standards.

Additionally, the Department of Education published the monthly community-oriented newsletter *Community Update* which was circulated to school systems and interested citizens to keep them informed of national progress, funding opportunities, and town meetings-many of which were rebroadcasted on the Discovery Network. By late 1994, 31 states had received funding under the *GOALS 2000* (Department of Education, 1994).

Funding opportunities under Title III of the *GOALS 2000*: Educate America Act (1994) allowed States to receive funding through the Department of Education. Title III supported the development and implementation of education improvement plans that aligned state standards with the national goals. Opportunities for partnerships with universities and other organizations for funding were also available.

## Reactions to *GOALS 2000*

There was considerable reaction to *GOALS 2000*. All but two states had participated in the program. Fully supporting the Clinton plan was Senator Edward Kennedy from Massachusetts, who asserted that the bill would change the way the federal government supports the local schools.

Now began the process of giving real support and encouragement to teachers, parents, and school administrators who were willing to roll up their sleeves and get down to the hard work of using these funds to improve their schools.

One of the first adverse reactions came from Senator Strom Thurmond of South Carolina. Senator Thurmond was quoted immediately after a failed Republican filibuster to defeat *GOALS 2000* that "it precludes state reform and could lead to a national curriculum" (Kaplan, 1993).

Jennings (1994) reported that there was much discussion in the U.S. Senate concerning *GOALS 2000*. The House version of the Bill passed in 1993 was different than the version that the Senate had examined earlier in that year. Several measures were added to the *GOALS 2000* legislation in the House. Proposals to use money for private school was included, but defeated. The House approved amendments outlawing guns and the use of tobacco on school property. Once the Senate completed the passage of their legislation, a Senate-House conference committee began to work toward agreement on the measure. This was difficult because the Senate and House were divided on two major issues. One issue was whether the states must have standards for content and student assessment as proposed by the House or be allowed to do whatever they desired with the federal funds as proposed by the Senate. Jennings noted that the most critical issue was whether the states should have opportunity-to-learn standards in order to receive federal funds.

Not surprisingly, the state governors agreed with the position of the Senate. They argued that the focus should remain on student outcomes and not move back to the opportunity-to-learn standards, fearing that this would move education back into more instructional inputs. Opportunity-to-learn standards were standards to assist students in poor school districts. The House felt that without these standards there would be no assurance that every student in America would have a fair or equal opportunity to meet the outcome-oriented standards.

The compromise which led to the completion of the act and to President Clinton's signature making the bill law was a requirement that any state wishing to receive federal funds for school reform have content standards and standards for performance and assessment, as required by the House version, and opportunity-to-learn standards.

One additional element that was included and passed into the *GOALS 2000: Educate America Act* was an inclusion of Clinton's Administration's *Safe School Act* which awarded the Department of Education with funding programs to make the public school safer.

Secretary Riley (1993) was pleased with the passage of *GOALS 2000*. He believed that this was an important step in President Clinton's educational reform efforts to establish "world class curriculum standards which challenge all students." In an article that he wrote for *Principal* on the reinvention of education, he warned of the great task before the nation. He explained the four titles under *GOALS 2000*. In *Title I: National Education Goals* the six national goals and objectives were described. He explained that under this title Congress became a "full partner with the President and the nation's governors" to provide the basic framework for a new system of public education. *Title II: National Education Reform Leadership, Standards, and Assessment* included the National Goals Panel. This panel was designed to monitor and report on state and national cooperation and success. *Title III: State Improvement* allowed for federal funding to states to implement programs at the local school level. *Title IV: National Skills Standards Board* called for the creation of a board composed of leaders from state and federal government, industry, business, and education to identify areas of major occupations, and to assist in the development of standards and assessments of skills in each of these areas."

Riley (1993) asserted that *GOALS 2000* required numerous partnerships to make the Act successful. He believed that in the new direction for education, it was going to take major cooperation among people to "reinvent education." This cooperation began to face a decline on January 4, 1995 with the induction of the 104th Congress with a new, conservative power. As the new Republican-controlled Congress took over the shift of legislative power for the first time in forty years and inducted the first Republican Speaker of the House since 1954, newspapers throughout America reported the GOP's latest triumph to power. *The Washington Post* reported the day after the induction several comments of members who were now in major power positions. House Speaker Newt Gingrich stated, "We owe it to our children and grandchildren to get this government in order."

Senator Robert Dole, returning to his seat as the Senate's majority leader, sounded his desire to roll back government regulations. He stated, "We will roll back federal programs, laws and regulation from A to Z— from Amtrak to zoological studies." It is worth noting that Mr. Dole was not elected president in the 1996 election.

The elementary school is an important breeding ground for the educational pursuits of children. It is the place where the schooling process begins, so the elementary school must be inviting and exciting to all students who attend. Its history dates back over two centuries in the United States and even further on the continent of Europe. The young child, between the entrance into kindergarten and the exit of 5th grade, experiences myriad developmental changes. The curriculum is crucial because it is the initial student encounter with an organized body of study. How this body of knowledge is aligned and taught may influence the academic success of the student. Some elementary schools have followed the paths of middle and high schools and have moved to block scheduling. This is an easy transition for elementary teachers in that many classes are already structured for extended periods of time. The reader will probably see more of the transformational and personalized designs of block scheduling in the early grades, K–2. Traditional and transitional block scheduling designs are more noticeable in Grades 3–5.

**Table 7.1** *America 2000* and *Goals 2000*

| America 2000 | Goals 2000 |
|---|---|
| 1. Every child will start school ready to learn. | 1. Every child will start school ready to learn. |
| 2. Raise the high school graduation rate to 90%. | 2. Raise the high school graduation rate to 90%. |
| 3. Students will leave Grades 4, 8, and 12 showing competence in core subjects. | 3. Students will leave Grades 4, 8, and 12 showing competence in core subjects. |
| 4. Our students will be first in the world in math and science. | 4. Our students will be first in the world in math and science. |
| 5. All citizens will be literate and able to compete in a global economy. | 5. All citizens will be literate and able to compete in a global economy. |
| 6. Schools will be free of drugs and violence. | 6. Schools will be free of drugs and violence. |
| 7. Teachers will have access to programs to enhance skills. | |
| 8. Increase parental involvement. | |

## ■ NO CHILD LEFT BEHIND

On January 20, 2001, George W. Bush became the 43rd president of the United States and Roderick Paige, the superintendent of the Houston Independent School District, the seventh largest school district in the country, was confirmed as the Secretary of Education.

Within days of his new administration, Bush released his plan for educational reform, No Child Left Behind. After becoming law, the new national program mandated a test-based system of accountability for educational achievement for all students. Central to the new law was a plan to close the achievement gap between high- and low-performing students. The law received major bipartisan support from Congress.

The law, which required states to finalize standards for reading and mathematics and mandated students in the grades three to eight from the elementary and middle schools be tested for yearly progress. Additionally each state is required to employ teachers who are (or must become) "highly qualified" as demonstrated by licenses, certifications, college education, and expertise in content areas. Known as adequate yearly progress (AYP) as determined by each individual state, failure of any school to meet their state's AYP goals for two consecutive years results in numerous sanctions including required expensive tutoring for failing students, allowing parents to transfer their children to higher performing schools. In the worst case scenario, the school's principal, teachers, and staff can be removed. In fact, the school can be closed. (U.S. Department of Education, 2008).

### Reactions to No Child Left Behind

Reactions to NCLB remain mixed with opponents citing several major problems. Rothstein (2008) argued that the forced focus on math and reading had limited the teaching process in that it has shifted time away from other academic areas. Others noted that the federal government's requirement that all core subject teachers be highly qualified by 2006 did not account for teacher shortages that school districts would continue to face then and now. Deadlines to meet standards were modified, but teacher preparation programs and other approved teacher education models such as lateral entry failed then and today to produce the number of classroom teachers needed to meet this criterion (Strawn, Fox, & Duck, 2008).

Higher academic performance standards became a problem for many school districts, and across the country many began to experience increased financial burdens associated with the new requirements. The federal government had forced NCLB mandates and deadlines on school systems without providing adequate funding. With continued escalating costs for meeting academic goals, some states began to reevaluate their education standards. One approach was to reduce the passing scores for tests, or to reduce the percentage of students who must pass statewide tests. For example, Michigan reduced the percentage of students required to pass statewide high school English tests, and in 2005 Connecticut used the federal Department of Education for not providing the state with adequate funding to meet the requirements of NCLB (Pendell, 2008).

As dissatisfaction with federal funding of the law continued, Democratic senators who previously supported the law became more vocal. Senator Edward Kennedy stated in a *New York Times* article written by David Sanger:

> No amount of soothing rhetoric by the president can hide the fact that he refuses to fund the bipartisan school reforms he signed into law with great fanfare a year and a half ago. These reforms will never happen without increasing the funds needed to pay for them. (September 9, 2003)

## A New Era?

After the 2008 election, most Americans are hoping for a new era in America with the election of Barack Obama as the 44th president. With the country in the worst economic recession since the Great Depression, and with the country at war, education may not rise to top priority for a few years. Prior to the 2008 election, many leaders in Congress were voicing for needed changes in NCLB (Congressional Digest, 2008; National School Board Association, 2008).

The author predicts that regardless of the direction of NCLB or any other educational reform efforts by Congress or President Obama, block scheduling will remain in the majority of middle and high schools. After an August 2008 conversation with Robert Canady, the father of block scheduling, the author also predicts that block scheduling will become the major reforming agent for the elementary school.

## ORGANIZATIONAL PATTERNS ■

The elementary school of today is typically arranged by grade, which is basically an age grouping. The students start kindergarten at age five and exit the elementary school around the age of 11 and most elementary classes are self-contained by grade with students having just one teacher. Even in these settings there are some great examples of teachers blocking for content or for the integration of content. Some teachers have a complete personalized program within the self-contained environment. In some of the block scheduling classes, students or perhaps teachers change classes every 90 or 100 minutes. This can be found more often in the upper elementary grades and the design is more traditional.

### Alternative Possibilities for Scheduling

*Looping*

Looping is generally defined as a teacher remaining with a group of students for more than one year. This practice is quite common in the elementary schools of the United States, and it greatly benefits the students and teachers. Because the teacher-pupil relationship has time to develop over a two-year time period, academic achievement tends to be greater (Forsten, Grant, & Richardson, 2000). Also, the teacher has an extended time frame in which to learn the strengths and weaknesses of the students and can differentiate instruction to better suit a group of learners (Crosby, 1993). The curriculum now can be dominated less by the notion of covering everything during the year, and the teacher can focus more on cooperative learning strategies and group project assignments (Burke, 1997). These processes give the learners more authentic activities that will greatly increase their retention of knowledge and information.

### Multiage Classrooms

Another alternative to the traditional graded program is the multiage classroom in which the teacher has students of different ages in the classroom working each at their own pace. A benefit from this arrangement is that students move from easy to more difficult material when they are ready, and peer tutoring is readily available because of the differing ages of fellow classmates (Leslie & Halpert, 1996). "Advancement to the next unit depends on the mastery of subject matter, regardless of age or attendance, and students who have mastered content can help those in need of additional assistance" (Kolstad & McFadden, 1998, p. 14). Students learn to take responsibility for their own learning because they work individually and in groups on a daily basis; this is necessary for classmates who work at different levels. The high rate of language skill development is evident because of the continuous interaction with older students who have mastered more complex skills (Kolstad & McFadden, 1998).

## ■ 4-BLOCKS MODEL

The 4-blocks model is an instructional model based on the premise that there are four fundamental ways that all children learn to read. The model ensures that students are exposed to all four methods every day, thereby addressing the individual learning styles of children. The four blocks are (1) guided reading, (2) writing, (3) working with words, and (4) self-selected reading. Most elementary teachers would agree that it is important to construct a balanced approach to literacy instruction that could address the individual needs of children to create a community of learners in a heterogeneous classroom setting.

The 4-blocks model is a literacy framework that can be used in isolation by an individual teacher in a school, even without the support of his or her peers and administrators, although the most successful teachers are those with a strong network of support from the staff and other faculty members.

Although it's important to use this model in a supportive environment, the 4-blocks model probably best serves a self-contained classroom. Keeping the blocks under one teacher's guidance is the best plan. One disadvantage of the model is that, often, teachers and or administrators change the design for various reasons. Sometimes the changes are minor; however, if the intent of the blocks is altered, the expected results may change as well (Sigmon, 2001).

## PARALLEL BLOCK SCHEDULING  ■

The elementary curriculum continues to evolve with more content being added and little subtracted. Teachers are required to teach more content in the same amount of time while incorporating such strategies and interdisciplinary instruction. Parallel block scheduling is a way of structuring time within a school day to facilitate instruction and to reduce the student-teacher ratio during designated time periods. Large and small blocks of time can be distributed among several teachers in a grade level by giving each teacher more minutes each day (i.e., 90 minutes) for whole-group instruction in language arts and social studies, with less time (i.e., 50 minutes) each for reading and writing in smaller groups.

During whole-group instruction, the teacher may use social studies content to teach a language unit on research skills. The students may reinforce those skills in small groups during reading or writing time and also in an extension center. Students may also be assigned to the library during extension center time where a media specialist will instruct them on effective use of the card catalog or an online computer search. There are many options for instruction in the parallel blocking model.

According to Canady and Hopkins (1997) parallel block scheduling produces the following instructional benefits: (1) smaller class size during critical instructional periods; (2) less reliance on strict ability grouping; (3) less fragmentation of the school day due to better integration of support programs such as special education, gifted education, and Title I; (4) more efficient and effective use of instructional staff; (5) significantly higher student engagement rates in learning activities; and (6) increased test scores.

With parallel block scheduling, the benefits of flexibility can be achieved with few additional expenditures. The schedule is built basically around half-class instruction groups in reading and mathematics. Homerooms are usually comprised of approximately 25 students, with reading and math taught in groups of fewer than 15, thereby magnifying instructional time and increasing student achievement (Canady & Hopkins, 1997).

## SUMMARY  ■

Restructuring of time occurs as educators capitalize on the potential of innovative scheduling as a means to improve schools, even in the elementary grades. From the latest reform efforts in reaction to *A Nation at Risk* to those reacting to No Child Left Behind, the elementary school has probably experienced the greatest success when compared to the middle and senior high schools. "With open minds and equal doses of creativity and technical expertise, school administrators, teachers, parents, and students can harness this power" (Canady & Rettig, 1995b, p. 12). It is estimated that every two of three schools, elementary through high school, are using some form of blocking or alternative scheduling practices. From the first one-room schools to the most modern schools-within-schools (often referred to as Student Learning Communities, SLC), educators have blocked a particular period of extended time for a specific subject. It may not have been called block scheduling, but in essence, it was blocking. This has been especially true in elementary schools where large sections of time exceeding 60 minutes have been used to block subject areas, especially language arts and mathematics.

Visit the author's Web site for using block scheduling in the elementary school.

# EIGHT

# Aligning Standards and Course Content

Curriculum alignment is an essential element in the total success of implementing the block. The first elements in curriculum alignment include scoping out and sequencing the units or content to be taught.

In sequencing, educators examine the order of information or skills that must be taught to achieve the desired outcomes. For example, in the language arts program, teachers instruct readiness skills in reading at kindergarten to basic skills in elementary and middle schools to English in the high school. Teachers strive to put content in a meaningful order. Some courses such as mathematics and science are sequential and require a step-by-step approach. In processing skills such as observing, comparing, and inferring, there can be a definite order in which higher-order processing skills are developed. In the sequencing, evident patterns emerge at various levels in the high school. In high school courses, the sequencing becomes extremely important, to include all of the desired content. Most subject content has been prescribed by the various state departments and the local boards of education. In most states, teachers will find biology being taught in the 10th grade; however, in other places, it may be taught in 11th or 9th grade. However, the scope of the content is similar. To be educationally sound, the material is taught in a sequence; the basic biology class is taught before advanced biology and usually before chemistry and physics courses. Once courses have been developed for scope and sequence, scheduling is the next step.

Scheduling is where administrators and curriculum leaders become involved in the process. Their role is to make sure that course offerings are presented at a particular time and offered on a regular basis to ensure all students the opportunity to take the classes. Scheduling becomes more important when moving from curriculum alignment to instructional alignment in that if the courses are not aligned in the schedule in the right fashion, it will be difficult to implement the desired curriculum.

# ■ MODELS FOR USE OF INSTRUCTIONAL TIME

As stated in Chapter 2, moving to a block schedule causes teachers to lose some overall instructional time that needs to be examined in the process of curriculum alignment. When realigning their courses with the curriculum, teachers can examine three basic models that will prove to be time wise and will allow for the maximum use of desired content. These include limiting content, assigning outside content, and integrating content.

## Limiting Content

In these three approaches for curriculum alignment, the one often used as default is limiting the content. A decision is made to limit what is to be taught and to focus on the priorities of the course. Teachers tend to spend more time on the content they like and less on content they either dislike or have limited instructional materials for teaching.

The concept is similar to the concept of abandonment found in the effective schools research of the 1980s. Researchers found that to succeed in designing an effective school, some part of the content had to be abandoned to allow time to implement the remaining content in an orderly and appropriate fashion. When examining the abandonment model, this is referred to as the prioritizing approach. When analyzing any curricular model, whether from the state department, the local board, or even the textbook alone, teachers begin to plan what to teach in a course. They begin by listing their intended topics, usually in the order they plan to teach. (These usually have a sequence and may be skill related.) Many topics are arranged by units.

What teachers should be striving to do is eliminate, move, or modify the competencies or guidelines in curriculum. The first step in prioritization is to list or group patterns of concepts, units, or mini-units. The teacher prioritizes these as shown in Table 8.1. In the table, 12 basic groupings of items are presented. (These numbers will be more or less in most cases.) Sometimes it is necessary to do a factor analysis on this and break down the content in particular areas. In most cases, these are listed in the local curriculum. A goal may be to abandon two or three in the list of 12. In the block schedule, 10% to 15% of class time will be lost in the course of a year. In comparison, research and observations show that teachers using traditional models often fail to use their time effectively and are teaching beyond the prescribed curriculum. Therefore, although some overall instructional time is lost in the block schedule, the abandonment model and the use of various instructional models will actually cause an increase in interactive learning time. For example, one can focus on a total of 12 concepts for the course and decide to abandon two components that could be eliminated from the course. Often, this is material that has been added by the teacher over the years. Teachers implement the curriculum but should not add to the curriculum. In a case where the curriculum is tightly outlined and the teacher strives to cover all material, he or she may choose one or two areas where similar competencies may be combined and taught simultaneously. For example, the Civil War and the Revolutionary War competencies may be taught together within the concepts of restoration. In the English classroom, epic poetry may be taught as a part of a general poetry unit. It is useful for teachers to find two or more concepts to abandon or combine with similar items.

**Table 8.1**  Prioritization in 9th-Grade English

| 9th-Grade English—Abandonment | | | |
|---|---|---|---|
| Speech | Epic Poems | Film | Advertising |
| Poetry | Technology | Drama | Short Story |
| Fiction | Nonfiction | Research | Novel |

*Notes to Remember*

1. Teachers must not use the abandonment model to cut required content or competencies. The only content that should be abandoned may include superfluous examples, excess content, or information outside the content area that teachers may have added over the years.

2. Group competencies together that may be taught in one unit instead of separate lessons, such as process skills or English short stories. Two or three short stories will enable students to understand selected literary terms and the general concept of short stories. It is not necessary to inundate them with 10 or more short stories.

3. Isolate the strengths and weaknesses of teaching styles, content examples, and student ability. Create recommendations to deal with the weaknesses.

## Assigning Outside Content

Assigning outside content is the second curriculum alignment model. With this approach, the teacher assigns content to students to investigate on their own or in pairs or groups outside class. Creative teachers use course contracts or instructional packages for students to complete this content by, for example, clarifying in their course syllabus specifically what must be completed outside class. Students often keep portfolios and/or journals to respond to share the content with the teachers. An excellent example would be that a student reads a novel that cannot be covered in class, but the teacher wants to hold the student responsible for the content.

Pretend there are 12 blocks of similar items, such as units or skills, content, and various situations or classes. In this model, the content is blocked and placed in order. Teachers can mark their use as "T" for teacher directed, "T/S" for teacher and student directed, and "S" for student directed (Table 8.2). Most will be teacher directed, meaning that the teacher plans to include this content within the course. The teacher will be responsible for preparing all the material. There may be an area where teachers and students can share teaching. The teacher could start a basic content, such as pollution, and have students research thermal, water, and air pollution. Learning stations, product or instructional packages, use of contracts, use of the library—all are helpful to responsible students and also serve as good tools. The teacher provides parameters and materials. This works well when students work on this over a period of time, alone or with peers. The student is held accountable for the content, and the assignments can be completed as cooperative projects. In the author's opinion, only 10% of the content should ever be taught in a student-directed manner. Another alternative would be to use the T/S, giving teachers more variety and flexibility in selecting contents.

**Table 8.2**  Assigning Outside Content in 9th-Grade English

| 9th-Grade English—Blocking | | | |
|---|---|---|---|
| Speech | Epic Poems | Film | Advertising |
| T/S | T | S | S |
| Poetry | Technology | Drama | Short Story |
| T | T | S | T/S |
| Fiction | Nonfiction | Research | Novel |
| T | T | S | T/S |

## Integrating Content: C–Clustering

The integrating model, which groups, or clusters, subject content, is shown in Table 8.3. The same 12 items are used as in Table 8.2. This model is known as the thematic approach. The 12 items are clustered into three categories or themes patterns, three basic sections of the course. These three major units may be carried over a long period of time.

**Table 8.3** Integrating Content in 9th-Grade English

| 9th-Grade English—Clustering | | |
|---|---|---|
| Unit 1 | Unit 2 | Unit 3 |
| Literature | Communication Skills | Media & Technology |
| Fiction | Research Writing | Advertising |
| Novel | Speech | Technical Writing |
| Nonfiction | Creative Writing | Electronic Research Methods |
| Poetry | Formal Presentations | |

Content is merged into a more meaningful pattern. For example, in a U.S. history course, there could be a grouping of wars. All the content of war can be taught in one long cluster to look for patterns of prewar climate, the political manifestations, causes, restoration, and postwar reconstruction. In a master plan or unit on war, timelines should be drawn and posted for students to see the sequence of time. To compare the similarities of the various wars, highlight mini-themes or curricular threads, such as politicians, taxation, and so on. In an English classroom, a cluster of media and technology could group together computer technology, advertising, and film. The cross correlation among these topics can result in student investigations into advertising on the Internet, in films, and in print media. Selecting content is difficult in the beginning; however, this approach is compelling when students see the relevance of what they are learning and how information may be linked. This approach can be implemented to focus on higher-order thinking skills. Weaknesses may occur in not being able to see the chronological order of events.

As teachers begin to redesign their courses from a traditional schedule to the block model, the following steps and related forms can be used. Sample models are included in the figures in Chapter 9 in the two subject areas of geometry and French II.

## CURRICULUM ALIGNMENT
## AND INSTRUCTIONAL PACING

### Curriculum Alignment Phase 1

*Step 1:* Scope out the course as it has been taught in the traditional schedule (see Figures 9.1–9.3).

*Step 2:* Place a minus sign over one or two areas or units on which you spent more time than you intended in the traditional model. Usually this happens when you have more materials or you like this part of the content more.

*Step 3:* Place a plus sign over one or two areas or units on which you spent less time than you intended or that you were unable to get to in the traditional model.

*Step 4:* Now mark the amount of time IN DAYS that you have used compared to time used for the traditional use for each unit. For example, 10 days on the introduction of the animal cell. Scope out each unit with respect to time needed for the traditional schedule.

*Step 5:* Now mark each unit using the following formula: For the areas in a unit not marked with a plus or minus sign, divide the number of days in a traditional schedule for the unit by half to determine how much time to spend in a blocked schedule on those areas; for the areas on which you spent more time (areas with a minus sign), divide by half and subtract one day to determine how much time to spend; and for the areas that you spent less time on (areas with a plus sign) divide by half and add one day to determine how much time to spend. This is one way to help teachers begin realigning their courses. This is refined in Phase 2.

## Curriculum Alignment Phase 2

*Step 1:* Further develop each unit according to the content on the Phase 2 form (see Figures 9.4–9.6). List content, vocabulary, and other material to be covered in the unit. Mark items that may be learned outside class in an alternative assignment. Make any notes that will help you organize your instructional plan or pacing.

*Step 2:* From the above formulas, begin further prioritizing content to be taught.

Mark areas where some content must be limited, assigned outside class, or integrated with other content. At this stage, don't worry about the instructional processes or activities that will be used in or out of class. You will complete this element in the pacing process, which follows. NOTE: Use a pencil with all of this because you will be making changes as you develop the plan.

## Instructional Pacing Phase 1

*Step 1:* Transfer the topics from Phase 2 of curriculum alignment to Phase 1 of instructional pacing. Use a day-by-day approach in the transfer (see Figures 9.7–9.9).

*Step 2:* Keep Days 3 and 8 as "safe days." These are days that no instruction is planned because over 90% of teachers are behind at these days, and this allows them to get caught up and feel less frustrated. A half-day for catching up should be included every week thereafter. If you are one of the few who are not too behind, just go to the next day of the plan and you are ahead. Keep the last three or four days as safe days for reviewing, catching up, and exams. Most teachers actually teach about 86 to 87 days per 90–day semester.

*Step 3:* Now that you have safe days to include, be sure to revisit the actual days planned and make adjustments. This may change again as you select specific activities to use for teaching. That is why it is important to be very process-oriented with this approach. Move now to the last stage, which is Phase 2 of instructional pacing.

## Instructional Pacing Phase 2

*Step 1:* Use this model as a weekly and daily lesson plan. Complete the content information as shown in the samples in Chapter 9, and then project activities that you will be using by minutes on a daily level (see Figures 9.10–9.12). It is important that you have the first three weeks of lessons completed before the students arrive and that you remain three weeks ahead throughout the semester or year. Most teachers use one day per lesson, but it is important to know that some lessons may exceed one day or that there may be two lessons in one day.

*Step 2:* As you learn more about interactive methods and assessment, you will have to make adjustments in your plan.

**Important Note:** This is a well-tested procedure that has been used by thousands of teachers in the United States to develop appropriate pacing of instruction. Do not take any of the steps lightly, or you will have difficulty pacing and being successful. Of equal importance, it will make your planning and teaching less stressful, and by the second and third time you teach the course and make appropriate modifications, you will have a master plan.

# NINE

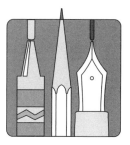

# Samples of Curriculum Alignment and Pacing

In this chapter, you will find blank forms and samples for curriculum alignment and pacing. The figures in this chapter are grouped according to phases. Each group of figures contains a blank form and two completed samples. Use them as shown or adapt them as necessary. Hopefully these pages will enhance the information presented in Chapter 8 and ease your journey into block scheduling.

The first step in aligning curriculum for block scheduling involves modifying a unit of study from the traditional schedule so that it can be taught in the block schedule. Figures 9.1, 9.2, and 9.3 address courses as they have been taught in the traditional schedule. Figure 9.1 is a blank form for teacher use and Figures 9.2 and 9.3 are samples of completed forms. For more detailed instructions, refer to Chapter 8, pages 69–70, Curriculum Alignment Phase 1, Steps 1–5.

**Figure 9.1** Curriculum Alignment: Phase 1 Form

| A | B | C | D | E | F |
|---|---|---|---|---|---|
|  |  |  |  |  |  |
|  |  |  |  |  |  |

| G | H | I | J | K | L |
|---|---|---|---|---|---|

**Figure 9.2** Curriculum Alignment: Phase 1—Geometry Sample

| A | B | C | D | E | F |
|---|---|---|---|---|---|
| Points, lines, planes, and angles | Deductive reasoning | Parallel lines and planes | Congruent triangles | Quadrilaterals | Similar polygons |
| Right triangles | Circles | Areas of plane figures | Surface area and volume | Coordinate geometry | Transformations |

| G | H | I | J | K | L |
|---|---|---|---|---|---|

Figure 9.3   Curriculum Alignment: Phase 1—French II

**Subject: French II**
**Grade Level: 10–12**
**Teacher(s):** _____

| A | B | C | D | E | F | G | H | I | J | K | L |
|---|---|---|---|---|---|---|---|---|---|---|---|
| Describing your city | Finding your way around | Describing your home and family | Making plans to do things in town | Talking about clothes | Discussing shopping plans | Buying clothes | Discussing leisure activities | Describing vacation travel plans | Narrating what happened | Talking about your favorite foods | Shopping for food |
| Planning a meal | Eating out with friends | | | | | | | | | | |

| M | N | O | P | Q | R | S | T | U | V | W | X |
|---|---|---|---|---|---|---|---|---|---|---|---|

Figures 9.4, 9.5, and 9.6 are for Phase 2 of curriculum alignment. They are used to further refine the content and materials of the unit of study. See page 102, Curriculum Alignment Phase 2, Steps 1 and 2, in Chapter 8 for detailed instructions.

**Figure 9.4**  Curriculum Alignment: Phase 2 Form

**Subject:** _____

**Grade Level:** _____

**Teacher(s):** _____

### Goal/Topic

| | | | |
|---|---|---|---|
| | | | |

| 1 | 2 | 3 | 4 |
|---|---|---|---|
| Notes: | Notes: | Notes: | Notes: |
| (a) | (a) | (a) | (a) |
| (b) | (b) | (b) | (b) |
| (c) | (c) | (c) | (c) |
| (d) | (d) | (d) | (d) |

**Figure 9.5** Curriculum Alignment: Phase 2—Geometry Example

## Subject: Geometry
## Grade Level: 9–12

### Goal/Topic

| Points, Lines, Planes, and Angles |
|---|
| |

| Points, Lines, and Planes | Segments, Rays, and Distance | The Coordinate Plane | Angles |
|---|---|---|---|
| 1 | 2 | 3 | 4 |
| (a) | (a) | (a) | (a) |
| (b) | (b) | (b) | (b) |
| (c) | (c) | (c) | (c) |
| (d) | (d) | (d) | (d) |

**Figure 9.6**   Curriculum Alignment: Phase 2—French Sample

**Subject: French II**
**Grade Level: 9–12**

## Goal/Topic

| Describing Your City |
|---|

| 1 | 2 | 3 | 4 | 5 | 6 | 7 | 8 | 9 | 10 |
|---|---|---|---|---|---|---|---|---|---|
| Streets and public buildings<br><br>28.B.2b | Places you often go to<br><br>28.D.2a | How you get around<br><br>28.B.3a | | | | | | | |

## Goal/Topic

| Finding Your Way Around |
|---|

| 1 | 2 | 3 | 4 | 5 | 6 | 7 | 8 | 9 | 10 |
|---|---|---|---|---|---|---|---|---|---|
| Asking and giving directions<br><br>28.B.3a | Indicating the floor<br><br>28.D.2a | | | | | | | | |

## Goal/Topic

| Describing Your Home and Family |
|---|

| 1 | 2 | 3 | 4 | 5 | 6 | 7 | 8 | 9 | 10 |
|---|---|---|---|---|---|---|---|---|---|
| Your address<br><br>28.D.2a | The inside and outside of your home<br><br>28.D.2a | Your family<br><br>28.D.2b | | | | | | | |

Figures 9.7, 9.8, and 9.9 are used for Phase 1 of instructional pacing. The topics from curriculum alignment Phase 2 are transferred day-by-day to this form. See pages 102–103, Instructional Pacing Phase 1, Steps 1–3 in Chapter 8 for detailed instructions.

**Figure 9.7**  Pacing: Phase 1 Form

**Subject** _____  **Teacher** _____

| Day | Topics/Goals/Objectives | Textbook/Materials/Resources |
|---|---|---|
| 1. | | |
| 2. | | |
| 3. | Safe day | |
| 4. | | |
| 5. | | |
| 6. | | |
| 7. | | |
| 8. | Safe day | |
| 9. | | |
| 10. | | |
| 11. | | |
| 12. | | |
| 13. | | |
| 14. | | |
| 15. | | |
| 16. | | |
| 17. | | |
| 18. | ½ Safe day | |
| 19. | | |
| 20. | | |

*(Continued)*

**Figure 9.7** (Continued)

| Day | Topics/Goals/Objectives | Textbook/Materials/Resources |
|---|---|---|
| 21. | | |
| 22. | | |
| 23. | | |
| 24. | | |
| 25. | | |
| 26. | | |
| 27. | | |
| 28. | Safe day | |
| 29. | | |
| 30. | | |
| 31. | | |
| 32. | | |
| 33. | | |
| 34. | | |
| 35. | | |
| 36. | | |
| 37. | | |
| 38. | | |
| 39. | | |
| 40. | | |
| 41. | | |
| 42. | | |
| 43. | Safe day | |
| 44. | | |
| 45. | | |

| Day | Topics/Goals/Objectives | Textbook/Materials/Resources |
|---|---|---|
| 46. | | |
| 47. | | |
| 48. | | |
| 49. | | |
| 50. | | |
| 51. | | |
| 52. | | |
| 53. | | |
| 54. | | |
| 55. | | |
| 56. | | |
| 57. | | |
| 58. | | |
| 59. | | |
| 60. | | |
| 61. | | |
| 62. | | |
| 63. | | |
| 64. | | |
| 65. | | |
| 66. | | |
| 67. | | |
| 68. | | |
| 69. | | |
| 70. | | |

*(Continued)*

**Figure 9.7**   (Continued)

| Day | Topics/Goals/Objectives | Textbook/Materials/Resources |
|---|---|---|
| 71. | | |
| 72. | | |
| 73. | | |
| 74. | | |
| 75. | | |
| 76. | | |
| 77. | | |
| 78. | | |
| 79. | | |
| 80. | | |
| 81. | | |
| 82. | | |
| 83. | Safe day | |
| 84. | Safe day | |
| 85. | Review | |
| 86. | Review | |
| 87. | Safe day | |
| 88. | Unit 8 Test | |
| 89. | Safe day | |
| 90. | Safe day | |

**Figure 9.8**   Pacing: Phase 1—Geometry Sample

**Subject: Geometry**                    **Teacher** _____

| Day | Topics/Goals/Objectives | Textbook/Materials/Resources |
|---|---|---|
| 1. | Points, lines, and planes | Geometry figures poster |
| 2. | Segments, rays, and distance | Geometry figures poster |
| 3. | Safe day | |
| 4. | The coordinate plane | |
| 5. | Angles | Protractors |
| 6. | Review | |
| 7. | Unit 1 test<br>If–then statements, converses | |
| 8. | Safe day | |
| 9. | If–then statements, inverses, and contrapositives | |
| 10. | Properties from algebra,<br>Introduction to proof | |
| 11. | Midpoint, angle bisector | |
| 12. | Special pairs of angles | |
| 13. | Perpendicular lines | |
| 14. | Mixed practice | |
| 15. | More on proofs | |
| 16. | Review | |
| 17. | Unit 2 test<br>Terms in parallel lines and planes | |
| 18. | ½ Safe day | |
| 19. | Properties of parallel lines | |
| 20. | Properties of parallel lines cont'd | |

*(Continued)*

**Figure 9.8** (Continued)

| Day | Topics/Goals/Objectives | Textbook/Materials/Resources |
|---|---|---|
| 21. | Proving lines parallel | |
| 22. | Angles of a triangle | |
| 23. | Angles of a triangle cont'd | |
| 24. | Angles of a polygon | |
| 25. | Review | |
| 26. | Unit 3 test<br>Congruent figures | |
| 27. | 3 ways to prove triangles<br>Congruent: SSS, SAS, ASA | |
| 28. | Congruent triangles and proof | |
| 29. | Congruent triangles and proof cont'd | |
| 30. | Isosceles triangles | |
| 31. | 2 more ways to prove triangle<br>congruent: AAS, HL | |
| 32. | Proving triangles congruent<br>practice | |
| 33. | Medians, altitudes, and<br>perpendicular bisectors | |
| 34. | Review | |
| 35. | Unit 4 test<br>Algebra review: quadratics | |
| 36. | Poperties of parallelograms | |
| 37. | Ways to prove quadrilaterals are<br>parallelograms | |
| 38. | Parallelogram practice | |
| 39. | Theorems involving parallel lines | |
| 40. | Special parallelograms | |
| 41. | Special parallelograms cont'd | |
| 42. | Trapezoids | |

| Day | Topics/Goals/Objectives | Textbook/Materials/Resources |
|---|---|---|
| 43. | ½ safe day | |
| 44. | Review | |
| 45. | Unit 5 test<br>Algebra review: fractions | |
| 46. | Ratio and proportion | |
| 47. | Properties of proportion | |
| 48. | Similar polygons | |
| 49. | Similar polygons cont'd | |
| 50. | A way to prove triangles similar: AA | |
| 51. | 2 more ways to prove triangles similar: SAS, SSS | |
| 52. | Proving triangles similar practice | |
| 53. | Proportional lengths | |
| 54. | Proportional lengths cont'd | |
| 55. | Review | |
| 56. | Unit 6 test<br>Algebra review: radicals | |
| 57. | Simplifying radicals<br>Similarity in right triangles | |
| 58. | Similarity in right triangles cont'd<br>Pythagorean theorem | |
| 59. | The converse of the Pythagorean theorem | |
| 60. | Special right triangles | |

**Figure 9.9**   Pacing: Phase 1

## Subject: French II        Teacher _____

| Day | Topic/Goal | Textbook/Materials/Resources | Strategies |
|---|---|---|---|
| 1. | Describing your city, directions, address, and your house | Lesson 21, pp. 188–197 | Diagram of house |
| 2. | | | |
| 3. | | | |
| 4. | | | |
| 5. | | | |
| 6. | | | |
| 7. | Things to do<br>Verb aller | Lesson 22, pp. 198–209 | |
| 8. | Places you go<br>How you get around | | |
| 9. | | | |
| 10. | | | |
| 11. | | | |
| 12. | | | |
| 13. | Asking others to come along | Lesson 23, pp. 210–219 | |
| 14. | Saying where you have been | | |
| 15. | Contradicting someone<br>Expressing surprise | | |
| 16. | | | |
| 17. | | | |
| 18. | | | |

| Day | Topic/Goal | Textbook/Materials/Resources | Strategies |
|---|---|---|---|
| 19. | Making plans to do things in town | Lesson 24, pp. 220–229 | |
| 20. | Expressing doubt Your family | | |
| 21. | Unit 6 | Lesson 24 (Suite) | |
| 22. | | | |
| 23. | | | |
| 24. | | | |
| 25. | Review | | |
| 26. | Unit 6 test | | |
| 27. | Padding | | |
| 28. | Padding | | |
| 29. | Talking about clothes | Lesson 25, pp. 246–255 | |
| 30. | What people are wearing | | |
| 31. | Whether their clothes fit | | |
| 32. | Where to go asking for help | | |
| 33. | | | |
| 34. | | | |

*(Continued)*

**Figure 9.9** (Continued)

| Day | Topic/Goal | Textbook/Materials/Resources | Strategies |
|---|---|---|---|
| 35. | Discussing shopping plans | Lesson 26, pp. 256–265 | |
| 36. | What to buy | | |
| 37. | Emphasizing a remark | | |
| 38. | | | |
| 39. | | | |
| 40. | | | |
| 41. | Paying for clothes | Lesson 27, pp. 266–273 | |
| 42. | What clothes look like | | |
| 43. | Deciding what to choose | | |
| 44. | Comparing time | | |
| 45. | Introducing an opinion | | |
| 46. | | | |
| 47. | Clothing | Lesson 28, pp. 247–285 | |
| 48. | Where to go | | |
| 49. | Finding out price | | |
| 50. | Talking about what you would like | | |
| 51. | | | |
| 52. | | | |
| 53. | | | |

| Day | Topic/Goal | Textbook/Materials/ Resources | Strategies |
|---|---|---|---|
| 54. | Review | | |
| 55. | Unit 7 Test | | |
| 56. | Padding | | |
| 57. | Discussing leisure activites | Lesson 29, pp. 296–305 | |
| 58. | Going out with friends | | |
| 59. | Sports | | |
| 60. | Helping around the house | | |
| 61. | | | |
| 62. | | | |
| 63. | Describing vacation plans | Lesson 30, pp. 306–317 | |
| 64. | How you and others feel | | |
| 65. | | | |
| 66. | | | |
| 67. | | | |
| 68. | | | |
| 69. | Narrating what happened | Lesson 31, pp. 318–327 | |
| 70. | How long to stay | | |
| 71. | What to see | | |
| 72. | | | |
| 73. | | | |
| 74. | | | |

*(Continued)*

**Figure 9.9** (Continued)

| Day | Topic/Goal | Textbook/Materials/Resources | Strategies |
|---|---|---|---|
| 75. | Narrating what happened | Lesson 32, pp. 328–337 | |
| 76. | Things you never do | | |
| 77. | Travel dates | | |
| 78. | Where you went and when you returned | | |
| 79. | | | |
| 80. | | | |
| 81. | Review | | |
| 82. | Unit 8 Test | | |
| 83. | Padding | | |
| 84. | Padding | | |
| 85. | | | |
| 86. | | | |
| 87. | | | |
| 88. | | | |
| 89. | | | |
| 90. | | | |

Notes _____

_____

_____

_____

_____

_____

Use the samples and blank forms to complete Phase 2 of instructional pacing. Phase 2 is completion of daily and weekly lesson plans. See page 103, Instructional Pacing Phase 2, Steps 1 and 2 of Chapter 8 for detailed instructions on completing the forms.

Figure 9.10  Pacing: Phase 2 Form

**Time Period**
**Day(s):** _____

| CONTENT FOCUS | REQUIRED RESOURCES |
| --- | --- |
| | |

| DESIRED OUTCOME(S)/OBJECTIVE(S) | ASSESSMENT/EVALUATION |
| --- | --- |
| | |

| DESCRIPTION OF ACTIVITIES/PROCEDURES |
| --- |
| |

# TIME LINE (Minutes)

| DAY | | | | |
|---|---|---|---|---|
| 0 5 10 15 | 20 25 30 35 | 40 45 50 55 | 60 65 70 75 | 80 85 90 |
| DAY 0 5 10 15 | 20 25 30 35 | 40 45 50 55 | 60 65 70 75 | 80 85 90 |
| DAY 0 5 10 15 | 20 25 30 35 | 40 45 50 55 | 60 65 70 75 | 80 85 90 |
| DAY 0 5 10 15 | 20 25 30 35 | 40 45 50 55 | 60 65 70 75 | 80 85 90 |
| DAY 0 5 10 15 | 20 25 30 35 | 40 45 50 55 | 60 65 70 75 | 80 85 90 |

Figure 9.11  Pacing: Phase 2—Geometry Sample

**Time Period**
**Dates:** _____

| CONTENT FOCUS (1) | REQUIRED RESOURCES (4) |
|---|---|
| Segments, rays, and distance | Geometry figures poster |

| SPECIFIC OBJECTIVES (2) | STUDENT ASSESSMENT (5) |
|---|---|
| Identify, name, and draw | Transparency questions<br>Decoding activity—distance on a number line |

## DESCRIPTION OF ACTIVITIES/PROCEDURES (3)

Review key points from previous lesson. Short lecture with transparency sample questions. Guided practice. Small assessment of transparency questions for groups of 3–4 students. Decoding activity dealing with calculating distance on a number line. Teacher points to a geometric figure on a large poster and asks students to name it without giving the students any information about the figures prior. Review of the day's lesson.

# DAY 1 IN MINUTE INTERVALS

| Time | Day 1 Activity |
|---|---|
| 0 | Review |
| 5 | |
| 10 | |
| 15 | Definitions and examples of terms |
| 20 | |
| 25 | |
| 30 | |
| 35 | |
| 40 | Student practice (transparency ?'s) |
| 45 | |
| 50 | Decoding activity (distance on a # line) |
| 55 | |
| 60 | Check student work |
| 65 | |
| 70 | |
| 75 | Poster |
| 80 | |
| 85 | Summary |
| 90 | |

DAY
0
5
10
15
20
25
30
35
40
45
50
55
60
65
70
75
80
85
90

DAY
0
5
10
15
20
25
30
35
40
45
50
55
60
65
70
75
80
85
90

DAY
0
5
10
15
20
25
30
35
40
45
50
55
60
65
70
75
80
85
90

DAY
0
5
10
15
20
25
30
35
40
45
50
55
60
65
70
75
80
85
90

Figure 9.12 Pacing: Phase 2—French II

**Time Period**
**Day(s): 1–5**

| CONTENT ANALYSIS AND FOCUS | REQUIRED RESOURCES |
|---|---|
| Describing your city<br>Finding your way home<br>Describing your home | Textbook<br>Workbook |

| DESIRED OUTCOME(S)/OBJECTIVE(S) | ASSESSMENT/EVALUATION |
|---|---|
| Students will learn to describe building, asked to give directions, describe their house | Graded interviews<br>Graded group exercises<br>Drawing of house<br>Composition—written description of house<br>Map of city |

| DESCRIPTION OF ACTIVITIES/PROCEDURES | |
|---|---|
| Lecture discussion<br>Paired exercises<br>Composition<br>Drawing | Generating conversations from drawings |

## DAY 1

| Time | Activity |
|---|---|
| 0 | Rules and expectations |
| 5 | |
| 10 | |
| 15 | |
| 20 | Students reintroduce |
| 25 | themselves—name, |
| 30 | where from, age, |
| 35 | interresting facts |
| 40 | Read over p. 188 |
| 45 | French cities |
| 50 | |
| 55 | |
| 60 | |
| 65 | |
| 70 | |
| 75 | |
| 80 | |
| 85 | |
| 90 | |

## DAY 2

| Time | Activity |
|---|---|
| 0 | Students draw bldgs. in |
| 5 | their citites |
| 10 | |
| 15 | |
| 20 | Identifying the building |
| 25 | in French |
| 30 | |
| 35 | |
| 40 | Vocab., p. 190 |
| 45 | |
| 50 | Ex. 1, p. 190 |
| 55 | |
| 60 | Work in pairs |
| 65 | Interviews |
| 70 | p. 190 |
| 75 | |
| 80 | Present interviews |
| 85 | |
| 90 | |

## DAY 3

| Time | Activity |
|---|---|
| 0 | Do Ex. 1, p 181 |
| 5 | Wrkbk. Cassette A–B |
| 10 | |
| 15 | |
| 20 | pp. 165–166 |
| 25 | Divide class in half—one |
| 30 | asks the other answers |
| 35 | |
| 40 | Ex. 3–4, p. 192 |
| 45 | Asking directions |
| 50 | |
| 55 | |
| 60 | |
| 65 | |
| 70 | Pairs Ex. 5, p. 193 |
| 75 | |
| 80 | Present group exercise |
| 85 | to class |
| 90 | |

# TEN

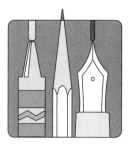

# Effective Instructional Strategies for Block Scheduling

To be a successful teacher in a blocked class, the author, with Robert Algozzine and Martin Eaddy (Queen, Algozzine, & Eaddy, 1997) concluded that the most important teaching skills for instruction are as follows:

1. The ability to develop a pacing guide for the course in nine-week periods, including weekly and daily planning

2. The ability to use several instructional strategies effectively

3. The skill to design and maintain an environment that allows for great flexibility and creativity

4. The desire and skill to be an effective classroom manager

5. The freedom to share the ownership of teaching and learning with the students

Another study (Queen, Algozzine, & Isenhour, 1999) showed that although it was important that all teachers master the preceding skills, beginning teachers need special attention from mentors and principals. This was most evident in the area of effective classroom management.

Principals and staff development personnel must provide initial and continuous training for teachers to master instructional strategies.

Cooperative learning, synectics, Paideia seminars, concept attainment, case method, inquiry methods, simulations, games, and role-playing strategies are excellent methods for teachers to use in blocked classes. The author, with Jenny Burrell and Stephanie McManus (Queen, Burrell, & McManus, 2000) identified and reviewed several strategies in *Planning for Instruction: A Year Long Guide.* However, just as a 90-minute lecture is inappropriate, a 90-minute discussion session may be too long. Changing activities every 15 to 20 minutes can prevent student boredom, encourage class interaction, and promote teaching to the needs of diverse learners. Instruction in these extended periods should begin with a review, include various activities, and conclude with an adequate summary. Briefly described below are some instructional strategies that teachers should be aware of and trained to use for teaching in the block. These instructional approaches are presented briefly here in the text, but the reader can find much greater details of these and additional approaches with numerous examples on the author's Web site, www.blockscheduling.com.

## Cooperative Learning

Cooperative learning, developed by Slavin in the early 1980s, is a very useful teaching method and classroom management tool (Slavin, 1987). A block schedule allows for group meetings, various grouping structures, and team presentations. Cooperative groups can include competitive subject reviews or timely coverage of material. Groups can be created by a random selection or a prescribed mix established by the teacher. For specialized activities, cooperative groups can be formed by the students. For optimal benefits, groups should stay together for at least four weeks. However, many class activities call for quick group formations. Limiting the time periods for groups can decrease problems resulting from personality conflicts within the groups.

For the most efficient use of time while grouping, teachers must inform students of the objective of their work together and explain the grading procedures that will be used for evaluating their performance. Group members should have an individual set of responsibilities and be held accountable for their actions in all activities. The teacher and students evaluate performance using self, peer, and teacher assessment in a cooperative evaluation model.

Cooperative learning can be structured in a variety of ways for a block schedule. However, inappropriate use of cooperative groups can lead to increased discipline problems and may result in excessive student competition. The author believes the most effective grouping structure is the Jigsaw II Method that uses Home and Expert grouping patterns. In a jigsaw, each student prepares an assigned activity, then meets with the group to teach or inform other members. Each student has individual accountability and special responsibility to listen and learn the new material from the other group members. Another approach used is the project groups. Groups are assigned a specified project to analyze completely or a specific problem to solve. Project groups conclude with a presentation to the class and, often, written documentation of the project. An advanced form of this approach is the case method.

## The Case Method

The case method is used to stress introspection, higher-order thinking, and individual accountability. It also creates the type of layered class structure needed in a block schedule. Once the initial narrative or case is presented to the class, individual students sign contracts for their roles in the case study. Groups negotiate with the teacher for final presentations, meet for daily discussions, or seek guidance for research. Portfolio development is possible on an individual and group basis. Many different activities can be incorporated into the case, which achieves the variability aim of teachers in the block. For example, a case study on Thomas Jefferson in a history class can include individual research projects, a jigsaw share of expert knowledge, group presentations on contemporary leaders, and Socratic seminars on several of Jefferson's accomplishments.

## Socratic Seminar

In 1982, Mortimer Adler introduced *The Paideia Proposal* by using a group discussion model that can be easily incorporated into a blocked class. Each member of the class reads a selection from the material provided by the teacher prior to the seminar. The teacher avoids directing the discussion of the seminar. The teacher's role is to record the participation and degree of preparedness of each participating student. Students are instructed to explore their ideas about a particular topic and question other members of the class in an open discussion. Students thrive in these seminars once they discover that their opinion is valued and that the teacher is not searching for a specific, "right answer." The teacher usually asks the first question, or it can be elicited from a student experienced with the seminar format. Teachers avoid evaluation, direct the discussion toward topic relevancy, and clarify arguments if there seems to be no solution. The Socratic seminar often leads to further issues, thus extending the learning opportunities beyond one classroom discussion.

## Synectics

Through the use of metaphor, Gordon in the early 1960s developed an approach by which students learn to associate a new topic with prior experience (Gordon, 1961). In analogy form, the teacher asks students to describe the similarities between a given topic (the concept) and some unrelated item (the analogue). For example, a biology teacher may ask her students to describe the similarities between the parts of an animal cell and the parts of a city. After reviewing these similarities, students are asked to "become" the concepts and analogues by using first-person statements of feeling. The teacher may elicit statements such as "I feel strong when my cell membrane keeps out impurities," or "I am the nucleus and I feel very powerful." If obvious differences exist between the topic and the comparative element, the teacher may address these differences while being careful not to destroy the link previously made. Finally, students create their own new analogies to better retain the original concepts. This method serves well as a review activity and can be a valuable tool in assisting students to retain facts and concepts.

## Concept Attainment

In the concept attainment model, initially developed by Bruner in the early 1960s, teachers prepare and present a series of positive and negative examples in order to lead students to a definition of a concept and its essential attributes (Bruner, 1966). After the teacher presents the students with the first set of examples, students brainstorm a list of similarities between the positive examples and formulate a definition of the concept. The teacher then presents the students with a second set of examples for the students to test their predictions. The final concept is gradually attained by students who develop a greater understanding of the concept than if they were merely expected to memorize it from a lecture or book. Joyce, Weil, and Calhoun (2008) 8th edition continue to advance different formats of the model.

## Inquiry Method

In using the inquiry method, the teacher presents students with a problem to solve using the scientific process. Students gather data by posing yes-no questions to the teacher and use their results to formulate a theory on relationships or the solution to the problem presented. Typically, as Eggen and Kauchak state in *Strategies for Teachers* (2001), inquiry is using facts and observations to solve problems. The teacher then directs the students to test their theories and discuss the steps used to solve the problem. Inquiry is an attention-getting approach useful as an anticipatory set and often works well at the beginning of an extended period. Teachers using inquiry can become masters at asking thought-provoking questions. Inquiry can lead to group or individual study and may serve as the motivational element for a case study.

## Simulations

Simulations can be used in a blocked class to create the effect or reality of a real situation or experience. Students participate in simulations of the real world by solving problems, completing developed packages of materials, or taking part in organized role-playing. Because of the extended time in a blocked class, students use short field trips to related sites as a part of simulations without being absent from an entire school day. Games, while more competitive than simulations and role-playing, are often included in the simulation family. Although it takes more time to plan, design, and implement a simulation, the increased student motivation and involvement are well worth the investment for greater student learning.

# RECOMMENDATIONS FOR IMPROVING BLOCK SCHEDULING FOR THE FUTURE  ■

Listed below are important recommendations for maximizing the positive effects of block scheduling:

1. Teachers must develop and follow monthly, weekly, and daily pacing guides.

2. Teachers must master a minimum of five instructional strategies that engage students directly in the learning process and should aim to master seven or eight strategies.

3. Teachers should pace each lesson by changing grouping patterns, varying presentations, and using different instructional activities every 15 to 20 minutes. In most cases, a teacher should use a minimum of three instructional strategies during any period.

4. Teachers should incorporate alternative and authentic assessment practices when evaluating students.

5. Teachers must use the entire class period for instruction. Every day. Period!

6. Teachers should strive to be creative and flexible in assigning activities.

7. Teachers should coordinate and incorporate outside assignments into regular classroom activities.

8. Teachers should monitor individual students consistently to be sure of total student participation.

9. Teachers should mentor, formally or informally, beginning teachers and veteran teachers having difficulty with instruction in block scheduling.

10. Principals (and/or staff development personnel) must provide continuous staff development for all teachers throughout the year on the topics of curriculum/instructional alignment, instructional pacing and strategies, and time management.

11. Principals must develop a monitoring team to verify that all teachers are using pacing guides, instructional strategies, and class periods effectively.

12. Principals must take appropriate disciplinary action with teachers unwilling to follow the basic principles and procedures necessary in block scheduling.

13. Principals should work with less effective teachers in the development of an instructional improvement plan.

14. Superintendents should contact colleges of education in their regions and demand that block scheduling methods be included in teacher and principal training programs.

15. Superintendents should require that before schools move to a block scheduling format that principals and teachers spend from one to two years in effective staff development. (Queen, 2000)

In essence, the success of block scheduling depends greatly on the professionals who implement the model in their schools. It is imperative that the teachers, principals, students, and parents give the same attention and effort to block scheduling that they would to any other school schedule. Using instructional methods effectively will assist students to learn at an optimal level, as affirmed by Joyce et al. in the 2008, 8th edition of their book *Models of Teaching*. Thoughtful planning, organization, implementation, and evaluation are imperative to maximize success in the block. All shareholders involved in education must provide the opportunity for the continued improvement of a scheduling format that has great potential for increased success in the future. Don't forget to visit the author's Web site for numerous examples of these methods in lesson formats that have been tested successfully with students.

# ELEVEN

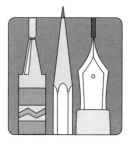

# Teacher-Directed Instruction

**D**irect instruction is a teaching method in which teachers direct the instruction from one lesson to the next within a fixed time period. It is sometimes referred to as a formal lesson. Direct instruction has come to have a number of different meanings, ranging from a type of classroom management system to any type of structured teaching to a set of specific steps to be followed in teaching a lesson. This instructional strategy is widely used and is a member of the behavioral systems family. In teaching models that have developed from the behavioral family, the focus is on the definition of the task and the analysis of the task. "Analysis of the task" refers, in this sense, to approaching the task from the perspective of the learner. The instructional design principles proposed in models such as direct instruction focus on (a) conceptualizing learner performance into goals and tasks, (b) breaking these tasks into smaller component tasks, (c) developing training activities that ensure mastery of each subcomponent, and (d) arranging the entire learning situation into sequences that ensure adequate transfer from one component to another and achievement of prerequisite learning before more advanced learning (Joyce, Weil, & Calhoun, 2008).

## DIRECT INSTRUCTION AS A TEACHING MODEL ■

Direct instruction is a teaching model that places a great deal of emphasis on the completion of academic tasks. Its purpose is to maximize student

**137**

learning and to achieve a high rate of student success. Direct instruction involves a high degree of teacher control and high expectations for student progress. One of the major goals of direct instruction is to maximize learning time. When using direct instruction, the teacher arranges the learning environment so that there can be a predominant focus on learning.

As mentioned earlier, direct instruction is primarily teacher directed, and that is a factor in determining how it is used. The teacher is responsible for asking the questions in the lesson and leading the student to the desired answers. This is one reason it is recommended that direct instruction not be used as the only method of instructional delivery. It is most applicable to teaching a well-structured body of knowledge or the steps in a process or skill. It was once thought that direct instruction was beneficial only to young students, but recent studies have demonstrated that direct instruction may be successfully used for teaching skills such as comprehension in reading to both elementary and secondary students (Klesius & Searls, 1990).

The most common applications of direct instruction are in the study of basic information and skills in the core curriculum areas (Joyce et al., 2008). Recently, there has been a resurgence of interest in direct instruction. It has been touted as a successful way to teach ESL students—those for whom English is a second language. Direct instruction has been seen as extremely beneficial for those students identified as being from low socioeconomic status homes and therefore "at risk." Jere Brophy (1996) has suggested that direct instruction of social skills is an appropriate way to work with shy or withdrawn students.

The phrase "direct instruction" has been used by researchers to refer to a pattern of teaching that consists of the teacher's explaining a new concept or skill to a large group of students, having the students test their understanding by practicing the skill or concept under teacher direction, and encouraging them to practice under teacher guidance. In a direct instruction lesson, structuring comments are made at the beginning of the lesson. The comments may take the form of introductory activities that capture the students' attention immediately, or they may simply involve a discussion of the objective for the day's lesson. During the lesson introduction, the teacher provides explicit instructions for how the work is to be done. Then students are informed about the materials they will use and the activities they will work on. Finally, the teacher provides an overview of the lesson.

In direct instruction, the teacher often models a "finished product." The purpose of these introductory comments is to provide clarification for the student about what the procedures will be and the actual content of the lesson that is to follow. The next step is for the teacher to present the lesson. The teacher has decided in advance what information students are to learn. In the presentation portion of the lesson, the teacher explains the new concept, providing demonstrations and examples, along with the rules or definitions that help students to remember the concept. The teacher directs the questioning, always bringing the student to the correct answer. When incorrect answers are given, there is immediate correction. After the presentation, the teacher demonstrates what he or she wants students to do in practicing what has just been taught. The teacher demonstrates each step in the correct order. When the teacher feels secure about the students' understanding, he or she assigns guided practice. This is an opportunity for students to practice the new learning under the teacher's guidance as the teacher circulates around the classroom, checking for student comprehension. The guided practice will be informally assessed so that the teacher is assured of student understanding. The aim is to master the skill. After this, independent practice is assigned. This is often done as homework. Whether the work is done as independent seatwork or at home, the objective is for the student to work independently. In a direct instruction lesson, the student works independently 50% to 75% of the time. The independent work is also assessed. The goal is 85% to 90% mastery.

The components of a direct instruction lesson design have appeared in other lesson designs as well. Dr. Madeline Hunter's (1982) research has shown that effective teachers have a methodology when planning and presenting a lesson. She has suggested various elements that might be considered in planning for effective instruction. In what has become known as the "Madeline Hunter model," the following elements are shown:

- Anticipatory set
- Purpose
- Input
- Modeling
- Guided practice
- Checking for understanding
- Independent practice
- Closure

It is not difficult to see the similarities in the design of a direct instruction lesson and the Madeline Hunter design. Others have also added to the basic lesson design of direct instruction, and direct instruction basics can be used in other teaching models. In fact, there are those who would argue that the components of direct instruction provide the background that is necessary before other models are used and that the lesson design can be used as a shell for any instructional lesson or unit.

The beginning of direct instruction is often credited to Siegfried "Ziggy" Englemann (Becker & Englemann, 1971). Englemann was a philosophy major who worked in the field of advertising. While exploring literature on the behalf of clients who marketed to children, he became interested in what type of input was required to induce retention of learning. Englemann began by working with small focus groups that included neighborhood children as well as his own sons. He outlined sequences of instruction that formed the nucleus for his later curricula. The early components of this sequence of instruction looked very much like the components of direct instruction today. Skills were precisely communicated in small bits, there was measurement to determine mastery, learners' mistakes were quickly corrected, learners adhered to a strict schedule, and there was continual and repetitive review for the purpose of incorporating old material with new material. Englemann's early focus was on computational skills and phonetic skills. Eventually, Englemann's research was purchased by Scientific Research Associates (SRA), a division of McGraw-Hill, and was published in the form of kits that contained everything needed for presenting a lesson. The material was marketed under the trade name of DISTAR.[1]

In 1968, direct instruction enjoyed national attention for a brief time. Nixon's White House initiated a federal study called Project Follow Through. The Office of Economic Opportunity and the Office of Education joined forces to organize and fund this endeavor. The study was the largest controlled comparative study in pedagogical techniques in history, and its purpose was to work to isolate the "best practices" in education. The cost of the study was $1 billion.

At the same time that Englemann was publicizing information about direct instruction, Jean Piaget was expounding his theory of developmental learning. The two ideas were in direct opposition to each other. Becker and Englemann (1971) were positing that regardless of a student's age, if information was transferred in small enough bites and with enough repetition, learning could be accomplished. Piaget believed that even with the very best instruction, student learning would not occur until the student was developmentally ready.

## ■ DIRECT INSTRUCTION AS A CONTINUUM OF TEACHING BEHAVIOR

Several studies have shown that a strong academic focus produces greater student engagement and subsequent achievement (Joyce et al., 2008). Direct instruction plays a limited but important role in a comprehensive educational program. Some proponents of direct instruction say it is a way to target specifics of learning and to teach children what you want them to know. But opponents argue that direct instruction thwarts the development of higher-order thinking skills. One way for an educator to examine direct instruction is on a continuum. At one end of this continuum is the very directed and carefully sequenced lesson. This would be the type of lesson that one finds in materials such as Mastery Reading or other SRA publications. The lessons are scripted, and the teacher is taught how to signal for correct responses from the student. The questions asked are not open-ended, and there is one right answer that the teacher is seeking. The middle of this continuum is where one finds lessons such as the ones included in most textbooks. The lesson is partially scripted, and the students may be encouraged to think of different responses to questions, but the lesson is teacher directed, and the students are acquiring information in small bits. The learning theory is that the acquisition of small pieces of knowledge can eventually be constructed into the larger concept. At the other end of the continuum is direct instruction used as an introductory mini-lesson in a writing workshop. The components of direct instruction are still there, but they are used as a part of the lesson, not as the whole lesson. The teacher directs the student to specific information that will assist in completing the rest of the lesson, which may actually use another instructional strategy.

Barak Rosenshine addressed the topic of direct instruction in 1978 at the annual meeting of the American Educational Research Association. He is credited with introducing the phrase "direct instruction" into the mainstream of educational research. When direct instruction was viewed at this time, Rosenshine said,

> Direct [a concept] is related to the concept of academic engaged time. The term is relatively new, and apparently was developed independently by a number of researchers in the last three years. The meaning of the term is still being developed, and the definition is still loose. I use it to refer to those activities which are directly related to making progress in reading and mathematics and to those settings which promote those activities.
>
> . . . Direct instruction refers to levels of student engagement within classrooms using sequenced structured materials. . . . [D]irect instruction refers to teaching activities focused on academic matters where goals are clear to students, time allocated for instruction is sufficient and continuous; content covered is extensive; student performance is monitored; questions are at a low cognitive level and produce many correct responses; and feedback to students is immediate and academically oriented. In direct instruction the teacher controls instructional goals, chooses material appropriate for the student's ability level, and paces the instructional episode. Interaction is characterized as structured, but not authoritarian; rather, learning takes place in a convivial academic atmosphere. (Rosenshine, 1985)

As Rosenshine continued to research student achievement, he and others found that students acquire structures for learning when the following take place.

- Information is presented in small steps so that the working memory does not become overloaded.
- Students are helped to develop an organization for the new material.
- Students are guided through practice and given opportunities for extensive processing.
- Students are provided with cognitive strategies as they approach higher-level tasks.
- Students are given opportunities for extensive practice.

Direct instruction is a highly structured approach to teaching content, whether for math, history, or biology, in a highly structured environment in which the information is given to the students and they learn by practicing their knowledge under the teacher's direction until the content and associated skills are mastered. For instance, a teacher provides the information on how to balance a mathematical equation, and the students learn by practicing their knowledge. Rosenshine (1985) describes the process in steps, such as reviewing, stating the objective, modeling, providing numerous examples and reteaching. He and others have attempted to identify those teaching behaviors related to student achievement for the purpose of improving the quality of learning that takes place in school.

There is often disagreement about what constitutes a pitfall or a promise with direct instruction, depending on whether or not one sees merit in direct instruction as a method. Some see scripted lessons as evils that destroy the creative nature of the classroom. Proponents of the scripted lesson argue that there is no doubt that what is important will be conveyed to the student. With lessons of this nature, lesson plans are also available. Again, for some, this is a disadvantage, while others see a constructed lesson plan as a great time-saver and advantage. Direct instruction is by definition, teacher-directed. Many educators feel that children learn best when the teacher tells them what they need to know. This kind of instruction has had a revival of popularity with the advent of high stakes testing. As one would expect, opponents of direct instruction include those who regularly employ instructional strategies such as cooperative learning, discovery learning, and group investigation. However, direct instruction, as stated earlier, can be viewed on a continuum that allows movement away from the "all or none idea" to understanding the ways that direct instruction can become a part of any lesson. Student mistakes are corrected quickly in a direct instruction lesson, but some educators would argue that this is a negative. Direct instruction is easily evaluated, which is usually seen as an advantage for two reasons. First, most people have been taught by this traditional method, so it is familiar. Second, most evaluation instruments "fit" with this model. The components of a direct instruction lesson are not hidden; they are very obvious. Parent involvement is not emphasized in direct instruction. Many see this as negative, but it is one reason that direct instruction is seen as a strategy to be used in low socioeconomic populations and in ESL settings. In both situations, parents are often not capable of helping their child. No technology is necessary to teach a lesson using direct instruction.

## ■ SUMMARY

Direct instruction is a teaching model that is beneficial to students and that certainly has validity. It is important to remember that it is not a model to be used for all instructional delivery. Students will benefit from direct instruction but only up to a certain point. It is beneficial to student learning to balance direct instruction with models that encourage discovery of concepts and ideas. Models that engage students in more sophisticated cognition should be used as well.

The chapter ends with a sample lesson related to direct instruction titled, "Our Mr. Jefferson."

**Note**

1. Direct Instruction, a packaged learning program published by SRA that was developed by Ziggy Englemann and supported by other researchers like Wes Becker (Becker & Englemann, 1971) should not be confused with direct instruction, a teaching strategy that has broad implications.

# OUR MR. JEFFERSON: ■
# A SAMPLE TEACHER-DIRECTED LESSON

Following is a sample teacher-directed lesson. When delivering a directed lesson, it is important to have visuals to maintain the students' attention as well as to accommodate the visual learners in your classroom. For this lesson, one could use slides or pictures of Thomas Jefferson, the Jefferson Memorial, the Declaration of Independence, Monticello, and so on as part of the presentation of the material, which is broken into short sections of boxed text. Remember that, to be effective, the lesson must be well planned and focused, should not be more than 30 to 45 minutes in length, and should maintain students' motivation. In addition, check frequently for understanding and modify the pace accordingly.

## Lesson Title: An American Enigma: Thomas Jefferson

Sources: *Thomas Jefferson: An Intimate History*, by Fawn M. Brodie (1915–1981) and *American Sphinx: The Character of Thomas Jefferson*, by Joseph J. Ellis (1943–   )

Who Was the *Real* Thomas Jefferson?
• If Thomas Jefferson were a monument, he would be the Sphinx
• If he were a painting, he would be the Mona Lisa
• If he were a character in a play, he would be Hamlet

Thomas Jefferson Was . . .
• A violinist, farmer, scientist, lover of fine wines
• A restless architect who couldn't bring himself to ever finish building his home
• A politician with a voice so soft that he could barely make himself heard from the podium but who founded the first political party
• A man who denounced the moral bankruptcy he saw in Europe, but delighted in the gilded salons of Paris
• A statesman who was twice elected president of the United States but didn't think it worthy for the listing on his gravestone

Thomas Jefferson . . .
- Brought about fiscal stability to the country but faced personal bankruptcy
- Was a lifelong champion of small government who took it upon himself to more than double the size of his country
- Endured the loss of nearly everything he held dear but somehow never lost his faith for the future
- Distilled a century of Enlightenment thinking into one remarkable sentence that began, "We hold these truths to be self-evident, that all men are created equal . . ." yet owned more than 200 human beings and never saw fit to free them

Early Life
- Born in Albemarle County, Virginia on April 13, 1743
- Mother—Jane Randolph Jefferson
- Father—Peter Jefferson

Schooling
- Received a classical education with the Rev. Maury
- Attended William & Mary in Williamsburg and was influenced by William Small (mathematics, science, and philosophy) and George Wythe (law)
- Governor Francis Fauquier (friend)

The Beginnings of a Patriot
- Colonists thought of themselves as British citizens with the privilege of British liberty
- Stamp Act of 1765—a dictate of a far-off parliament that had no colonial representatives
- Jefferson in the Virginia House of Burgesses—signed a boycott of British goods to end the "enslavement" of the colonists

As a Young Adult . . .
- Practiced law for 7 years
- Married Martha Wayles Skelton on New Year's Day 1772
- Received land, slaves, and debt from his father-in-law

**The American Revolution**

Before the Revolution
- 1774—Summary of the Rights of British America
- June 1775—Left for Philadelphia
- The Continental Congress and committee work
- Declaration of Independence: "We hold these truths to be self-evident, that all men are create equal, that they are endowed by their creator with certain inalienable rights, that among these are life, liberty and the pursuit of happiness."

During the Revolution
- House of Delegates in Virginia: Sponsored the law to overturn primogeniture and wrote the Establishment of Religious Freedom in Virginia
- Governor of Virginia
- Mentor of the next generation of statesmen: James Madison, James Monroe, William Short

After the Revolution
- Martha Jefferson died in September 1782
- 1784: Wrote Notes on the State of Virginia

Jefferson in Paris
- Went to Paris in 1784—took daughter Patsy and slave James Hemings
- Friendship with John & Abigail Adams
- Paris: A close view of monarchy and the salon society
- Daughter Polly comes to Paris, accompanied by slave Sally Hemings
- Maria Cosway: "My Head and My Heart" (letter to Maria on a dialogue between his head and his heart)
- Mentor of the next generation of statesmen: James Madison, James Monroe, William Short

Secretary of State
- 1789: Secretary of State for Washington's administration
- Conflict: Alexander Hamilton
- Political parties: The Federalists vs. the Democratic-Republicans

Home to Monticello: Before Returning to Politics
- Monticello—his home and safe haven
- Focused on his farm, his home, and his inventions
- 1786: Ran for president—became John Adams's vice president
- Opposed the Alien & Sedition Acts of 1798

Revolution of 1800
- 1800: Candidates for president: Adams, Pinkney, Jefferson, and Burr
- Election thrown into the House of Representatives
- A legacy of Federalists judges for the Jefferson administration

Jefferson as President . . .
- Worked to decrease federal spending
- Negotiated the Louisiana Purchase
- Sent Lewis & Clark and the Corps of Discovery to explore the West
- James Callender publishes rumors about Jefferson and Sally Hemings
- Daughter Polly dies—1804
- Imposed an embargo on exporting American goods and the economy suffers
- Endured a tormented second term
- Left Washington in 1809 for Monticello, never to return

Did He or Didn't He?
- Sally Hemings had five children: Tom, Beverly, Harriet, Madison, and Eston; all were reported to be mulattos
- Jefferson was present at Monticello nine months prior to the births of Sally's last four children; Sally was said to be in Paris when she became pregnant with her first child
- Jefferson's descendents claim that the father was one of the Carr brothers

Genetic Evidence
- A man receives a "Y" chromosome from his father and an "X" chromosome from his mother.
- The Y chromosome has polymorphisms—the "glue" holding the actual genes together.
- Fathers pass on polymorphisms (the "glue"), which have specific characteristics, to their sons.
- If two men have identical polymorphisms, the chances are great that they have a common ancestor.
- Field Jefferson and Eston Hemmings had identical polymorphisms.

Retirement at Monticello
- His plants and garden
- Constant visitors
- A household with grandchildren


The North and South Poles of the Revolution
- 1812: James Madison negotiated a "truce" between John Adams and Jefferson
- 1812–1826: The most important correspondence between public figures in U.S. history


University of Virginia
- Founded the University of Virginia—an "academic village" in Charlottesville
- First university in the world that did not begin as a religious or theology school


Mounting Debt
- 1815: Forced to sell his library—became the nucleus of the Library of Congress
- At the end of his life, owed over $100,000 and knew that Monticello would be lost to his descendents


"Is It the 4th?"
- July 4, 1826, was the 50th anniversary of the Declaration of Independence.
- Thomas Jefferson died on July 4th around 1:00 p.m. at Monticello.
- John Adams died in Massachusetts the same day around 5:00 p.m.—his last words were, "Jefferson still survives."

Indeed he does.

# TWELVE

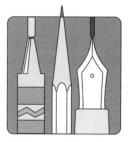

# Discovery and Inquiry

## DISCOVERY LEARNING ■

Although the phrase "discovery method" has been used to describe a variety of instructional techniques, most definitions include the learner's discovering what is to be learned without much assistance from the teacher. After discovering the rule that underlies the example, the student must apply that rule to a new example or concept. Because of its many uses, discovery learning is sometimes called the inductive method, guided discovery, problem solving, activity learning, or learner-centered instruction (Blake, 1984). Although these are used as synonyms for discovery learning, there does exist a difference between it and the inductive, guided discovery, and problem-solving methods. The inductive method is a mental process, whereas discovery learning is an instructional strategy. In guided discovery, the teacher guides students by using hints, questions, and other devices. This differs from pure discovery in that students receive no help. Finally, problem solving requires students to discover or find many different rules they may have already known in isolation and craft them into a solution (Blake, 1984).

Discovery learning can be broken into the following two parts: (a) the amount of guidance and (b) the sequence of rules and examples. The variable regarding guidance is straightforward and deals with how much assistance a teacher gives a student in the learning process. This can range from providing no help to providing many clues and hints. To understand the second variable in sequence, it is important to understand what a rule is and where it came from. In Bloom's domains and categories of learning behaviors, the three domains are psychomotor, affective, and cognitive (Bloom, 1959). Discovery learning is located within the cognitive domain and primarily deals with the last three categories of learning behaviors—concept, rule, and problem solving. A concept is a class of objects, things, or events. A rule is the interaction of two or more concepts. Problem solving involves selecting, combining, and/or generating rules to solve a problem (Blake, 1984). Therefore, in discovery learning, the student is trying to discern the rule having to do with the interaction of the concepts in the example. The sequence of rules and examples in discovery learning is always example, then rule—referred to as "egrule." This contrasts with the sequence in the expository method. Here, the teacher supplies the student with all of the content to be learned, and the student applies that knowledge to an example. Expository learning results in a rule-to-example sequence—"ruleg" (Blake, 1984).

David Ausubel stated that the rationale for discovery learning was that all true knowledge is self-discovered (Blake, 1984). This echoes an earlier belief of John Dewey, whose rationale for discovery learning lay in the distinction between knowledge and the record of knowledge. To Dewey, knowledge was gained when students created or discovered that knowledge for themselves while being actively engaged (Davidson, 1971). Proponents claim that by experiencing the example first, abstract ideas become more concrete and easier to understand (Blake, 1984).

The lesson design for discovery learning is simple. First, students are presented with an example. This can be an interaction between any two or more concepts. The students study the example and attempt to discern a rule. During this process, the teacher plays a very limited role and does not provide content. Once the rule has been established, students are then asked to apply this rule to a new example or concept.

## History and Research

The discovery method has been around for many centuries. Socrates engaged in a dialog of questions to the slave boy in an effort to help him discover the principle of geometry. In more modern times, discovery learning grew out of the progressive education movement. The method saw a large growth in interest during the post-Sputnik era when schools were encouraged to use discovery methods so students could become more "scientific" (Blake, 1984).

Although other proponents for discovery learning included Rousseau and Montessori, the two major designers of the method were John Dewey and Jerome Bruner (Blake, 1984). Dewey believed that education should be based on personal experience and that knowledge should be discovered. His book *Experience and Education* (1938) proved a major force in discovery learning (Blake, 1984). Bruner's works in the 1960s helped to give discovery learning a boost in popularity (e.g., see Bruner, 1966). He has been credited with starting the experimentation necessary to establish discovery learning as a valid instructional method (Blake, 1984).

One of the loudest critics against discovery learning was Ausubel. His main contention had to do with whether discovery learning was more efficient in helping students learn given the large amount of time necessary for the method. He argued that if students could learn the material without discovery learning in less time, then discovery learning was inefficient (Hermann, 1969).

Research findings in discovery learning have often been contradictory. The primary reason is that researchers have been unable to agree on a single definition for discovery learning. Taking this into consideration, Hermann (1969) and Blake (1984) conducted two extensive meta-analyses of discovery learning research. Most of the research compared discovery learning with expository learning. Both researchers found that discovery learning assisted students in transferring the knowledge to a new problem. It was also more effective when the transfer task was more complex or when background knowledge was limited. They also found that discovery learning resulted in better long-term retention. In addition, research showed that discovery learning was appropriate for all subjects. It was more effective with low-ability groups than with high-ability groups. Finally, guided discovery was more effective than pure discovery.

## Promises and Pitfalls

Discovery learning has several advantages. It is appropriate for all subjects and ages and uses students' own personal associations as a basis for understanding. It also allows students the opportunity to reconcile any misconceptions about a topic. Discovery learning has also proven easier for beginners in a field since understanding is constructed and not received. This learning method places the responsibility of learning on the learner (Svinicki, 1998).

A disadvantage of discovery learning is that it is time-consuming and does not lead to immediate retention. In addition, it is difficult for administrators to observe, and it demands teacher creativity.

## Summary

The discovery learning model is designed to let the learners realize knowledge for themselves. Although there has been conflicting research, this method has been shown to be effective when the background knowledge is limited and the transfer task is difficult. It is more efficient than expository learning for overall task transfer. This method is a good way to begin a lesson and can serve as an advanced organizer.

NOTE: See the end of this chapter for a sample discovery learning lesson titled "How Do We Build the Tower?"

# ■ THE INQUIRY TRAINING MODEL

The inquiry training model (inquiry) is designed to teach students how to learn an inquiry process by asking questions and developing hypotheses concerning a puzzling problem, called a "discrepant event." Inquiry is a model of teaching in the information processing family. This model specializes in causal reasoning that helps students sharpen their scientific inquiry skills. Information processing models assist students to make sense of their world by acquiring and organizing data, identifying problems, and generating solutions. These models are designed to help students develop a conscious awareness of strategies for learning that will help them reflect on the world in which they live.

Inquiry builds on a child's natural curiosity. Students develop skills that are relevant and useful in helping them become autonomous learners. Using this method, students solve problems by asking a series of questions, collecting and verifying data, developing concepts, and building and testing hypotheses. With practice, students develop into independent, autonomous learners who become increasingly conscious of their process of inquiry. Students participate in the process of scientific inquiry, questioning why events happen, logically processing and analyzing new data, and in the process, developing intellectual strategies to use in the acquisition of knowledge. Although inquiry training is not in the social family of teaching models, students do collaborate with others to solve problems, and this collaboration helps them enrich their thinking and tolerate views other than their own.

There are five stages in the lesson design structure of inquiry training. In Phase 1, confrontation of the problem, the teacher explains the inquiry procedures and then presents a discrepant event. Teachers and students must use the language of the inquiry process. Students are told that they will be able to ask the teacher questions with a "yes" or "no" answer. If the questions require more than "yes" or "no," students will be asked to rephrase them. Because students may feel uncomfortable asking questions and developing theories on their own, the teacher will not evaluate student theories; teachers will encourage students to make precise statements and will ask students to support their theories with facts. Interaction among students will be allowed during the inquiry process. Once the inquiry procedures are explained, the teacher presents the discrepant event. A discrepant event is anything that is puzzling or unusual. Joyce, Weil, and Calhoun (2008) state that "the ultimate goal is to have the students experience the creation of new knowledge, the confrontation should be on discoverable ideas. . . . bending a metallic strip held over a flame begins the inquiry process" (p. 177). An example of a discrepant event is the following scenario: You are traveling across the Golden Gate Bridge in San Francisco, and you realize that there is nothing under the bridge. What is holding it up?

In Phase 2, data collection, verification takes place. This is the stage in which students begin asking questions such as "What holds the bridge up?"

The teacher answers the students' questions to verify the nature of the objects and conditions and to verify the occurrence of the problem situation. Phase 3, data gathering and experimentation, requires students to isolate relevant variables and begin to restate their questions in the form of a hypothesis that could explain the discrepant event. To continue the example, an explanation may be, "Is the bridge held by the steel cables that are anchored at both ends?" A fact sheet, used in Phase 4, organizing, formulation, and explaining, is useful in helping the students understand the explanation for the discrepant event.

Phase 5, analysis of the inquiry process, has the teacher questioning the students regarding the process of inquiry. The main purpose of inquiry training is not to help students acquire knowledge; instead, the purpose is to teach the process of inquiry. In this final stage, the teacher might ask these questions: What questions were most effective in leading you to a hypothesis? What questions were not effective? What have you learned about this process? What suggestions do you have that would make this inquiry more effective? Students continue to use inquiry methods to learn more about their world because new knowledge is continuously available. Both teachers and students are engaged in a never-ending quest for new information. The inquiry training model is one tool teachers and students need in their acquisition of knowledge.

## History and Research

In 1962, Richard Suchman developed the method of teaching called inquiry training. Suchman defined inquiry as "learning that is directed and controlled by the learner." All students should be responsible for their own learning. Since he believed that "all knowledge is tentative," students need well-developed inquiry skills so they can become life-long learners. Students begin to understand that there is not always only one right answer. When questions are asked using new tools and technology, knowledge once considered a "truth" might turn out to be false or inaccurate. In the inquiry technique, students learn the art of asking questions and the science of searching for answers. The tools of inquiry include an inquiring mind, the ability to ask questions to collect more data, and the ability to analyze findings to determine possible reasons or discover solutions to a problem. Since students are naturally inquisitive, teachers should present information in such a way as to help students increase their power of inquiry. Most of Suchman's work dealt with children of high intelligence. Using inquiry training, highly verbal students more than doubled their ability to inquire effectively to solve problems, and they increased their use of analytical procedures when learning new information (Suchman, 1962). Suchman's research showed that inquiry training was very beneficial to gifted students, but other research studies showed that all students could benefit from inquiry training.

Another researcher, Howard Jones (1966), studied the effects of planned guidance on the problem-solving abilities of elementary-age students. The results showed a significant relationship between inquiry training and changes in the problem-solving behaviors of elementary students, but there was no significant relationship between inquiry training and concept transfer or changes in recall of factual knowledge.

Ivany (1969) and Collins (1969) studied two modes of teaching science—the expositional and the hypothetical. The Illinois Inquiry Training Program developed by Dr. Suchman was implemented with their experimental treatment groups. Their study showed that inquiry training worked best when the discrepant event was strong and the topics under consideration were especially instructional. For example, in determining how a suspension bridge works, students' knowledge deepens if they can build a model of a suspension bridge. One of the instructor's responsibilities prior to the lesson is to select appropriate puzzling events for inquiry—discrepant events suitable for capturing the students' interests. The selection of the discrepant event is crucial for the success of the lesson.

Emily Elefant, a science teacher at a school for the deaf, conducted a study to determine the strategies that would be acquired by deaf students involved in an inquiry training program modeled on Suchman's design (Elefant, 1980). As in Suchman's study involving gifted students, behaviors exhibited by the deaf students were no different from those of the hearing students. The actual number of inquiry behaviors and experimenting behaviors increased over an eight-week period.

Studies by Schlenker (1986) showed that inquiry training increased the understanding of science, creative thinking, and skills for obtaining and analyzing information. Inquiry training proved as effective as recitation or lectures accompanied by laboratory experiences, but not more effective than any other information processing method.

Donald Hansler (1985) conducted a series of studies over a three-year period to determine whether inquiry was effective for teaching problem solving, thinking, and decision making. He concluded that inquiry training was a potentially highly effective method of teaching cognitive skills and was appropriate for use with elementary-level to college-level students. Although many educators feel inquiry methods of teaching are best in science courses, Hansler's studies showed that inquiry could be used with almost any subject. With some modifications and teacher training, inquiry can be one of several strategies in a teacher's repertoire.

## Promises and Pitfalls

Implementing inquiry training as a teaching strategy has numerous advantages. Inquiry can be used successfully with elementary, secondary, and college-age students. It is adaptable to all elementary and secondary curriculum areas, although inquiry training seems most suitable for science curricula. Like the social family models of teaching, inquiry encourages cooperation, although it provides students with more intellectual freedom. Because the teacher does not evaluate students' questions and theories, students feel a greater sense of equality in the learning process.

Where inquiry training is a prevalent method of teaching, schools report an increased use of their school libraries.

Disadvantages of implementing inquiry training are important considerations. First, the method takes time—time to train students in the process and time to train teachers in the method. Inquiry is not one of the most familiar of the teaching methods, especially among teachers of non-science curricula. Second, inquiry training involves risk taking on the part of students, who must develop the skills and courage to question and verbalize possible theories. It also involves risk taking on the part of the teacher, who must be willing and able to turn over the direction of the learning process to the students. Third, lower-level students may have difficulty generating questions. In addition, some students in all ability levels have difficulty working with and expressing theories. Since the major focus of inquiry is on students' developing inquiry skills, some teachers and administrators may have difficulty using a model that emphasizes the process over the acquisition of specific facts or concepts. However, if implemented correctly, inquiry training could do both—teach the inquiry process as well as the content.

## Summary

All teachers need a selection of teaching tools from which to choose to meet the various needs of their students. Inquiry training is not a model of teaching with which many teachers feel comfortable, but that should not be a reason for not using it. Administrators should create a school environment in which teachers are willing to take risks and try new methods of teaching. Some teachers teach only the way they were taught or teach only the way they learn best, but not all their students learn best using these methods. Traditionally, teachers have felt responsible for directing instruction and learning, but current thought is that students should be accountable for their own learning, although this paradigm shift may be difficult for some educators and students to accept. All students in all curriculum areas need to possess inquiry skills. Since research shows that students of all abilities and ages can benefit from inquiry training, this method should be used in all classrooms. As our society enters the 21st century, more and more jobs require employees to be problem solvers and analytical thinkers. Schools have the responsibility to equip students with the skills they will need to be productive citizens. If all knowledge is tentative, as Suchman believed, citizens will have to be lifelong learners whether they want to be or not.

## BUILDING THE TOWER: ■ A SAMPLE DISCOVERY METHOD ACTIVITY

This activity is one that covers all the components inherent in the discovery method. It is learner centered and requires brainstorming and the formation and testing of hypotheses. The conclusion of the activity is a debriefing process that requires learners to evaluate their performance.

The materials needed for this activity are several packs of 100 4x6 index cards and a yardstick. The learners are grouped into teams and given an unopened pack of cards. They are told that they will have five minutes to build the highest-standing structure using only the index cards that they have been given. No "tools" of any sort are allowed; they can fold the cards, but that is all.

The first round of "play" is a five-minute planning stage. The learners cannot yet open the package of cards, but they can strategize and determine how best to build their structure. After the five-minute planning stage, the instructor gives the students a 10-minute experimental phase. The participants are able to open their cards and test the strategies they devised in the planning session. After 10 minutes of experimentation, the instructor takes up the used index cards and provides each team with a new unopened package. The students are then given five minutes to build the tallest structure they can. At the end of the building stage, the structures are measured and the winners are announced. Then the participants are given a 15-minute debriefing stage in which they determine what they could have done differently, what went well, and so forth. Finally, a reporter from each team takes a turn discussing the knowledge gained in the debriefing session.

# THIRTEEN

# Simulations and Role Play

## SIMULATIONS ■

Simulations belong to the behavioral family of instructional strategies. They are constructed using real-life situations in a simulated environment. Simulations can be used to learn how to fly a plane, develop international negotiations skills, or resist peer pressures. Their applications for classroom use are numerous and are designed to enhance the cognitive and affective domains of learning.

Simulations are considered a form of experiential learning. Although they are sometimes called games or role playing, a distinction needs to be made between role playing, games, and the simulations model. Games and role play are forms of simulations. Simulations can involve games, using rules and competition, but they do not use drama as is the case in role play. The learner is himself or herself, perhaps serving in another role in a simulated environment, but is still himself or herself. Any reaction from the simulated environment should be the learner's own natural behavior so that the consequences of actions can be learned while experiencing the simulation. Simulations are experiential learning, not direct instruction or rehearsed events. In simulations, mistakes are inevitable and desirable because the participants learn through these mistakes. In fact, sometimes the greater the disaster, the greater the learning (Jones, 1987).

## Forms for the Simulation Model

There are several forms of the simulation instructional model. Simulations can use machines or people. For example, there are machine simulations for flight instruction, driver education, military combat, or simply trekking through the Oregon Trail. Most simulations are used to teach technical skills for learning to drive a car or to use machinery that can be both expensive and dangerous. Simulations teach technical skills in a safe, inexpensive way. Some simulations teach personal skills. Examples might be having students keep an imaginary bank account or play the stock market with fake money. Furthermore, some simulations have more of a gaming flavor, such as Monopoly or Trivial Pursuit. Today, several simulations can be used on the computer. Educators are split on the definitions and consider simulations, games, and role playing all to be the same or to have similar characteristics. Call them what you like, but use them. Students love them and they learn a great deal from them.

Machine simulations involve simulators or readily available software. The simulator is a type of training device that represents reality but that has controlled events. An example of this would be a driving simulator with which students learn to drive in a simulated automobile. The automobile simulator has the same mechanisms as an automobile—namely, a steering wheel, brakes, a clutch, and a gearshift. A moving picture represents the road, and realistic noises accompany the driving. This type of driving simulator mimics actual events that could occur while driving without the consequences in real life, thus enabling the student to acquire the skills needed later for actual driving. A flight simulator is another example; students can learn how to fly and master certain aspects before actually piloting a plane (Joyce, Weil, & Calhoun, 2008). Less complex machine simulations include computer games, such as the popular Where in the World or USA Is Carmen Sandiego?, Oregon Trail, or SimCity software programs.

There are simulations involving both aspects of a game (roles and competition) with the components of a simulation. In gaming simulations, roles are defined for the players, a scenario is used to describe the situation, and a type of accounting system is used. The accounting system monitors and records the status of the players and provides appropriate feedback. In simulation games, success is defined in terms of player's goals with a prescribed criterion for winning (Dukes, 1978). These gaming simulations are usually competitive in nature, involving both the accumulation of points and clear winners and losers.

All-people simulations are another type of simulation. These simulations extract certain elements of a social or physical reality in such a way that students can interact with and become a part of a simulated reality (Dukes, 1978). True simulations represent a real-life situation, which duplicates selected parts of an environment along with its interrelationships. A common mistake is to believe simulations involve role playing. In simulations, students are not performing in a dramatic role. It is the environment that is simulated. The students participate as themselves in a role and are given the key facts, not asked to invent them (Jones, 1980, 1987).

Reality can be manipulated in numerous ways. Simulations can be used to demonstrate how governments work, teach economic concepts, or gain career knowledge. Simulations can be structured to demonstrate the adverse effects of prejudices, socioeconomic power, or unethical decisions. Simulations can help students learn about competition or cooperation and empathy or apathy (Joyce et al., 2008).

Joyce et al. (2008) describe the following four components of the simulation instructional model: orientation, participant training, simulation operation, and debriefing. In the orientation phase, the teacher presents the topic and concepts to be explored and explains the type of simulation in which the students will participate. In the second phase, the rules and procedures are established. The third phase involves the actual simulation activity. The students participate, and the teacher serves as a referee or coach. The final stage is the participant debriefing, in which the events are summarized and analyzed by the teacher and students.

Simulations are based on social situations so that cooperative interaction can flourish. The overall success of the simulation depends on the cooperation and participation of members. While some simulations can be disconcerting to individuals because they have the potential to reveal negative characteristics, the overall social system should be non-threatening and one of mutual cooperation.

## Rationale for Appropriate Use

Simulations can be used in numerous contexts and to teach numerous process skills, especially in the affective domain. Simulations have the unique ability to help students achieve attitudinal objectives more effectively than any other instructional model. It is possible for students to observe emotions through the use of texts or other media; however, no other instructional design format is capable of permitting participants to actually experience them (Thiagarajan & Stolovitch, 1978).

Thiagarajan and Stolovitch (1978) recommend the use of simulation games as a way of introducing instructional content; they consider it especially applicable for the social studies curriculum. Students become interested in the variables influencing an individual's behavior, making them eager to learn the background or content of the simulation's real-life counterpart. A simulation may also be used as the cumulative activity to provide students an opportunity to try out the skills and knowledge they have acquired during the unit of study. Maximum effectiveness can be achieved through the participation in the same simulation prior to and preceding the unit of study.

Simulation games are effective ways to assess the student's ability to transfer content skills and knowledge in a realistic context. The teacher will need to observe students and use an evaluative rubric, which can be somewhat complex; however, simulations are valid and authentic assessments.

Thiagarajan and Stolovitch (1978) found that they can also be used for instructional improvement. Used as a pre-assessment tool, educators can determine which skills need to be emphasized or de-emphasized depending on the observation and analysis of the performance of students during the simulation. By identifying student's strengths and weakness, the instructional delivery can be tailored to meet individual needs.

Simulations have a practical value for the classroom and, used correctly, can help students achieve affective objectives as well as introduce and integrate authentic learning and assessments for meaningful long-term learning.

## Lesson Design

Simulations can be structured into three basic areas for the lesson design: the *briefing*, the *action*, and the *debriefing*. These are the terms commonly used in all simulation models. The teacher can serve as the controller-facilitator or referee-coach and is responsible for moving the students through the three stages of the lesson.

The briefing should be used to provide an overview of the simulation. The rules, roles, procedures, scoring, goals, and levels of decisions should be discussed. Roles should be assigned, followed by a short practice session to check understanding. During the briefing stage, the teacher should be cautious about disclosing too much information. If answers are available in reading materials or documents for the students, more learning will occur if they are encouraged to investigate on their own. One of the functions of simulations is to provide students with the opportunity to find out the facts. The teacher-facilitator will also need to explain the rules sufficiently for the students to carry out the simulation, but it is not essential for students to have a total understanding of the simulation at the start. Rules can be revealed as needed, imitative of real life (Joyce et al., 2008). Should the simulation involve various stages, a briefing should be included with each consecutive stage.

The action stage involves the actual simulation. Students participate in the simulation, and the teacher functions as a coach. Occasionally, the simulation may need to be stopped to provide feedback or evaluate performances and clarify tasks. If a new stage or round is required, the teacher briefs the class prior to starting it.

One possible danger involves inappropriate behavior by the students. This may happen if the facilitator fails to clearly explain the rules of the simulation. In ordinary teaching, the instructor will step in and correct the behavior or mistakes. There are arguments suggesting that this makes the activity ineffective and an instructor-controlled exercise (Jones, 1980). Additional arguments state that students should have the opportunity to make mistakes, take the consequences, and learn (Joyce et al. 2008).

After the action, the debriefing stage occurs, during which the events are summarized and analyzed. During the debriefing, students explain their parts, their perceptions of the problem, and how they dealt with it.

Each participant contributes without any comments from the others. The teacher then leads an open discussion. The teacher should structure questions in advance to guide students to the expected outcomes. The simulation is compared with the real world and related to the curriculum content.

The debriefing is a crucial stage and one that should not be rushed through, especially if the simulation had a hidden agenda. Simulations dealing with prejudices, ethics, or power plays can sometimes stir up emotions, with the participants feeling exposed or humiliated. These individual insights may not be pleasant, requiring a supportive teacher to guide students through the process.

## History and Research

Simulations can be traced back to ancient war times. Ancient China had a war game called Wei-Hai, and Chaturanga was a war game first played about 1,500 years ago in India. Chess, developed during the Middle Ages, simulates battles between nations with the game pieces representing competing forces with various degrees of strength and flexibility. In these games, which were played primarily for enjoyment until the 18th century, the game pieces were useful in planning and predicting war outcomes. Following its defeat by Napoleon, Prussia pioneered the development and refinement of war gaming. Chess pieces were replaced by pieces representing actual infantry, artillery, and cavalry units. Teams of players replaced two single opposing players, and judges monitored the game activity (Heitzman, 1983; Maidment, 1973).

During the 20th century, the U.S. military refined the Prussian model, and the development of the computer led to technical improvements in national security efforts. During the 1950s, experimentation began with other social simulations. Economists and business theorists used quantitative models of simulations. Soon, political scientists, sociologists, and psychologists discovered the practical value of simulations. Crisis games were developed that created possible future international disasters in various parts of the world. This simulation provided foreign policymakers with a set of alternatives in the event of an actual crisis (Maidment, 1973).

Harold Guetzkow and his colleagues at Northwestern University created an international relations simulation during the late 1950s and the early 1960s. Guetzkow introduced simulations into the educational arena. This simulation was known as the 'Inter-Nation Simulation.' It re-created the main structural and dynamic features of an international system. His model was used to explain the operation of a system, and it advanced the theory of international relations. Student teams represent countries and act as decision makers. Information is provided to the teams about the nation's economic, consumer, and military bases. Then trading and the development of various agreements begin. Organizations can be established or trade agreements made. Nations can make war, with the outcome being determined by the military force of the group. The negotiation stage helps students develop an understanding of the principles in international relations (Joyce et al., 2008; Maidment, 1973).

Simulations are designed using cybernetics, a branch of psychology. Cybernetic psychologists compare humans to machines and conceptualize the learner as a self-regulated feedback system. Cybernetic psychology operates on the principle of sense-oriented feedback that is intrinsic to the individual, in which the ability to feel the effect of one's decisions is the basis for self-corrective choices. According to this theory, human behavior has covert behaviors, such as thinking and feeling, and overt behaviors, or actions. Actions are created by the received feedback. When the choices are played back, the consequences can be felt. Simply put, simulations in cybernetic terms are designed to create an environment in which feedback is given that results in self-corrective behavior.

Numerous books and research articles recommend the use of simulations; however, there is no recent empirical research to substantiate the claims of the effectiveness of the simulation model for instruction. Several documents state that more research is needed; however, none is forthcoming. Jones (1988) offered this reasoning for the shortage of empirical data, claiming that the studies are confined to one simulation only, making it difficult to measure results. Furthermore, Jones contends that the articles are full of hypotheses and statistics from the tests but usually say little about what actually happened.

Boocock and Schild (1968) also identify several research issues that confound studies. A simulation evaluation requires the use of experimental and control groups, which Boocock and Schild find difficult to implement in school settings. Likewise, they cite a variance in the degree of teacher capability, claiming that researchers cannot be sure that sample teachers are using the same techniques or are presenting the materials in the same way. Boocock and Schild hypothesized that teacher bias or preference for one teaching method would also confound the results.

Boocock and Schild conducted a study on the use of simulation techniques in the fall of 1964, as simulations were being introduced in the schools. The purpose of the study was to test students' role empathy and feelings of efficacy after participation in the simulation. Pre- and post-tests were used to compare responses and measure the effectiveness of simulation activities. The study involved the use of two games. *Life Career* introduced students to labor, school, and marriage decisions and the consequences of those decisions, and the *Legislative Game* allowed collective decisions to be reached on issues with which members of society have differing interests.

Boocock and Schild concluded that the career game provided role empathy, especially with the boys who took the feminine role or role of the high school dropout. The male students developed a sympathetic attitude toward those roles after their experiences. The image of political roles was not changed by the legislative game, although feelings of political efficacy were greater. The most convincing evidence supporting the use of simulations was produced by the career game, for which actual cognitive learning gains were measured. Boocock and Schild stated that although their study was far from conclusive, they believed the results showed promising effects for positive results of the simulation, based on the stated objectives for the learner.

## Promises and Pitfalls

Simulations hold much promise as an instructional method because they incorporate both the cognitive and affective domains of learning. Simulations help students develop process-thinking skills. Simulations can enhance decision-making abilities, communication skills, the use of persuasion, or to influence resisting. Simulations can be used for learning in general or be designed to integrate ideas and information students already have. A simulation experience leads students to see the interconnectedness of political, social, interpersonal, cultural, economic, and historical factors. Simulations are especially useful to help students understand the idea of social systems.

Simulations can be designed to affect attitudes. Participants can gain empathy for real-life decision makers, learn that life is more complicated than ever imagined, or decide that they can do something important about affecting their own personal lives or the lives of others. Simulations provide participants with explicit and experiential ideas and with concepts and words to describe human behavior. They act as an information retrieval device to help bring dormant knowledge to consciousness.

Simulations affect the social setting in which learning takes place. The physical format alone produces a more relaxed natural exchange between teacher and students. During simulations, the control of the classroom goes from the teacher to the structure of the simulation, allowing for better student-teacher relations. Simulations are engaging, helping students to drop their usual interpersonal facades, which leads to a more open classroom atmosphere.

The use of simulations leads to personal growth (a) through the discovery of personal skills, abilities, fears, and weakness that weren't apparent before and (b) by providing opportunities to express affection, anger, and indifference without suffering permanent consequences.

Joyce et al. (2008) claim that simulations have several advantages. One is the practice of complex activities prior to the application in real life. Simulations have the ability to help students learn from self-generated feedback and, consequently, learn necessary corrective behaviors, another distinctive feature of this instructional strategy.

Dukes and Seidner (1978) describe how simulation activities reach cognitive and affective educational objectives. They contend that simulations can incorporate a body of factual knowledge in the structure and functioning of the game so that the knowledge can be transmitted to the student through participation in the simulation. Simulations can be designed for students to use higher-order thinking concepts, principles, and processes.

Maidment and Bronstein (1973) state that simulations have three advantages over other teaching methodologies: (a) an increase in student motivation and interest brought about by (b) the creation of a favorable learning environment by having the teacher behave in a non-authoritative role and (c) the presentation of realistic and relevant learning experiences.

Although simulations are a promising instructional strategy, possible drawbacks should be considered. First, there is a lack of evidence to support the effectiveness of simulation activities in the classroom, especially for cognitive skill attainment. A careful study of the practicalities of this model may suggest that in this day of high-stakes testing and accountability, there is no time to use models that do not guarantee success. For this argument, an assertion can be made that numerous instructional standards require the use of process skills, which can be obtained through simulation activities. In addition, there is a strong need for our schools to have a positive influence on students' character building and value systems—something that may be achieved only through participation in simulation activities.

Experts note other potential problems with this instructional strategy. First, simulations can be defective, producing a lack of validity or playability. According to Maidment and Bronstein (1973), there is little educational value in a simulation game that does not in some way accurately reflect events in the real world or that creates a false sense of reality. The lack of playability refers to the lack of clear directions, or rules that are too complex or confusing, requiring the teacher to continuously interrupt the flow of the simulation.

Jones (1987; see also 1980) also cautions educators on the use of correct terminology for simulation activities, stating that the wrong wording can lead to wrong expectations, which in turn can lead to wrong student behavior. Words can often be interpreted in numerous ways based on prior knowledge. For example, telling students they are going to play a game and having the students expect fun and games may create disappointment because it wasn't their expectation, or students may decide to interject a little fun through inappropriate behavior. Jones also warns that saying the simulation is a role play can be interpreted as a need for students to play a role and so not behave as they naturally would. Simulations are simulated environments, not simulated behaviors. To avoid confusion, it is helpful for educators or the simulator presenters to use appropriate terminology. Jones recommends the words *simulation, event, participant, behavior, action, issues,* and *ethics* and not the use of the words *game, drama, play, player, act, winning,* or *losing* to describe simulations.

No matter which terms are used, simulations provide active and engaged learning for students. The lesson at the end of this chapter should validate this model as an effective instructional strategy for helping students attain learning objectives.

## Summary

Simulations provide relevant learning opportunities for real-life situations. They have numerous applications for classroom use—all designed to enhance the cognitive and affective domains of learning—and should be a regular part of a master teacher's instructional strategies.

NOTE: See the end of this chapter for a sample lesson titled "The Gifted and Talented Simulation."

## ROLE PLAY ■

Role play is a method of learning based on role theory. In this instructional method, students adopt assumed positions and interact in a simulated life situation. Role play takes on different meanings for different people. These range from highly controlled, guided conversations to improvised drama activities to highly complex simulated scenarios (Ladousse, 1987).

Role play has roots in both the personal and social dimensions of education. On a personal level, it helps students find personal meaning within their social worlds and resolve personal dilemmas. Socially, it allows students to work together to analyze social issues and develops democratic ways of coping with these situations (Joyce et al., 2008).

To really understand the instructional model of role play, one must understand the concept of *role,* one of the central theoretical underpinnings of the role-playing model. Students must understand roles and how they are played to truly understand themselves and others. It is the teacher's responsibility to teach students to recognize different roles and to think of their own and others' behaviors using the concept of roles.

The role of the teacher is critical to the success of the instructional model of role play. It is not the time for teachers to check papers or do remediation with students while students participate in role playing. First, teachers may need to provide initial props to support the role play. These props make the role play more realistic and will engage the students in the instructional model. Teachers should also challenge the children to use the skills they are learning in other curriculum areas to apply them during the role play to assist in the problem-solving process. Sometimes, it may be necessary for teachers to enter into the role play to encourage the students to think more deeply and play their roles more realistically. By intermittently assuming roles in the children's play, a teacher can assess the students' understanding of their roles and their ability to solve problems.

Finally, it is important for teachers to provide enough time for the children to interact with the materials and with one another. Teachers should not rush the children; they need time to build understanding (Jarrett, 1997).

The instructional value of role playing is that students learn to analyze their personal values and behaviors. They learn empathy and respect from participating in the nine steps involved in the Shaftels' (Shaftel & Shaftel, 1967) model of role-play (see Table 13.1 later in this chapter). In addition, students learn strategies for solving interpersonal and personal dilemmas they encounter. Role playing also has nurturing effects as students learn skills in negotiating and comfort in expressing their own opinions (p. 73).

A teacher may use role play for two basic reasons. First, it can be used to develop a social program that teaches children to problem-solve as they work through social issues students will experience as they develop into adults. Teachers may also use role play to counsel a group of students who are experiencing a human relations problem (Shaftel & Shaftel, 1967, p. 70). This instructional method can also be used to increase the efficiency of academic learning through the portrayal of current events or historical circumstances or through the use of the dramatization of plays or novels (Chesler & Fox, 1966).

## History and Research

Many people have designed models for role play. Each model has its own series of steps for conducting a role play. Fannie and George Shaftel, Mark Chesler and Robert Fox, and Gillian Ladousse are just a few names associated with the instructional model of role-play.

Mark Chesler and Robert Fox (1966) argue that role playing in the classroom works best when there is an attempt to follow a definite sequence of steps. The steps allow for a logical ordering and development of the role-playing session. The first step is preparation and instruction. During this step, the problem is selected, a warm-up is conducted, and instructions and roles are given to the students. The second major step involves dramatic action and discussion. The actual role playing itself and the subsequent discussion and interpretation of the action are conducted during this step. Evaluation is the final step in Chesler and Fox's model. This is the time for the students and the teacher to review the successes and failures of the role-playing experience.

Fannie and George Shaftel's (1967) model of role play has nine steps that involve assigning students to be either role players or observers during the enactment. Each of the steps has a clear purpose that contributes to the richness and focus of the learning activity. The collection of steps ensures that a line of thinking is maintained throughout the role play, that roles are assigned and understood, and that the discussion is rich.

Gillian Ladousse's (1987) model of role play is structured around a lesson design for teachers to follow while using the instructional model. First, teachers decide the aim of their role play, which focuses the children's attention. An example may be to encourage students to interpret a scene in different ways through the use of photographs. Once the teacher explains the aim to the students, he or she warms up the group with an activity that introduces the students to the aim for the day. For example, in a lesson on the three branches of the government, the teacher may do an activity about how we would make a new rule for the class. Following the warm-up, the teacher moves onto the procedure part of the lesson. At this point, the teacher explains the problem and passes out role cards that describe the roles students are to take during the role play. The students then participate in the role play using their role play cards to support them. The lesson ends with the teacher conducting a follow-up discussion to allow the students to debrief the role play.

In their book *Models of Teaching*, Bruce Joyce, Marsha Weil, and Emily Calhoun (2008) describe the role play model created by Fannie and George Shaftel. The Shaftels' model of role play includes nine steps (Table 13.1). To begin the role play, the teacher should warm up the students. To support the children in their understanding of the problem, the teacher should assist the children in expressing the problem vividly through the use of examples that the students generate based on reality, imagination, or literature. The Shaftels (1967) wrote *Role-Playing of Social Values: Decision Making in the Social Studies*, which presents problem stories that can be used by teachers to support Step 1 of the model. The problems the Shaftels present in their book are open-ended problems without solutions. It is the job of the students to use role play to generate solutions to the problem presented. Step 1 concludes with the teacher asking probing questions that will require the students to make predictions concerning the outcomes of the problem story.

Following the presentation of the problem, a brief discussion of examples that relate to the problem, and predictions about the outcome of the problem, the teacher moves on to Step 2. In this step, characters involved in the role play are clarified and students are assigned roles. The teacher can assign roles or students can volunteer for them. Once the roles are assigned, the next step involves the students and the teacher creating the setting to support the problem that has been presented. Next, in Step 4, the students who are not assigned roles in the role play are assigned as observers who are responsible for examining how students are playing their roles, the solutions that the role play demonstrates, and the feelings and emotions shown by the role players.

In Step 5, the role players conduct the role play in front of the observers. The role play should be short and allow for the role players to respond to each other. The purpose of this step is to ensure that the role players and observers really understand the problem they are dealing with. A discussion and evaluation of the role play that was just conducted make up Step 6. The observers discuss what they observed, how the role players solved the problem, and the consequences of the way the problem was solved during Step 5.

Following the discussion and evaluation of the first enactment of the role play, the students reenact it, which is Step 7. This time, the information that was discussed and evaluated in Step 6 is incorporated into this reenactment. Once again, a discussion and evaluation is conducted on the reenactment that just took place (Step 8). The role play ends with Step 9 as the teacher helps the students produce generalizations that can be made about the problem and the appropriate solutions to the problem presented by the teacher. The teacher may have to guide the students to the generalizations and how they can apply to their personal lives.

**Table 13.1** Components of Role Play

| | |
|---|---|
| Step 1 | Warm up the group |
| Step 2 | Select participants |
| Step 3 | Set the stage |
| Step 4 | Prepare the observers |
| Step 5 | Enact |
| Step 6 | Discuss and evaluate |
| Step 7 | Reenact |
| Step 8 | Discuss and evaluate |
| Step 9 | Share experiences and generalize |

## Promises and Pitfalls

Role play has many advantages over traditional ways of problem solving. First, the traditional approach to problem solving involves only having the children think about the possible solutions. Role playing requires the students to use cognitive and affective skills to generate solutions to problems. For children who are bored and find school a waste of time, role playing simulates the real conflicts of the child's world, which makes school more meaningful and relevant for them. Children who are engaged in role play are not involved in competition activities, so children feel more relaxed and friendly while they are learning. In traditional instruction, students learn concepts from listening to their teacher lecture to them. In role play, students learn by doing. It converts ideas into direct experiences. One of the most important advantages of role play is that it makes students aware of the possibilities of alternative choices as they observe and participate in ways other than their own of resolving problems. Finally, role play allows students to examine their own values, defend them, and possibly make changes to their values as a result of looking at a problem from a variety of perspectives (Furness, 1976).

Role play does have disadvantages that administrators and teachers need to be aware of when using this instructional model. First, compared with traditional instructional models, the teacher turns over a lot of the responsibility of learning to the class and individual students. The teacher presents a problem, but the students generate solutions to the problems through the role play. The teacher can indirectly influence the solutions through the discussions that follow the first and second enactment, but he or she turns over most of the control of learning to the students. Role playing does take a lot of time. Students need time to fully explore the problems, problem-solve solutions, and enact their role play. If a teacher rushes this process, the purpose of the role play can be lost because insufficient time was provided. Many times, role play may be seen as too entertaining or frivolous. It looks different from the traditional classrooms where students sit in their seats and do their work without any noise. Finally, if the students have not had many experiences with problem solving, the solutions generated during the enactments may not be what the teacher wants the students to learn. Problem solving is a skill that needs to be worked on prior to engaging in role play so that students have prior knowledge of generating and supporting solutions to problems presented to them (Van Ments, 1999).

## Summary

Role play leads students to understand social behavior, their role in social interactions, and ways of solving problems effectively. The model involves students acting out conflicts, learning to take the roles of others, and observing social behavior (Joyce et al., 2008).

Role play is best used when the teacher wants students to experience and become involved in the situation they are studying and to formulate their attitudes toward it. It is an excellent way for students to develop interpersonal and communication skills, and it provides highly motivating and memorable lessons.

In the following staff development activity for teachers, there are 10 applicants who have applied for the National Gifted Program in Washington, DC. This is a free school that selects only three or four new students per year. The school is nongraded and defines gifted and talented loosely. Tell the teachers that the objective of the simulation is to devise their own selection criteria and procedure and then select the top three applicants. They must be able to defend their choices. Next, the teachers should rank order the applicants from 1 to 10, with 1 being the top selection and 10 being the last. They should then defend their positions for this ordering. Finally, share with the group what these selections grew up to become (1. university professor in physics; 2. brilliant scientist; 3. famous wife of a president; 4. congressman; 5. satirist; 6. most famous president; 7. famous inventor; 8. famous dancer; 9. inventor; 10. famous congresswoman).

The following abbreviations are used in the exercise:

AQ = achievement quotient

IQ = intelligence quotient

SQ = social quotient

CQ = creative quotient

For the sake of the simulation, 100 is average for all four quotients. As a follow-up activity, have the teachers try to figure out who the individuals really were. Variations can be done with students on who would be the best scientist, the best artist, best farmer, and so on.

## ■ GIFTED AND TALENTED SIMULATION: A SAMPLE LESSON USING SIMULATION

### Applicant #1

**FATHER**

**Name:** Bill Grost
**Address:** Lansing, Michigan
**Age:** 30
**Race:** Caucasian
**Place of birth:** East Lansing
**Nationality:** American
**Occupation:** Accountant
**Religious preference:** Catholic
**Educational level:** M.S.
**Interests:** Sports, reading

**MOTHER**

**Name:** Audrey Grost
**Address:** Lansing, Michigan
**Age:** 28
**Race:** Caucasian
**Place of birth:** East Lansing
**Nationality:** American
**Occupation:** Housewife
**Religious preference:** Catholic
**Educational level:** B.A.
**Interests:** Sports, music

### Applicant #1
### Child Applying for N.G.P

**Name:** Mike Grost    **Age:** 10    **Educational level:** Grade 6
**Height:** 4'11"    **Weight:** 75 lbs.    **Appearance:** Average

**IQ:** 180    **SQ:** 140    **AQ:** 170    **CQ:** 165

**School adjustment:** Aloof from age peers, organizer
**General physical health:** Excellent
**General emotional health:** Excellent
**Congenital concerns:** Requires glasses
**Family status:** Above average
**General political beliefs:** Conservative but futuristic
**Special interests:** Chess, math
**Special skills:** Eidetic memory
**Vocational goals:** Make a commitment to education
**Personal goals:** Personal fulfillment and make significant contribution to society
**Vocational contributions:** Published an original mathematics theorem (Accepted by the American Association of Mathematics)

## Applicant #2

**FATHER**

**Name:** Herman Edder
**Address:** Gary, Indiana
**Age:** 31
**Race:** Caucasian
**Place of birth:** Germany
**Nationality:** American
**Occupation:** Self-employed
**Religious preference:** Agnostic
**Educational level:** High school
**Interests:** Reading

**MOTHER**

**Name:** Anna Edder
**Address:** Lansing, Michigan
**Age:** 30
**Race:** Caucasian
**Place of birth:** Germany
**Nationality:** American
**Occupation:** Housewife
**Religious preference:** None
**Educational level:** High school
**Interests:** Music

## Applicant #2
## Child Applying for N.G.P

**Name:** Sam Edder     **Age:** 9     **Educational level:** Grade 4
**Height:** 5'1"     **Weight:** 74 lbs.     **Appearance:** Homely

**IQ:** 82     **SQ:** 74     **AQ:** 82     **CQ:** 110

**School adjustment:** Very poor, considered unsociable, disturbed
**General physical health:** Often sickly
**General emotional health:** Certified emotional breakdown,
                 removed from school temporarily
**Congenital concerns:** None
**Family status:** Average
**General political beliefs:** Quiet child, beliefs not known
**Special interests:** Frequently withdraws into fantasy world
**Special skills:** Plays violin, likes to be alone to read
**Vocational goals:** No evidence
**Personal goals:** Independence from family
**Vocational contributions:** None

## Applicant #3

**FATHER**

**Name:** William Hall (deceased)
**Address:** Lives with grandmother
**Age:** —
**Race:** Caucasian
**Place of birth:** New York
**Nationality:** American
**Occupation:** Itinerant
**Religious preference:** Presbyterian
**Educational level:** B.A.
**Interests:** —

**MOTHER**

**Name:** Rosemarie Hall (deceased)
**Address:** Lives with grandmother
**Age:** —
**Race:** Caucasian
**Place of birth:** New York
**Nationality:** American
**Occupation:** Chores
**Religious preference:** Catholic
**Educational level:** High school
**Interests:** —

## Applicant #3
### Child Applying for N.G.P

**Name:** Mary Hall     **Age:** 10     **Educational level:** Grade 5
**Height:** 5'8"     **Weight:** 76 lbs.     **Appearance:** Unattractive

**IQ:** 110     **SQ:** 76     **AQ:** 83     **CQ:** 95

**School adjustment:** Erratic, withdrawn, seeks attention, fails often
**General physical health:** Sickly, bedridden, hospitalized often
**General emotional health:** Bites nails, phobias, attention-seeking behavior, dominates
**Congenital concerns:** Wears back brace from spinal defect
**Family status:** Average or better, father alcoholic
**General political beliefs:** Conservative
**Special interests:** Daydreams, prefers to be alone, wants to be center of attention
**Special skills:** Patience with children, elderly or infirm
**Vocational goals:** None
**Personal goals:** Altruistic, prefers to help elderly or poor
**Vocational contributions:** None

## Applicant #4

**FATHER**

**Name:** James Horn
**Address:** Indianapolis
**Age:** 29
**Race:** Caucasian
**Place of birth:** Philadelphia
**Nationality:** American
**Occupation:** Banker
**Religious preference:** Protestant
**Educational level:** B.A.
**Interests:** Sports, chess

**MOTHER**

**Name:** Jane Horn
**Address:** Indianapolis
**Age:** 29
**Race:** Caucasian
**Place of birth:** Philadelphia
**Nationality:** American
**Occupation:** Housewife
**Religious preference:** Protestant
**Educational level:** B.A.
**Interests:** Swimming, reading

## Applicant #4
## Child Applying for N.G.P

**Name:** William Horn  **Age:** 10  **Educational level:** Grade 5
**Height:** 5'4"  **Weight:** 125 lbs.  **Appearance:** Attractive

**IQ:** 169  **SQ:** 155  **AQ:** 166  **CQ:** 128

**School adjustment:** Good, organizer, and leader
**General physical health:** Excellent
**General emotional health:** Excellent
**Congenital concerns:** None
**Family status:** Above average
**General political beliefs:** Conservative
**Special interests:** Basketball, math
**Special skills:** Leader, self-motivated
**Vocational goals:** To teach math
**Personal goals:** Wants to make a personal contribution to society
**Vocational contributions:** None

## Applicant #5

### FATHER

**Name:** Van Gunther
**Address:** Oklahoma
**Age:** 51
**Race:** Am. Indian
**Place of birth:** Oklahoma
**Nationality:** American
**Occupation:** Rancher
**Religious preference:** None
**Educational level:** High school
**Interests:** Ambitious

### MOTHER

**Name:** Mary Gunther
**Address:** Oklahoma
**Age:** Deceased
**Race:** Am. Indian
**Place of birth:** Oklahoma
**Nationality:** American
**Occupation:** Housewife
**Religious preference:** —
**Educational level:** High school
**Interests:** Religion/philosophy

## Applicant #5
### Child Applying for N.G.P

**Name:** William Gunther  **Age:** 11  **Educational level:** Grade 4 (3 times)
**Height:** 4'11"  **Weight:** 135 lbs.  **Appearance:** Unkempt

**IQ:** 110  **SQ:** 85  **AQ:** 82  **CQ:** 115

**School adjustment:** Dislikes school, does not mind, has caused extensive damage to schoolyard and building through carelessness
**General physical health:** Good
**General emotional health:** Shy and bashful, prankster
**Congenital concerns:** None
**Family status:** Healthy, low-middle class
**General political beliefs:** Inconsistent and critical
**Special interests:** Horse riding, roping
**Special skills:** Good sense of humor
**Vocational goals:** Perform in wild west show (parents want him to be a minister)
**Personal goals:** Wants to see world, perform for people
**Vocational contributions:** Participates in local rodeos

## Applicant #6

**FATHER**

**Name:** Joseph Wright
**Address:** Indiana
**Age:** 45
**Race:** Caucasian
**Place of birth:** Virginia
**Nationality:** American
**Occupation:** Rancher
**Religious preference:** Baptist
**Educational level:** Uneducated
**Interests:** Horses

**MOTHER**

**Name:** Mary Wright (deceased)
**Address:** Indiana
**Age:** Deceased
**Race:** Caucasian
**Place of birth:** Virginia
**Nationality:** American
**Occupation:** Housewife
**Religious preference:** Baptist
**Educational level:** Uneducated
**Interests:** Cooking, state fairs

## Applicant #6
## Child Applying for N.G.P

**Name:** Albert Wright **Age:** 17      **Educational level:** High school dropout

**Height:** 6'4"      **Weight:** 170 lbs.  **Appearance:** Plain

**IQ:** Unavailable **SQ:** Unavailable **AQ:** Unavailable  **CQ:** Unavailable

**School adjustment:** Good, well-liked, respected, attendance irregular
**General physical health:** Good, large for his age
**General emotional health:** Pleasant, easygoing, poor self-concept
**Congenital concerns:** Opthamuscular weakness (eye wanders)
**Family status:** Mother illegitimate, father involved in several law-suits
**General political beliefs:** Very conservative
**Special interests:** Physical sports, wrestling, practical jokes
**Special skills:** Likes to argue, fairly well-read, good debater
**Vocational goals:** Interested in retailing
**Personal goals:** Wants to own his own business and have a good family
**Vocational contributions:** Manual labor, clerked in store, long-shoreman, considered lazy by employers

## Applicant #7

**FATHER**

**Name:** Sam Ridell
**Address:** Michigan
**Age:** 54
**Race:** Caucasian
**Place of birth:** Nova Scotia
**Nationality:** Canadian
**Occupation:** Unemployed
**Religious preference:** Baptist
**Educational level:** None
**Interests:** None

**MOTHER**

**Name:** Nancy Ridell
**Address:** Michigan
**Age:** 49
**Race:** Caucasian
**Place of birth:** Ontario
**Nationality:** Canadian
**Occupation:** Teacher
**Religious preference:** Baptist
**Educational level:** B.A.
**Interests:** Literature, crafts

## Applicant #7
## Child Applying for N.G.P

**Name:** Bill Ridell    **Age:** 11    **Educational level:** Withdrawn
**Height:** 4'5"    **Weight:** 75 lbs.    **Appearance:** Pleasant

**IQ:** 81    **SQ:** 79    **AQ:** 87    **CQ:** 110

**School adjustment:** Withdrawn from school after three months, considered backward by school officials
**General physical health:** Enrolled in school two years late due to scarlet fever, respiratory infections, going deaf
**General emotional health:** Stubborn, aloof, shows little emotion
**Congenital concerns:** Enlarged head at birth
**Family status:** Father lower class, mother intelligent
**General political beliefs:** Unconcerned
**Special interests:** Mechanics, likes to build things, flying, likes to play with fire (burned down father's barn)
**Special skills:** Manual dexterity, reads well, poor grammar
**Vocational goals:** Scientist or railroad mechanic
**Personal goals:** Works hard, wants to earn money
**Vocational contributions:** Sold magazines

## Applicant #8

**FATHER**

**Name:** Bill Hawkins
**Address:** Los Angeles
**Age:** 55
**Race:** Caucasian
**Place of birth:** California
**Nationality:** American
**Occupation:** Entrepreneur
**Religious preference:** Catholic
**Educational level:** Not known
**Interests:** Writing

**MOTHER**

**Name:** Valerie Hawkins
**Address:** Los Angeles
**Age:** 51
**Race:** Caucasian
**Place of birth:** California
**Nationality:** American
**Occupation:** Teacher
**Religious preference:** Catholic
**Educational level:** B.A., music
**Interests:** Traveling, sewing

## Applicant #8
## Child Applying for N.G.P

**Name:** Elaine Hawkins  **Age:** 12  **Educational level:** Elementary
**Height:** 5'2"  **Weight:** 99 lbs.  **Appearance:** Attractive, mature

**IQ:** 108  **SQ:** 84  **AQ:** 94  **CQ:** 115

**School adjustment:** Dropped out at age 10, claimed to be 16 years old
**General physical health:** Very good
**General emotional health:** Talked back, stubborn, rebellious, behavior problem
**Congenital concerns:** None
**Family status:** Broken home, mother works, rarely home, migrants
**General political beliefs:** Radical, outspoken
**Special interests:** Reading, art
**Special skills:** Dancing
**Vocational goals:** To teach dance
**Personal goals:** Wants a career in dance
**Vocational contributions:** Likes to play at being a dance teacher with neighborhood children

## Applicant #9

**FATHER**

**Name:** Samuel Krebbs
**Address:** Indiana
**Age:** 34
**Race:** Caucasian
**Place of birth:** Indiana
**Nationality:** American
**Occupation:** Farmer
**Religious preference:** Methodist
**Educational level:** High school
**Interests:** Playing the fiddle

**MOTHER**

**Name:** Sally Ann Krebbs
**Address:** Indiana
**Age:** 32
**Race:** Caucasian
**Place of birth:** Indiana
**Nationality:** American
**Occupation:** Housewife
**Religious preference:** Methodist
**Educational level:** Junior high
**Interests:** Sewing, canning

## Applicant #9
### Child Applying for N.G.P

**Name:** Lloyd Krebbs   **Age:** 11   **Educational level:** Grade 5
**Height:** 4'11"   **Weight:** 142 lbs.   **Appearance:** Pleasant

**IQ:** 108   **SQ:** 98   **AQ:** 112   **CQ:** 105

**School adjustment:** Good average performer
**General physical health:** Very good
**General emotional health:** Good
**Congenital concerns:** None
**Family status:** Conservative, rural family, active in church
**General political beliefs:** Mostly conservative
**Special interests:** Sports, fiddle
**Special skills:** Active in 4-H
**Vocational goals:** Farming
**Personal goals:** Get married and own good farmland
**Vocational contributions:** None

**Applicant #10**

**FATHER**

**Name:** Ben Jackson
**Address:** Texas
**Age:** 47
**Race:** Black
**Place of birth:** Texas
**Nationality:** American
**Occupation:** Minister
**Religious preference:** Baptist
**Educational level:** High school
**Interests:** Music

**MOTHER**

**Name:** Arlyne Jackson
**Address:** Texas
**Age:** 46
**Race:** Black
**Place of birth:** Texas
**Nationality:** American
**Occupation:** Housewife
**Religious preference:** Baptist
**Educational level:** High school
**Interests:** Wants daughter to be a music teacher

**Applicant #10**
**Child Applying for N.G.P**

**Name:** Pearl Ruth Jackson    **Age:** 16    **Educational level:** Grade 10

**Height:** 5'11"    **Weight:** 195 lbs.    **Appearance:** Heavy, unattractive

**IQ:** 138    **SQ:** 126    **AQ:** 149    **CQ:** 108

**School adjustment:** Top 5% of class, ghetto school
**General physical health:** Good, obese
**General emotional health:** Good, confident
**Congenital concerns:** None
**Family status:** Conservative parents, opposed to program
**General political beliefs:** Politically active in school
**Special interests:** Rock music, student government
**Special skills:** Debate team
**Vocational goals:** Wants to be a lawyer
**Personal goals:** Ambitious, hardworking, wants to participate in National Gifted and Talented Program
**Vocational contributions:** Has participated in local "get out and vote" efforts

# FOURTEEN

# Cooperative Learning

Cooperative learning has been attributed to gains in three major areas—academic achievement, intergroup relations, and social and affective development (Gillies & Ashman, 2000; Slavin, 1996). Academic achievement has been expressed in terms of higher grades, better retention of information, and more long-term learning; it benefits both high and low achievers, and it benefits all races and genders. The success of cooperative learning strategies is evident; moreover, it has been shown to cross all barriers of race, gender, and ability. It aids in the cognitive growth of all children at all levels.

The intergroup aspect of success is exhibited by better race relations in desegregated settings, more tolerance of different cultures, and an appreciation of diversity. Cultural diversity is an issue confronting all of society, and cooperative learning can assist in more positive interactions between the races in the future.

Students also display substantial affective development by showing higher self-esteem, an increased "liking" of school, better attendance, increased socialization skills, increased ability to work effectively with others, and a better understanding of people as individuals. It is important for schools to impart cognitive knowledge and skills to students, but it is also crucial for students to become contributing members of society. Cooperative learning can make these social processes second nature to children, and they, in turn, can become better citizens making positive impacts on society.

The literature identifies essential components necessary for successful implementation of the cooperative learning model. Lyman and Foyle (1998) and Ngeow (1998) contend that seven elements contribute to the whole of cooperative learning.

1. Designed learning tasks based on shared learning goals

2. Groups consisting of two to six members

3. Prior teaching of effective group processes

4. Teacher initiation of concept

5. Cooperative learning behavior within the groups

6. Positive interdependence within groups

7. Individual accountability of all group members for the final outcomes

The teacher and student develop the intended learning task based on the shared goals of the school and the classroom. This allows students to take ownership in their learning through the establishment of the task. An essential aspect of cooperative learning is the structure of the group itself. A teacher must be aware of the situational aspect of group assignment and place students accordingly. The situational aspect refers to the role that each student has within a group. For example, different students within a group have different areas of academic strength. In most group situations, the teacher needs either to assign or approve individual, specific roles in cooperative learning settings for the purpose of balancing the group dynamic. The group task also contributes significantly to the composition of the group, and the potential group structures are innumerable—homogeneous, heterogeneous, mixed ability, equal ability, culturally diverse, and ranging in size from two to six members.

The teacher is responsible for the next two processes in the continuum of cooperative learning. Before group learning is to happen, the teacher must model and discuss certain group processes for students to be successful in the assignment. Communicating with others and being able to work well in groups are topics that must be explored and explained. The initiation of the cooperative learning task will occur when the teacher introduces the concept. This process provides students with some amount of prior knowledge or cognitive structure on which to base their group learning. Although the teacher is not directly involved in the cooperative learning, he or she initiates the concept discussion and establishes the framework on which the learning is built.

True cooperative learning can happen only when collaboration among all members of the group is required to accomplish a given task. This cooperative behavior and positive interdependence among the group members are crucial for successful learning. The promises of this method are rooted in these two factors. Students are "forced" to cooperate and establish positive relationships as a means of reaching that predetermined end.

Finally, individual accountability must be used to ensure that all students are learning and contributing. Within this strategy, it is too easy for a student to become passive and allow the other members to provide the learning, but teachers who encourage and mandate accountability for every student will find the most success with cooperative learning.

Cooperative learning has established its effectiveness across grade levels and curricular areas. Gillies and Ashman (2000) contend that "it has been used successfully to promote learning achievement in collaborative writing, problem solving in mathematics, comprehension in reading, and conceptual understanding in science" (p. 19). The affective domain has also shown positive growth, and Gillies and Ashman point out that "it promotes socialization and positive student interactions, improved attitudes to learning, and improved acceptance of children with disabilities by their nondisabled peers" (p. 20). These findings signify gains and growth in multiple cognitive and social domains.

Often, cooperative learning is viewed solely as an elementary strategy that works only with younger students. But this teaching model can promote growth in middle and high school students, who many times are attempting to establish independence from adult authority figures. Cooperative learning gives adolescents some degree of independence within their groups and creates a situation in which the progress of each member contributes to the group's success (Slavin, 1996). The adolescent is searching for an identity that conforms to the peer group, and cooperative learning can help the student with this quest.

Similar to other teaching models, cooperative learning has a "best" structure by which to organize the lesson. Stahl (1994) outlines five basic parts for a well-developed cooperative learning lesson.

1. A clear set of outcome objectives

2. A complete set of task completion instructions

3. Heterogeneous grouping

4. Individual accountability

5. Time for reflection and debriefing of the learning

Students must know beforehand exactly what they are expected to learn from the activity. This may be basic knowledge, social skills, or cognitive processes, but the teacher should dictate this information to students prior to initiation of the lesson. How are students supposed to accomplish the learning objectives? The teacher must provide concise and clear instructions for the activity so that students will be cognizant of the means with which to meet the end. This also has to be done before any group activity is started to avoid infinite questions after the activity begins.

The groups should be as heterogeneously mixed as possible. Academic ability, race, gender, ethnic backgrounds, and socioeconomic status are characteristics to consider when grouping. Students will learn how to work effectively with different students and with classmates who probably are not "regular" friends. The diversity of the group exposes all students to viewpoints different from their own and provides the opportunity to appreciate the differences present in the human race.

The rationale for cooperative groups is to have the whole be greater than the sum of its parts. However, each member must be held personally accountable for the work completed and for internalization of the content. The teacher should develop appropriate devices to assess the learning and long-term retention of each student.

The last step is to allow time for reflection on the group process as a whole. This forces students to analyze not only the group dynamics used to achieve a goal but also how they individually contributed to the group's success. The stage is now set for improved cooperative learning in the future because students have reflected on the past "mistakes" and can use them as a springboard for continuous improvement.

## ■ HISTORY AND RESEARCH

John Dewey (1910) was the first to advocate the teaching methods combining academic inquiry and democratic learning. "Dewey viewed the school as a miniature democratic society in which students could learn and practice the skills and tools necessary for democratic living" (Ornstein & Hunkins, 1998, p. 46). Dewey also contended that one of the philosophies of education is not only to learn to acquire information but to bring that learning to bear on our everyday actions and behaviors (Ngeow, 1998).

More recently, renewed research efforts have been made to further develop cooperative learning models. Researchers and theorists who currently study the effects of cooperative learning are David and Roger Johnson, Robert Slavin, and Shlomo and Yael Sharan.

David and Roger Johnson, based at the University of Minnesota, have published numerous articles and books on the effectiveness of cooperative learning models. They contend that the education of cooperation is an important aspect of the entire schooling process. Their "learning together" (Johnson & Johnson, 1994) model, where groups hand in a single assignment and receive a group grade based on this product, has proven beneficial to student learning (Slavin, 1996). They have also searched for the effects of cooperative tasks and reward systems, the effect of peer teaching, and the improvement of intergroup relations and behavior (Johnson & Johnson, 1994).

Robert Slavin, co director of the Center for Research on the Education of Students Placed At-Risk at Johns Hopkins University, has studied how cooperative learning can benefit children for which traditional teaching methods have been unsuccessful. The focus of his research is to find "best practices" for teachers to use to enhance student learning. Slavin has experimented with various types of grouping and differing group tasks. His efforts have also focused on the implementation of heterogeneous groups and the importance of both intrinsic and extrinsic rewards for students.

At the University of Tel Aviv, Shlomo Sharan studies the impact of cooperative learning with regard to student achievement. His "group investigation" model (Sharan & Sharan, 1992) involves students in the planning, researching, and presentation of information to the class on a topic chosen by the group (Slavin, 1996). Students take ownership of the learning process because they are given the opportunity to chose interesting topics to study. Shlomo and Yael Sharan, along with Rachel Hertz Lazarowitz, have intensely studied the outcomes derived from the group investigation model (Hertz-Lazarowitz, 1990; Sharan & Sharan, 1992).

## PROMISES AND PITFALLS ■

Although the strengths or promises of cooperative learning are evident, educators are also identifying the negative consequences of using this method. Randall (1999) has contended that this model contains the following three challenges to learning:

1. The responsibility of members for each other's learning

2. The design of the cooperative learning group

3. A tendency toward lower-level fact-based activities

That students have responsibility for other members' learning may be too much for younger children who struggle themselves to learn. Also, if this arrangement is in place, students may work equally, or they may rely too much on their peers to provide conceptual understanding.

Frequently, the membership of the cooperative learning group includes one high achiever, one low achiever, and two average achievers. The result is that the high achiever becomes bored because he or she has to explain the information many times for the entire group to understand. Consequently, the lowest achiever can become a passive learner simply waiting for the other members to provide the needed information and learning.

In addition, the general nature of the cooperative learning activity is basic lower-level knowledge acquisition. Students need to develop and train their minds to be critical thinkers and problem solvers, and group work traditionally neglects this need. Simply stated, cooperative learning does not address the higher-level cognitive structures that students need to be a successful, contributing citizenry in the future.

### The Case Method

It is important to note in this chapter on cooperative learning an offshoot of this instructional strategy—the case method. Case studies are a special form of the cooperative learning technique. In this instructional method, students study individual cases representative of a type of institution, issue, problem situation, or the like, in order to draw conclusions about the type as a whole (McBurney, 1995, p. 36). Examples of topics suitable for case studies include the following: the similarities of the causes of wars; the formation of clouds; the structure and function of the Krebs Cycle; the measurement of angles in a circle; effects of a recession on the economy; investigating the concept of the corruption of power; comparing Julius Caesar with Alexander the Great, Napoleon Bonaparte, George Patton, and Dwight Eisenhower; the mechanics of writing; the elements of literature; comparing synonyms with metaphors. Case studies allow students to focus on a situation or topic that is a prime example of its type. In this way, they learn specifics about individual cases and learn about the overall type as well. In addition, case studies offer opportunities to deal with specific diversity issues in the classroom such as prejudice, gender bias, poverty, and cultural misunderstandings. By acknowledging students' previous experiences and attitudes in response to multicultural and diversity issues, the teacher gains a clearer picture of strategies to use to introduce and integrate additional information and heighten cultural awareness. The case method also promotes and advances students' ethical and moral reasoning (Sudzina, 1993, p. 5). Meaningful learning occurs when a learner has a knowledge base that can be used with fluency to make sense of the world, solve problems, and make decisions. Higher order thinking skills are important for all students; teaching them is not a frill, nor is it a skill that only *gifted children* can or need to develop (Lewis & Smith, 1993, p. 42). An important benefit of the case study method is its responsiveness to the varying developmental differences of students (Sudzina, 1993, p. 4). There are a variety of differences in today's classrooms. The case study method is responsive to all student reflections and opinions.

Prior to assigning case studies, it is important for teachers to discuss evaluation procedures with their students. Teachers should prepare students before lessons so that they will have a clear understanding of the teacher's expectations. If students are going to be tested on their grasp of the concepts discussed in a case study, they need to know. Ground rules are a necessity. Teachers may choose to let students set their own goals and work to meet them. Goal setting requires both creative and critical thought, as well as a sense of evaluation of what is important and what is not. Goal setting also requires time management and an organization of ways to assess whether the goals have been met at the end of the assignment (Parsons & Smith, 1993, p. 21).

After selecting a topic for study and materials, students can be divided into groups or pairs. Ground rules must be established. The teacher must clearly state the case, so students will not be confused during the lesson. If cases have been previously assigned, it is a good idea to briefly summarize the facts of the case for the benefit of those who may not have prepared. Teachers should emphasize the importance of reasoning during the assignment, rather than emphasizing the solution of the case study (McBurney, 1995, p. 37). Once students begin discussing the case, teachers should remain silent so that they don't give their conclusions or opinions. The teacher's role is to pose questions, draw out incomplete answers, and probe inconsistencies (McBurney, 1995, p. 37). So often, students will become anxious and sometimes dispirited when a teacher refuses to tell them the right answer. The case study method is designed to teach students that there is no one right answer, an important lesson unto itself.

## Summary

Cooperative learning is an instructional model adaptable to all grade and cognitive-ability levels. The effective teacher can propose the specific modifications needed in a particular classroom setting, and if this is duly accomplished, the lesson will extend knowledge and learning to students. An understanding of group processes is desperately needed for one to function effectively in society, and the more opportunities that students have to practice these processes, the more success they will experience in school and in life.

Cooperative learning has been proven to foster academic achievement, better intergroup relations, and social and affective development. These three areas give students an excellent knowledge and skills base that will help them develop into productive, contributing citizens ready to meet the future.

# BUILDING THE PERFECT SCHOOL: ■
# A COOPERATIVE STAFF DEVELOPMENT ACTIVITY

Every educator at some point in his or her career has said or thought, "I could do things better. If only I ran this place, things would be done differently." This staff development idea allows teachers that opportunity, if only for a short while.

Divide teachers and staff members into groups and tell them that they are in a committee for the purpose of designing the perfect school. They need to determine roles and make sure that each committee member has an equal part. At the end of a set amount of time, they are to come to a mutual decision as to the perfect school. The key word is, of course, *mutual*. This activity allows teachers to see the cooperative method in action while they are actually involved in it. The relevancy of the activity to their real life experience is obvious. It also puts them in their students' shoes for a change. Teachers can present their "perfect schools" upon completion, making sure to rationalize to the audience the choices they made during synthesis. This activity also gives teachers a chance to focus on and refine their educational philosophies. See Table 14.1 for a sample handout for participant consideration during this activity.

**Table 14.1**  Educational Philosophies

| Educational Philosophy | Method of Teaching | Exam | Preferred Architecture | Seating | Educational Outcome | Root Philosophy | Rationale | Curriculum | Teacher |
|---|---|---|---|---|---|---|---|---|---|
| Perennialism | Lecture Discussions Seminars | Essay | Classical | Students grouped around teacher (philosopher) | Philosopher | Idealism | Deals with that which is lasting—stresses intellectual attainment | Great books liberal arts | Philosophically oriented—knowledges about great ideas |
| Essentialism | Lecture Teaching Machines | Objective | Efficient Functional | Students grouped around teacher (scientist) | Technician Scientist | Realism | Deals with basic knowledge—facts | 3 Rs, history, science, foreign language, English | Fact oriented Knowledgeable about scientific and technical data |
| Progressivism | Discussion Projects | Gauge how well people can solve problem | Flexible Natural | Group | Good problem solver | Pragmatism | Search for things that work—experimental—democratic | Core, flexible Revolves around interests and needs, student-centered | Guide one who can present meaningful problems with skill |
| Reconstructionism | Real-life projects Action projects | Gauge ability as activist | Nonschool setting "Schools without walls" | Outside involvement | Social activist | Pragmatism | Seeks to reconstruct society through education | Current events Social problems | Social activist Utopian oriented |
| Existentialism | Learner is encouraged to discover the best method for himself or herself | Student should learn to examine himself or herself | Individual preference | Individual preference | Innerdirected person "Authentic individual" Committed, involved person | Existentialism | Importance of the individual—"existence precedes essence"—paradox, subjectivity, anxiety | Individual preference | Committed individual I Thou—person who is both teacher and learner—one who provides a free environment |

# FIFTEEN

# Synectics

Synectics is a teaching model for information processing that stimulates creative thought and problem solving through the use of metaphoric activity, attempting to break set ways of thinking to address familiar material in new ways, or to introduce new material through previously learned concepts (Rettig & Canady, 2000). The word *synectics* is derived from the Greek *son,* meaning "to bring together," and *ectos* or *ectics,* meaning "diverse elements" (Weil, Joyce, & Kluwin, 1978). There are two main strategies or approaches in the synectics model. The first, making the familiar strange, seeks to assist students in looking at tasks or ideas in new ways. The second, making the strange familiar, is used to connect prior learning with new concepts. Synectics is rooted in metaphoric activity and seeks to increase students' capacity for creative thought.

Each strategy—making the familiar strange and making the strange familiar—attempts to help students connect prior knowledge with new concepts. Both strategies involve numerous steps that must be followed to elicit the desired metaphoric activity and conceptual distance needed to be creative. Both involve the three analogy types—direct analogy, personal analogy, and compressed conflict—although variations of each do exist.

Also called "creating something new," the first method, making the familiar strange helps students see familiar things in new ways, to view old problems or ideas in a more creative light. Possible objectives include developing new understanding, empathizing, designing a new product, addressing social or interpersonal problems, and prewriting. Analogies are used to create conceptual distance, and steps are followed to ensure that students cycle through Gordon's stages of creativity, discussed later in this chapter.

## ■ HISTORY AND RESEARCH

William J. Gordon, known for his work in creativity, developed the synectics model, publishing *Synectics* in 1961 (Joyce, Weil, & Calhoun, 2008). The method was originally used for business and industry in "creativity groups." It was believed that by participating in creative exploration, new ideas could be formed and creative solutions for problems could be found. The model was later modified for the classroom. Synectics has deep roots in creativity, metaphoric activity, and Gordon's assumptions about the creative process.

Citing that creativity is important in everyday activities, Gordon proposes three assumptions about the creative process (Weil et al., 1978). First, the creative process is not mysterious; it can be described, and it is possible to train persons to increase their creativity. Gordon believes that teachers can directly train students to be aware of their own creative processes and that students can be taught to engage in metaphoric and creative activity on their own to assist in understanding topics and ideas. Next, creative invention is similar in all fields. Although most people associate creativity with artists, writers, and musicians, Gordon argues that we all possess the ability to be creative. Scientists call it invention; writers, inspiration; others, creativity. Finally, individual and group invention (creative thinking) are similar. The same processes that individuals go through to tap their creative potential are mimicked in creative group interaction.

A scholar in the psychology of creativity, Gordon posits additional holdings to his assumptions to further describe the creative process. He states that by bringing the creative process to consciousness and by developing explicit aids to creativity, we can directly increase the creative capacity of both individuals and groups. Gordon contends that in creative thought, the emotional component is more important than the intellectual, the irrational more important than the rational. He does explain that the rational mind should be used to evaluate alternatives and make decisions but that the creative process affords the individual or group a wider range of solutions. Gordon also argues that emotional and irrational elements must be understood in order to increase the probability of success in a problem-solving situation. From these holdings and assumptions, Gordon introduced metaphoric activity as paramount in the synectics model.

Metaphors establish a relationship of likeness, the comparison of one object or idea with another object or idea by using one in place of the other. By engaging in such activity, participants are able to make connections between prior knowledge and new concepts. Metaphor introduces "conceptual distance" between the student and the object or concept and prompts original thought. This distance is presumed to increase the mental flexibility of participants. Just as the two strategies in synectics imply, metaphoric activity can make the familiar strange and make the strange familiar, offering participants a new view of an old topic or a way of relating new information to prior learning.

There are three basic types of metaphoric activity: direct analogy, personal analogy, and compressed conflict. A direct analogy is a single comparison of two objects or concepts (Joyce et al., 2008). The comparison need not be identical in all respects, and students would be expected to identify similarities and differences between concepts to strengthen the analogy. Direct analogies function to transpose the conditions of the real topic or situation to another topic or situation to afford new perspectives. Differing levels of strain are involved in analogical activity. Comparing oneself to a dog is a lesser degree of strain than comparing oneself to a car engine or other inanimate object. Participants involved in direct analogy are said to progress through stages of creative activity. Detachment from the situation, deferment of easy or obvious holdings, speculation about different approaches and framing, and finally, a return to the original situation make up these stages.

Personal analogy requires students to become involved empathetically with the ideas or objects compared (Weil et al., 1978). There are four levels of empathetic involvement: (1) first-person description of facts, (2) first-person identification with emotion, (3) empathetic identification with a living thing, and (4) empathetic identification with a nonliving object. The greater the conceptual distance attained through each type of analogy, the more likely that students have been creative or innovative in their thinking and in their work. Synectic success depends on the quality of analogies developed and mental stretching that students achieve.

"Compressed conflict" is generally a two-word description of an object in which the words seem to be opposites or contradict each other, sometimes called an *oxymoron* (e.g., "organized chaos"). Gordon maintains that these contradictory terms provide the broadest insight into a new subject (Weil et al., 1978). Compressed conflict incorporates two frames of reference in viewing a single object and encourages the distance desired in the detachment and speculative stages. The greater the conceptual distance achieved, the greater the mental flexibility.

There is a paucity of research on synectics, aside from the studies commonly mentioned by instructional methods texts. In one study of college students, synectics was found to enhance both immediate and long-term learning (Joyce et al., 2008). Another study makes similar findings about learning and adds that although synectics is effective across domain boundaries, specific training in some domains increases the likelihood that students will master concepts. A study done in science revealed that the use of synectics with text materials bolsters short- and long-term learning (Glynn, 1994).

# ■ GORDON'S STAGES OF CREATIVITY

In Gordon's model, creativity includes seven stages, or phases. Phase 1 is the description of a present condition. The teacher has students describe a situation as they see it now. Students should be encouraged to flesh out the concept or topic and note specifics that can be used for comparison later in the lesson. Phase 2 is direct analogy, and the teacher prompts students to suggest direct analogies, select one, and explore and describe it further. Phase 3 involves personal analogy during which students are to "become" the analogy they selected in Phase 2. Empathetic involvement and a focus on the other three types of personal analogy is important because students must move through more pronounced levels of strain to flex their creative muscles. Phase 4 is compressed conflict. Students take their descriptions from Phases 2 and 3, suggest several compressed conflicts, and choose one on which to focus, preferably a grouping that reflects the truest ring of conflict. Phase 5 is direct analogy; in this phase, students generate and select another direct analogy, based on the compressed conflict and explore it in detail. The students then come to Phase 6, which is the reexamination of the original task. Finally, students move back to the original task or problem and use the last analogy or the entire synectics experience to create new products or solutions. Students should exhibit more creative artifacts or solutions as a result of the model. Differences in perceptions, writings, and thinking should be noticeably different than at the beginning of the lesson.

Alternatively, aimed at increasing understanding and internalization of new or difficult material, the strange-to-familiar strategy makes use of similar phases but involves a different end. Metaphoric activity is used for analyzing, not for creating "conceptual distance," and while the first method involves a great deal of divergent thinking, this second method encourages students to converge thinking in creative ways (Lasley & Matczynski, 1997). Making the strange familiar involves defining or citing both the characteristics that are present and those that are lacking in analogies and comparisons. Through these comparisons, students gain a better understanding of new concepts because they have prior knowledge to build on, even though it may be seemingly unrelated in the beginning.

Phase 1 of making the strange familiar involves the provision of substantive input about the new topic by the teacher. Phase 2 is the direct analogy step; the teacher suggests a direct analogy and asks students to describe the analogy in as much detail as possible, in hopes of achieving some conceptual distance in the process. Phase 3 moves the students into a personal analogy, one in which the teacher has students "become" the direct analogy in the previous step. Phase 4 involves a comparison of analogies. Students identify and explain the points of similarity between the new material and the direct analogy. Phase 5 is concerned with explaining differences. To contrast the two frames of reference, students explain where the analogy does not fit. In Phase 6, exploration, students re-explore the original topic on its own terms, applying what they have learned from the experience. Finally, Phase 7, generating an analogy, requires students to provide their own analogy and explore the similarities and differences found in the new pairing. Students should exhibit the ability to make connections and point out discrepancies in creative ways. The goal of this strategy is to make the strange familiar, and students should be able to evidence a more comprehensive understanding of the new material or concept.

Teachers have much to consider when tackling a synectics lesson. First, they must master the process and operational procedures of each method. They must also take care to avoid premature analyses and limited mental stretching (Queen & Isenhour, 1998b). Teachers should explain the vocabulary to students and give them an idea of the purpose of each phase, as well as taking students through the process numerous times to build familiarity with the model. Teachers employing this method should strive to be well versed in evocative questioning and ready in advance to facilitate lesson flow and encourage spontaneity. Because of the "playful" nature of the activities, teachers must be proficient in time and behavior management. They must be sure to involve all students and accept all responses, and they should be prepared for nontraditional student and teacher interaction and dialogue. Done correctly, this model is fun and immediately productive. Results are obvious, and teachers can begin to ascertain the increase in student creativity fairly quickly. Done poorly, the model is a nightmare and will likely prove counterproductive.

In evaluating a synectics lesson, administrators or evaluators must understand the difficulty inherent in mastering all the steps and in stretching students to think divergently. The evaluator should be aware of what to look for in lesson presentations. Administrators should provide ongoing staff development in synectics and should be aware that the methods take time to master. Synectics is not direct instruction and may appear to be fluff during valuable instructional time. Evaluators not privy to the model and its form are likely to dismiss creative learning as "silly banter." This method requires strong classroom management skills. Evaluators observing teachers consistently using this model should develop an approach to instructional evaluation for this method and perhaps obtain forms or guide sheets to assist them.

Synectics does not require that a canned curriculum be purchased or that teachers bring in tons of equipment and materials. The two main resources necessary for success in the model are time and operational skill, both of which are necessary to realize all the benefits of the model. This method also requires an open and inviting classroom climate in which all students feel comfortable in contributing. Most of the time, needed materials will already be present. Although synectics is possible with large groups, smaller groups are recommended, and the classroom and teacher must support this type of grouping.

Peer teaching and observation is widely recommended in synectics literature as a way to train staff and help teachers master the method. The model is difficult, and care must be taken to offer thorough and continuing staff development. Synectics materials and training groups are available as resources for schools or groups interested in learning the model. Training for synectics should include focus on the questioning and classroom management skills necessary for successful implementation, as well as training in the theory and processes under girding the model. Short, brief introductions to this model may cause frustration and attrition.

## ■ PROMISES AND PITFALLS

There are many purported promises in the synectics method. Proponents argue that synectics stimulates and promotes creativity, encourages divergent thinking, addresses higher-order thinking skills, and bolsters students' ability to problem solve (Dallman-Jones, 1994). Synectics can be used in any subject or content area or for any activity, and the strategies work with all student types—high or low achievers, withdrawn or outgoing personalities, and students with varied learning styles. Synectics combines easily with other models and affords both instructional and nurturant effects. Users of the model claim that it promotes empathy and interpersonal closeness because all students are allowed to participate without fear of delivering an "absurd answer" and students gain deeper understanding of classmates and their views. Synectics requires students to synthesize and analyze, and the strategies can be used to introduce new concepts or to expand or review previously learned material. Synectics is alleged to bolster self-esteem because there is no "right" answer, and the model can be used individually or in groups. Finally, synectics improves self-expression—in oration, writing, and other areas.

Synectics has its drawbacks as well, and many teachers find themselves unhappy with the number of steps and the "weird" nature of the students and their interactions with metaphor and analogy. The methods, with their phases and steps, take some time to master and much preparation to implement. Younger children may have trouble with emotional expression or understanding the process and will probably have difficulty understanding the terms and activities involved. All levels of students may find the steps cumbersome and the operational vocabulary intimidating (Dallman-Jones, 1994). Students partial to left-brain, concrete, sequential thinking may be stretched out of their comfort zone in synectics, and teachers may be uncomfortable with letting student thinking "run free" or the fact that there is no "right answer."

## ■ SUMMARY

Synectics is not for the faint of heart. It involves a great deal of time and energy both in mastering the method and in instruction. Synectics is effective if it is implemented correctly and is useful in almost any setting, for any content, and at any point in the teaching of a unit. Synectics activities often transfer to students who pick up the processes and begin to use them on their own, ultimately producing students who can use the approach as a system to create or remember any time they want. At the very least, synectics offers a viable alternative for instruction and addresses many of the skills and processes that educators want to deliver to students. Whether making the familiar strange or making the strange familiar, synectics stimulates creative thought and helps students make connections that may not normally go together well. Synectics, although involved and difficult to master, promises to continue to be an effective instructional method and alternative.

Following is a sample synectics lesson. Remember that the foundation of the synectics method includes developing various types of analogies—direct, personal, and new. This metaphoric activity is the central concept of this instructional method. *To Kill a Mockingbird* is especially appropriate because even its title is metaphoric.

After reading the book, students view the movie starring Gregory Peck. The presentation is used to help the students determine the direct analogy in a general way. First, students should consider the following question, "Who would be like the mockingbird?" Then the lesson moves to the second, personal, phase in which students empathize with the character by "becoming" him or her. Finally, the students can compress their own feelings into a new analogy in order to better understand the concept.

## *TO KILL A MOCKINGBIRD*: ■
## A SYNECTICS SAMPLE LESSON

Harper Lee
• Born in 1926 in Monroeville, Alabama
• *To Kill a Mockingbird* was her first and only novel
• Was awarded the Pulitzer Prize in 1961
• Now lives a very private life in Alabama and avoids press interviews

### Characters

Atticus Finch
• Lawyer in Maycomb, Alabama, in the 1930s
• Widower and father of two children, Scout and Jem
• Defends Tom Robinson, a black man who is accused of raping a poor white woman

Jean Louise "Scout" Finch
• Narrator of the novel
• An intelligent six-year-old tomboy
• Younger sister of Jem and daughter of Atticus

Jem Finch and Dill Harris
• Jem is Scout's ten-year-old brother who is fascinated with "Boo" Radley, their neighbor
• Dill is a "goin' on seven" friend of Jem and Scout who visits during the summer

## Characters

Arthur "Boo" Radley
- A mysterious and reclusive neighbor of the Finches
- The children are terrified of him because of untrue rumors, but they try to get him to come out of his house

Tom Robinson
- A black farmhand who is wrongly accused of raping a poor white woman
- Defended in court by Atticus Finch
- His only "crime" was saying that he felt sorry for a white woman

Bob Ewell
- The main "villain" in the novel and known as the "trash" of Maycomb
- Charges Tom Robinson with raping his daughter, Mayella
- Threatened to get even with Atticus after the trial

## Major Themes in *To Kill a Mockingbird*

Racial Injustice
- A man's guilt or innocence was determined by his skin color
- Atticus demonstrates moral courage by defending Tom Robinson

To Kill a Mockingbird
- "Mockingbirds don't do one thing but make music for us to enjoy. They don't eat up people's gardens, don't nest in corn-cribs, they don't do one thing but sing their hearts out for us. That's why it's a sin to kill a mockingbird."
- Tom Robinson and "Boo" Radley were "mockingbirds"—they didn't harm anyone but were victims of injustice and cruelty.

## *To Kill a Mockingbird:* The Movie

- The movie was filmed in 1962 in black and white.
- Gregory Peck won an Oscar for Best Actor for his portrayal of Atticus Finch.
- Robert Duvall, who played "Boo" Radley, made his film debut in this movie.
- Harper Lee was pleased with the movie and the portrayal of its characters.

# SIXTEEN

# Socratic Seminar

In 1982, Mortimer Adler introduced *The Paideia Proposal,* using a group discussion model that can be easily incorporated into a blocked class. Each member of the class reads a selection from the material provided by the teacher prior to the seminar. The teacher avoids directing the discussion of the seminar. The teacher's role is to record the participation and degree of preparedness of each participating student. Students are instructed to explore their ideas about a particular topic and question other members of the class in an open discussion. Students thrive in these seminars once they discover that their opinion is valued and that the teacher is not searching for a specific, "right answer." The teacher usually asks the first question, or it can be elicited from a student experienced with the seminar format. Teachers avoid evaluation, direct the discussion toward topic relevancy, and clarify arguments if there seems to be no solution. The Socratic seminars often lead to further issues, thus extending the learning opportunities beyond one classroom discussion.

## GROUP DISCUSSION AND STUDENT PARTICIPATION ■

The success of the Socratic seminar can be attributed to the stark contrast it provides to the normal classroom setting. Students are used to teachers being in front of them, perhaps at a podium, whereas the teacher is literally on the same level as the students in the Socratic method. Students are also typically seated in rows but are placed in a circle during a Socratic seminar. Rather than teachers talking for the majority of the class time, students talk approximately 95% of the time during this instructional method.

In a comparison of a typical class discussion and the Socratic seminar method, student responses increase from 2 to 3 seconds in a typical discussion to 8 to 12 seconds in a Socratic seminar. Teachers are not to provide feedback during the seminar to ensure maximum student discussion time. This "silence" tactic works well in getting even those students who do not typically speak up to contribute. It also encourages students to think their way through their own ideas and speak up without concern about being incorrect; open exploration of thoughts is paramount.

Following is a list of the nine steps the author structured to help classroom teachers in implementing the Socratic seminar.

*Step 1:*  Students arrive and form a circle prepared for the assignment
*Step 2:*  The teacher presents opening question
*Step 3:*  Students respond to each other (Phase 1, about 15 minutes)
*Step 4:*  The teacher probes or clarifies *only*
*Step 5:*  The teacher asks core questions
*Step 6:*  Students respond to each other (Phase 2, about 30 minutes)
*Step 7:*  The teacher presents closing question
*Step 8:*  Students personalize discussion (Phase 3, about 30 minutes)
*Step 9:*  Seminar evaluation (Phase 4, usually 15 minutes)

## ■  WHAT HAPPENED: A SOCRATIC SEMINAR

This activity is one that may begin simply and in an unassuming way, but as so often happens in the Socratic seminar method, the relevance becomes serious and encourages deep introspection.

In preparation for this activity, the book *The True Story of the 3 Little Pigs* by A. Wolfe (Scieszka, 1999) should be read aloud. This book, available in any library or bookstore, is a twist on the traditional fairy tale in that it is told from the point of view of the wolf, who believes himself to be innocent of the crimes of which he has been accused. Prior to reading the story the teacher should read or tell the traditional story of the Three Little Pigs. Use the version of the story where the first two pigs are killed and eaten by the wolf and the third Little Pig keeps the wolf out of the brick house and calls the police.

To begin the seminar, the opening question is presented: Should the wolf be charged for the crimes? After approximately 15 minutes, in which the students have control and the instructor merely clarifies or probes only when absolutely necessary, a core question is asked, such as, "What should the punishment be?" or "Do you believe in capital punishment?" In the next phase, the teacher asks a closing question, such as, "Should

Osama bin Laden be executed?" It is important to personalize the closing question in some way, such as having the students pretend, if necessary, that they lost a loved one in the terrorist attacks on the World Trade Center and the Pentagon on September 11, 2001 (using the bin Laden example from before).

Most teachers have thought that the Socratic seminar could be used for limited areas in English and perhaps the arts. As a teacher, the author has found that the Socratic seminar can be used in any subject. It is great for the social sciences and even the sciences. The author knows of teachers who even do specific problems in advanced mathematics. Feel free to modify the time periods, and in some cases, math for example, only the first and third questions can be used, omitting the second question. One thing is important: Experiment—and then experiment some more. What works for one teacher will not always work for another. Visit www.block-scheduling.com to share examples of lessons used for Socratic seminars.

# SEVENTEEN

# Instructional Assessment

Instructional evaluation, or assessment, was once exclusively the teacher's domain. It consisted mainly of predetermined paper-and-pencil testing. Periodically, the students read a book, wrote a report, or gave an oral presentation, activities that all had to live up to the expectations of the individual teacher. Now, assessment is not necessarily based on the sole, personal judgment of the teacher. Students are included. As the community demands more student accountability, students are becoming more involved in their own learning process, including evaluation and assessment.

Instructional evaluation occurs through the assessment of student achievement, which often depends on the effectiveness of the instructor. For example, does the teacher choose the right delivery system? Are the teacher's objectives clear? Do test items relate to objectives? Evaluation of instruction is also evaluation of the curriculum. It reveals the success of one dimension—how much the student achieves in areas that are assessed. It may also indicate whether the content has been adequately covered. Evaluation of instruction does not answer curricular concerns as to whether the subject matter was the right choice, whether its content is relevant, whether it meets student or societal needs, and whether it has been selected wisely.

# ■ METHODS OF INSTRUCTIONAL EVALUATION

Measurement is the means of determining the degrees of achievement of a particular competency. Testing is the use of instruments for measuring achievement. The three phases of instructional evaluation are (a) preassessment, evaluation that takes place before instruction; (b) formative evaluation, evaluation that takes place during the instruction process; and (c) summative evaluation, assessment that takes place at the end of instruction.

## Preassessment

The tool used in preassessment is the criterion-referenced test or pretest. The criterion-referenced test measures the entry skills that have been identified as critical to beginning instruction. This is also known as a pretest. The pretest is criterion-referenced to the objectives the designer intends to teach. A pretest by itself is not sufficient to address all needs at the beginning of instruction. If students perform poorly on a pretest, the instructor may not be able to gauge whether they did poorly for lack of general knowledge or for lack of the knowledge required for entry-level instruction.

A second type of test is designed to help students measure their skills against the skills of others. These types of tests are called norm-referenced tests. Norm-referenced measurement compares a student's performance on a test with the performance of other students who took the test. Norm-referenced testing is necessary when a limited number of spaces are to be filled from a pool of applicants. Norm-referenced measurement permits comparisons between people, with the primary purpose of making decisions about the qualifications of individuals.

## Formative Evaluation

Formative evaluation consists of formal and informal techniques of assessing the learning of students. Formative evaluation occurs during the process of instruction. It may include questions at different points during the instruction or checking students' responses to parts of the instruction. Instructors use formative evaluation to determine if the skills to be learned are being addressed. It allows instructors to determine whether they need to provide remedial instruction to overcome difficulties.

## Summative Evaluation

Summative evaluation is the assessment that occurs at the end of a course or unit. The tools used are final exams, a posttest, or an actual demonstration of a skill or operation. It is used to determine whether students have mastered the instruction.

# ASSESSMENT OF STUDENT ACHIEVEMENT    ■

Several new ways are available to evaluate student achievement. The new tools are called performance-based or authentic assessment. *Authentic* means "worthy of acceptance or belief, trustworthy" (Engel, 1994, p. 24). Assessments are authentic because they are valuable activities within themselves and involve the performance of tasks directly related to real world problems. Brookhart, Moss, and Long (2008) found that this type of assessment can be an empowering event for students and assists in the communication process between teacher and student.

*Portfolios, authentic assessment measures,* and *alternative assessment activities* are the latest buzzwords used to describe activities other than standardized tools for determining a student's achievement. Educators, parents, and students have come to realize that standardized tests do not truly represent a student's academic growth in the content knowledge, skills, and instructional activities in the classroom. Following is a more detailed explanation of these methods of assessment, beginning with a definition of *assessment.*

An *assessment* is an exercise such as a written test, portfolio, or experiment that seeks to measure a student's knowledge in a subject area.

*A portfolio* is a systematic and organized collection of a student's work throughout a course or school year that measures the student's knowledge and skills and often includes some form of self-reflection by the student.

*Alternative assessment* is any form of measuring what a student knows and is able to do, other than traditional standardized tests, including portfolios, performance-based assessments, and other means of testing students. These alternative assessments show actual growth over a period of time that the students, parents, and teachers can physically see. Tests do not show this growth as it occurs.

*Authentic assessment* allows the student to "become progressively self-disciplined as a thinker . . . (and) to acquire the habit of inquiring and engaging in discourse with care and thoroughness" (Wiggins, 1993, p. 211). Its purpose is to get students to take control of their own learning while maintaining relevance and a meaningful connection to what they are learning. Student contracts, for example, enable students to take responsibility for their own learning while giving them freedom to explore; these contracts also teach organizational control of the lesson content.

## Portfolio

The portfolio, a collection of student writing samples assembled over a period of a course or longer, is the most popular form of alternative assessment and is authentic assessment when done correctly. It is like a collection of photographs of a student's writing. Analyzing each writing sample singularly does not give one a complete picture. The portfolio allows for a comprehensive evaluation of a student's growth and the creation of individual goals for future work.

A portfolio is called a performance-based assessment because the intent of the portfolio is for students to assemble a collection of samples of their work, which in essence, shows evidence of their accomplishments. Portfolios may contain creative writing, tests, artwork, exercises, reflective essays, notes on topics, and whatever other materials portray achievement. Standards and criteria for achievement in portfolios should be set. Some of the criteria may include completeness, effort, neatness, and creativity. Portfolios reveal students' patterns of learning and thinking as the year progresses; they also allow both teachers and students to work in the most productive ways possible. There are almost as many approaches to compiling and evaluating portfolios as there are proponents of this form of assessment. Portfolios can be used both formally and informally. Ideally, the portfolio captures the evolution of the student's ideas and can be used instructionally and as progress markers for the student, teacher, and program evaluator.

Portfolios are adaptable to a variety of educational settings. In Fort Worth, Texas, a 5th-grade teacher used them in his math class. Kentucky and Vermont educators have made portfolios a part of their statewide assessment of students. Pittsburgh educators have used portfolios to assess learning in imaginative writing, music, and visual arts.

A portfolio has three major parts: biography, range of works, and reflections. The biography shows the developmental history of the child's progress and gives the reader an impression of how the student has progressed from the beginning to that point. The portfolio contains a range of assignments. These could be the student's "best," "most important," "satisfactory," and "unsatisfactory" pieces of work, as well as revisions. The student critiques his or her work by reflecting on how his or her performance has changed, what he or she has learned, and what he or she needs to do to improve. See Box 17.1 for three portfolio models.

Educators who use portfolios in the block schedule believe that these are practical and effective assessment tools for several reasons. Portfolios are easy to design, durable, and reusable. This form of assessment influences the teacher's way of teaching and testing by problem solving, communication, application, and so on, and promotes worthwhile learning while expanding the dimensions of education. It provides a developmental perspective that is easily observed by students, parents, and teachers. Finally, it documents a student's progress through school until graduation. Members of the NEA (National Education Association) support the portfolio's use because it accurately reflects what the student has learned.

Not all educators support the portfolio. Some teachers use it to display the best of a student's work. Used this way, it will not accurately reflect performance and rate of progress and cannot be called an assessment measure because, rather than including a representative sampling of a student's work, teachers may guide students about what to write and include. Storage is difficult because a portfolio, if used appropriately, can be big and bulky. Scoring is time-consuming as well as inconsistent, and even if the scorers do agree, that does not guarantee that the portfolio measures what it was supposed to measure (Viadero, 1995). In Vermont, for example, it took more

**Box 17.1** Three Portfolio Models

**Model 1**

I.   Introduction—title page
II.  Student Portrait—photo or video montage of student
         Attendance record
         Discipline record
         Self-esteem rating
         Test scores
III. Educational Goals
         Student goals for the year
         Career goals
         Copies of exceptional work—all discipline areas
IV.  Conclusion—reflection
         Evaluation of portfolio
         Summary paper at end of year—student self-evaluation

**Model 2**

I.   Writing
         Submissions from English: literature response, personal
             essay, research paper
         Submissions from history: cause-and-effect paper,
             defense paper
         Submissions from science: classification paper, lab report
         Submission of student choice
II.  Reading List
III. Conclusion
         Self-evaluation of writing and reading goals
         Teacher analysis of writing ability—establish goals for
             next school year

**Model 3**

I.   Student Goals for the School Year
         Writing goals
         Reading goals
         Communication goals
II.  Writing Samples
         Literature response
         Comparative analysis
         Journal entry
         Research paper
         Essay test
         Creative writing—poem, short story, etc.
         Student choice
III. Editing
         Peer evaluation
         Self-evaluation
IV.  Future Goals for Writing and Reading
         List of future goals
         Summary of career goals

than 160 scorers five days to assess 7,000 portfolios. In addition, these scorers were, understandably, influenced by their personal beliefs.

Teachers participating in block scheduling seminars expressed the following suggestions for evaluation success:

## Student Assessment and Instructional Evaluation

- Reports
- Team competitions, research projects
- Skills
- Role playing
- Portfolios
- More oral response time, debates
- Team projects
- Self-assessment
- Individual
- Pre- and posttests
- Teacher-student evaluation, one-on-one
- Practical hands-on skill evaluation, theory into practice
- Peer evaluations
- Standardized testing
- Parent conferences
- Ongoing evaluation of program, formative evaluation
- More home involvement
- Nonthreatening evaluations for teachers, opportunities to try things without fear of failure or accountability

## Unit Evaluation

Unit evaluation includes two major types of evaluation: diagnostic and summative. Diagnostic evaluation allows the teacher to learn what the students' learning potential and level of related knowledge are prior to the start of the instruction. Product evaluation measures what the students have learned through implementation of the unit. The usual form of evaluation is a written test. The unit test can contain a mix of objective (answer with the facts) and subjective (essay) questions. These two types of evaluation assist with the planning of future methods of teaching a unit by providing, through student response to test items, information about how the instruction can be organized to become more effective.

## Lesson Evaluation

Lesson evaluation occurs daily. Informal and formal evaluation occurs while the lesson is going on as well as at its completion. Some informal ways of evaluation are observations of the students both individually and as a group, assessment of students' contributions, review of homework, and overall impressions of the level of student understanding and success. Some formal methods of evaluation are quizzes, debates, and rating scales.

These evaluations are done constantly throughout the lesson to verify that the lesson is being comprehended by the students. They allow for modifications to be made at any point in the lesson.

## A POSITIVE CLASSROOM ■
## CLIMATE THROUGH INSTRUCTION

Students and teachers learning in a classroom using block scheduling or extended learning time become more active and engage in hands-on activities. The classroom climate is positively affected by this active learning. During the lengthened class period, students and teachers have the opportunity to get to know one another better. Teachers have fewer students in one day and spend longer periods of time with individual students. This one-on-one time helps to build strong relationships between students and teachers.

To improve the classroom climate, a strong management program is important. The classroom management program puts boundaries and limits on student behavior and gives opportunities for the students to learn in a safe environment. Along with more engaging and hands-on learning, students benefit from a warm and inviting environment and build responsible behavior. Queen and Algozzine (2009) provide research and a step-by-step schoolwide discipline program that has proven to be extremely effective in the block scheduled school. The classroom climate will improve if teachers have a positive attitude, are approachable, can create learning activities that are student-friendly, and decorate the classroom in a pleasing and educational manner. The school building itself can also be a warm and nurturing place. Bulletin boards that clearly display upcoming events, lists of students with perfect attendance, and lists of awards and honors. Honor roll lists and athletic achievements are both visually interesting and communicative. Giant calendars, club-sponsored bulletin boards, and festive holiday decorations make the school more personal and aid in creating a positive learning environment.

# EIGHTEEN

# Relationship and Purpose of Program Evaluation and Student Assessment

**E**valuation is the process of determining the worth of any given thing. Evaluation of school programs and of the curriculum is done in order to establish their value. Throughout the history of education, evaluation in these areas has been assessed either formally or informally. Many trends and issues affect evaluation. Evaluation must be carefully considered before, during, and after implementation of a block schedule. This chapter will address the "how" and "why" of evaluation in general since the methods and reasons can be applied to any type of program.

Evaluation has many definitions. It can be seen as a product of the work of evaluators, but it is more commonly viewed as a process. The process of evaluation primarily involves two basic acts. First, the process by which data are gathered so that decisions will be informed. Second, the process of applying criteria to the available information in order to arrive at justifiable decisions. In *Perspectives of Curriculum Evaluation,* Michael Scriven (Tyler, Gagné, & Scriven, 1967) explains that evaluation itself is an activity that is essentially similar whether we are trying to evaluate coffee machines or teaching machines, plans for a house or plans for a curriculum. The method for the activity consists simply in the gathering and combining of performance data with a weighted set of goal scales to obtain either comparative or numerical ratings and in the justification of (a) the data-gathering instruments, (b) the weightings, and (c) the selection of goals.

When evaluating a curriculum or a program, it is necessary to distinguish between the roles associated with evaluation and the goals associated with evaluation. When discussing roles, distinctions must be made as to the role of the principal, the role of the teacher, and the role of the evaluation itself. What will the evaluation be used for? What evaluative instrument will be used? When the question is asked, "What is the goal of evaluation?" the question "Whose goal?" must be answered. The point is that when discussing evaluation, it must be acknowledged that this is a complicated, multifaceted subject, and the terms and their particular usage must be clearly defined every step of the way. Evaluation should be a continuous process that is part of every stage of curriculum development and program development, and during implementation of the two.

## ■ REASONS FOR EVALUATION

Evaluation provides the information needed to make changes. Evaluation gives (or should give) direction to everything that is done in school. Evaluation should guide decisions about staffing, materials and equipment, facilities, and scheduling. Evaluation of curriculum and of programs must be done systematically in a way that can be easily explained and replicated. Only then can all involved stakeholders learn from the process. Too often, only those conducting the evaluation have knowledge of the instrument and, later, of the findings. If the information is not shared and understood, there was little reason for conducting or imposing an evaluative process in the first place. In the book *Supervision and Instructional Leadership*, Glickman, Gordon, and Ross-Gordon (2001) discuss the importance of evaluation in education and the way it has recently changed. The public demand for accountability and the advent of high-stakes testing has added new interest to the subject of evaluation. National reform efforts such as No Child Left Behind have drawn attention to education. There is great concern over what the children of the nation are learning. Right now, the focus with regard to student learning is performance on standardized tests. Administrators, teachers, and parents want to know how to enable their students to achieve higher test scores. Evaluation is a large part of this. An example shared by the authors of *Supervision and Instructional Leadership* (Glickman et al., 2001) is a look at 15 exemplary elementary and middle schools in three districts that all made significant improvements in mathematics and reading over a three-year period. The common characteristic of these schools was found to be that information about student progress was regularly gathered, and the information was used schoolwide to make decisions about changing curriculum. Every school did not change curriculum in the same way but changed based on the determined needs of the students. The information obtained was also used to guide professional staff development.

# DEFINING PROGRAM EVALUATION     ■

The terms *curriculum* and *program* are sometimes used interchangeably but are usually not considered the same thing. A program is often viewed as a specific component of a curriculum. A program can mean an organized set of ideas and plans within a certain discipline that may be used to provide information for students. For example, the term may be used to detail what will be done with a particular group of students in reading. The reading program is only a component of the total curriculum. The word *program* may also be used to mean the overall instructional program. It is acceptable to use the terms in either way as long as the definition used in a particular instance is made clear and the definition is used consistently.

Evaluation must be applied to the programs used within a curriculum. As evaluation is used to determine the worth of anything, evaluation of a program is used to see if the programs have merit, if the programs are working for the students for whom they are used, and if changes need to be made. Glickman et al. (2001) discuss six components that may be considered as one conducts a comprehensive program evaluation. The components are as follows:

*Evaluation of Needs Assessment.* It is important to determine whether or not there is a need for a program. While this may seem obvious, there is evidence that schools often succumb to good salesmanship and "bandwagon" popularity rather than responding to actual need when choosing programs. Teachers report the frustration that occurs when asked to implement new programs without old programs first being phased out. Layering program on program is confusing. The needs assessment will assist in determining what should continue to have a valid place in the curriculum and what has outlived its usefulness.

*Evaluation of Program Design.* An essential part of program evaluation is to look at the written plan of a program. It is important to ask if the goals and objectives are consistent with the needs the program is to meet. And it is critical to determine *before* implementation of the program what human and material resources have been committed to the program.

*Evaluation of Readiness.* When a program fails, it is usually because one or more of the stakeholders (principals, teachers, students, parents, and/or other community members) were not prepared to support implementation of the program. This lack of support may stem from disagreement with the program, lack of understanding about how to implement the program, or a lack of communication about the program. Many times, a good program has had no success because a stakeholder did not understand, like, or feel competent to implement the program as designed.

*Implementation Evaluation.* The key question to be asked here is, "Was the program implemented as planned?" If the answer to this question is no, then what was responsible for the error? When a program is implemented, three phases should be considered: (1) the initiation of the program, (2) the continuation of the program, and (3) integration of the program with the school culture. Implementation according to the directives of the program is key. Many programs fail to produce desired results because they are not executed as intended. School principals and other educational leaders must fully understand the programs that are to be put into operation within the total school and individual classrooms. Regular monitoring of instruction and program implementation can control what evaluators refer to as "loss of program fidelity."

*Evaluation of Outcomes.* Two types of outcomes can be measured with program evaluation. *Intended outcomes* are the goals and objectives of the program. *Unintended outcomes* are results that came about but that were not planned for. Unintended outcomes can be positive or negative. Unintended outcomes should be carefully studied, for they provide valuable insight as the "next step" is contemplated.

*Cost-Benefit Analysis.* When an analysis is applied, evaluators are comparing the benefits of the programs to the cost in terms of the use of human resources, material resources, and dollars spent. Most schools operate with limited resources in all areas, so this is very important.

Program evaluation may be used effectively to make the changes that benefit students whether the changes are for a short time or are more permanent. A principal in North Carolina whose elementary school had adopted a popular mathematics program tells a story about the importance of program evaluation. A prepackaged mathematics program was chosen for use because (a) most of the elementary school leaders in his particular district felt that the program would raise end-of-the-year test scores and (b) the program, since it incorporates the use of many manipulatives and "real-life" situations, would improve math instruction in the school. Teachers follow a script to deliver instruction with this particular package. The program was implemented at the beginning of the school year. The training for how to use the program was very brief because all the material did not arrive until a few days after school had started. Teachers were told to "read the script" and to "stay a couple of days ahead of the kids." After a few weeks of using the program, the 4th-grade teachers approached the principal with the disturbing news that 12 children in the grade level could not keep up with the program. Parents had been contacted about the problem, and the students had been supported in a variety of ways, but the difficulty remained. These particular students had learning difficulties in mathematics, but the discrepancy between ability and performance was not substantial enough to allow them to qualify for diagnosis of a specific learning disability. Therefore, the students could not be placed in a separate learning environment, which would have helped to address their needs. A few of the students struggled because of very low IQs, but again, that alone did not allow them to receive services outside the regular education classroom.

These boys and girls were the students with whom educators constantly struggle. They were the children who fail to meet any criteria for additional services. These were the children who are often referred to as "at-risk" or "falling through the cracks." Their math skills were significantly below grade level, and after two of the program assessments, it was apparent that a change must be made for the struggling students. The principal supported the teachers in their request, trusting in their collective professional abilities to recognize that a change needed to be made. A great deal of time was spent as the principal and the teachers, along with the special education teacher, discussed solutions to the problem. At the heart of each discussion was the desire to create a situation that would provide for the needs of the students who were experiencing such difficulty. The principal provided support as classes were reorganized. He also provided an extra teacher to work in the classroom with the 12 students. The important lesson to be gleaned from this case study is that (a) teacher input was valued, (b) the children for whom the program *was* working were not affected, (c) teaching support was provided so that the group of students working below grade level could make progress faster, and (d) the integrity of the mathematics program was not compromised. The outcome of this program evaluation was that the school gained valuable knowledge about the ability level of these at-risk students. The decisions to act and to support student learning were made, and as a result, there were increased skills for those students as well as significant gains on the end-of-year standardized tests.

When evaluating the overall instructional program, many areas within the school must be looked at because the areas are appreciably related to the success of the program. Glickman et al. (2001) address this issue in *Supervision and Instructional Leadership.* Box 18.1 illustrates the areas they recommend be considered.

## INSTRUCTIONAL EVALUATION ■

A program has been defined as a component of the curriculum. A program may be further broken down into a unit of study. Classroom teachers implement and present information to students in units of study. This presentation is commonly referred to as instruction. Instruction of a unit must also be evaluated. In *Curriculum Practice in 21st Century Schools* (Queen, 2009), reference is made to the two major types of evaluation— diagnostic and summative. Through diagnostic evaluation, the teacher identifies what the learning potential of a student is prior to the start of an instructional unit. An authentic assessment evaluation is a way of measuring what a student has learned from the presentation of an instructional unit. These methods of evaluation are valuable to the classroom teacher and should not be overlooked by the instructional leader of the school. Regular instructional evaluation is the piece of the evaluation process that should regularly inform classroom teachers about how to proceed so that the needs of students are met.

**Box 18.1**    Areas to Consider When Evaluating an Overall Instructional Program

Educators must ask themselves . . .

What are the characteristics of the community, parents, teachers, and students?

What programs are in place that involve parents, the community, and professional development?

What are the standards for student achievement, and are students meeting those standards?

What is the climate and culture of the school?

How is the school governed?

What kind of relationships exist between other schools, the central office, and external organizations?

SOURCE: Glickman, Gordon, and Ross-Gordon (2001).

The focus today for most school principals is "alignment." This refers to the prescribed objectives of the curriculum "matching up" with instruction delivery, textbooks, and scheduling. There may be the perception that in a state where there is a standard course of study, very specific curriculum and program objectives, and an evaluation that measures these objectives, there is very little that the principal has any control over, at least in the area of curriculum and instruction. This is certainly not the case. An instructional leader in this instance is responsible for knowing the course of study. While it would be ridiculous to imagine a building administrator who has detailed knowledge of the content objectives for every subject area or grade level, the principal must have an overall knowledge of what is to be taught. This is important in all instructional settings but imperative in the school using block scheduling. Today and in the future, the author believes from numerous observations in classrooms throughout the nation that the principal or the designated instructional leader in the school must have a working mastery of several effective instructional strategies.

Important in this expanded or continued era of accountability and reform is the principal who has the ability to communicate a vision and purpose to all members of the school community so that students get the best possible education. This is sometimes referred to as the ability to transform.

Principals interested in becoming the instructional leaders of their schools must consider three key features, according to Henderson and Hawthorne (2000) in *Transformative Curriculum Leadership*. The first item to consider is action research. When principals examine their own practices and encourage teachers to do the same, there is a greater understanding within the entire community about what is happening and why. The second item to consider is dialogue. Good dialogue can help educators avoid the type of instructional activity that serves no purpose. When dialogue is focused around the needs of the students and teachers of the school, then everyone is supported in doing the best possible work. Finally, principals and other members of the educational community recognize the ongoing nature of evaluation.

The challenge for the aspiring instructional leader facing problems related to block scheduling will be to know when and how to lead the faculty to transform the school and classrooms to be environments where greater focus is placed on student learning over teaching. The block schedule is rapidly turning into an environment where the ownership of learning must be the students.

Evaluation is an important part of the issue of school reform and school transformation. All stakeholders of the school must be a part of any change that is to take place. Decisions must be based on careful and intentional evaluation. The instructional leader must also understand the dynamics that occur when change is introduced into an organization. Evaluation means assessing the value of something. Regularly determining the value and the effectiveness of not only the curriculum, the programs, and the instruction in a school but the best scheduling format for maximum effectiveness.

Two tools for evaluation before and after a school implements block scheduling. Evaluation Resource 1 is a preassessment survey that can be used to determine a school's interest in and attitudes toward block scheduling. Evaluation Resource 2 can be used to assess the use of, preference for, and training in classroom instructional practices for teachers from schools that use block scheduling.

# EVALUATION RESOURCE 1
## Block Schedule Teacher Survey

Please take a few minutes to complete the items on both sides of this sheet. Thank you.
Use the following scale to answer each question:
1 = Very High (VH), 2 = High, 3 = Average, 4 = Below Average, 5 = Low, 6 = Very Low (VL).

|  | VH | | | | VL | |
|---|---|---|---|---|---|---|
| 1. Effectiveness of block scheduling relative to student achievement? | 1 | 2 | 3 | 4 | 5 | 6 |
| 2. Effectiveness of block scheduling relative to use of instructional time? | 1 | 2 | 3 | 4 | 5 | 6 |
| 3. Effectiveness of block scheduling relative to instructional pacing? | 1 | 2 | 3 | 4 | 5 | 6 |
| 4. Effectiveness of block scheduling relative to "completeness" of course? | 1 | 2 | 3 | 4 | 5 | 6 |
| 5. Overall rating of the effectiveness of block scheduling? | 1 | 2 | 3 | 4 | 5 | 6 |

Use the following scale to respond to these items:
1 = Very Strongly Agree (VSA), 2 = Strongly Agree, 3 = Agree,
4 = Disagree, 5 = Strongly Disagree, 6 = Very Strongly Disagree (VSD)

As a result of block scheduling,

|  | VSA | | | | VSD | |
|---|---|---|---|---|---|---|
| 6. Fewer class changes result in safer and more secure school | 1 | 2 | 3 | 4 | 5 | 6 |
| 7. I am able to vary the instructional methods I use to keep students actively engaged. | 1 | 2 | 3 | 4 | 5 | 6 |
| 8. I am more involved in my school's curriculum and decision making. | 1 | 2 | 3 | 4 | 5 | 6 |
| 9. I am better able to meet the needs of students at differing levels of ability. | 1 | 2 | 3 | 4 | 5 | 6 |

Tell us about yourself and how you teach:

10. Total years of teaching experience?
    a. first-year teacher    b. 2–5 years    c. 6–10 years    d. 11–20 years    e. more than 20 years

11. Typical percentage of time spent in interactive instruction with students?
    a. less than 20%    b. 21–40%    c. 41–60%    d. 61–80%    e. more than 80%

12. Typical percentage of time spent monitoring independent work of students?
    a. less than 20%    b. 21–40%    c. 41–60%    d. 61–80%    e. more than 80%

13. Typical percentage of time spent handling classroom management problems?
    a. less than 20%    b. 21–40%    c. 41–60%    d. 61–80%    e. more than 80%

Tell us what you think of block scheduling.

14. List in priority order characteristics or teaching skills of a master teacher in block scheduling.

    a. _____    b. _____

    c. _____    d. _____

    e. _____    f. _____

15. List some benefits of block scheduling.

    a. _____    b. _____

    c. _____    d. _____

    e. _____    f. _____

16. List some problems with block scheduling.

    a. _____    b. _____

    c. _____    d. _____

    e. _____    f. _____

17. What kind of assistance do teachers need to better deliver instruction when using a block scheduling model?

_____

_____

# EVALUATION RESOURCE 2
## Teacher Survey: High School Instruction

The following sections request information about your classroom instructional practices, your recent staff development experiences, and your teaching experience/workload. Please provide answers directly on the survey.

### I. Classroom Instructional Practices

Please select the statement that *best describes* your level of use, preference, and training for each of the following instructional practices.

**Cooperative Learning** (*Cooperative learning is the practice of grouping students in small, mixed-ability learning teams. The teacher presents the group with a problem to solve or task to perform. Students then work together to achieve a group performance score by helping one another and praising and criticizing one another's contributions*)

### Level of Use
A.  I *do not use/do not have time to use* cooperative learning in my classroom.
B.  I use cooperative learning activities *very seldom* (e.g., once or twice during the course I teach).
C.  I use cooperative learning activities *seldom* (e.g., once or twice during each grading period).
D.  I use cooperative learning activities *often* (e.g., once a week).
E.  I use cooperative learning activities *very often* (e.g., every day).

### Level of Preference
A.  I do not prefer cooperative learning as a teaching practice for my subject.
B.  Cooperative learning is an appropriate practice that can be used occasionally in my subject area.
C.  Cooperative learning is a practice that is well suited to my course content.

### Level of Training
A.  I have had *no training* in cooperative learning.
B.  I have had *some training* but not enough to implement.
C.  I have had *extensive training* in cooperative learning and understand it well.

**Discovery Learning** (*Discovery learning involves hands-on, experiential, intentional learning through teacher-directed problem solving activities*)

### Level of Use
A.  I *do not use/do not have time to use* the discovery learning in my classroom.
B.  I use discovery learning *very seldom* (e.g., once or twice during the course I teach).
C.  I use discovery learning *seldom* (e.g., once or twice during each grading period).
D.  I use discovery learning *often* (e.g., once a week).
E.  I use discovery learning *very often* (e.g., every day).

### Level of Preference
A.  I do not prefer discovery learning as a teaching practice for my subject.
B.  Discovery learning is an appropriate practice that can be used occasionally in my subject area.
C.  Discovery learning is a practice that is well suited to my course content.

### Level of Training

A. I have had *no training* in the discovery learning.
B. I have had *some training* but not enough to implement.
C. I have had *extensive training* in discovery learning and understand it well.

**Lecture** *(A lecture is an instructional practice in which the teacher gives an oral presentation of facts and principles, with the students frequently being responsible for note taking.)*

### Level of Use

A. I *do not use/do not have time to use* lecture in my classroom.
B. I use lecture *very seldom* (e.g., once or twice during the course I teach).
C. I use lecture *seldom* (e.g., once or twice during each grading period).
D. I use lecture *often* (e.g., once a week).
E. I use lecture *very often* (e.g., every day).

### Level of Preference

A. I do not prefer lecture as a teaching practice for my subject.
B. Lecture is an appropriate practice that can be used occasionally in my subject area.
C. Lecture is a practice that is well suited to my course content.

### Level of Training

A. I have had *no training* in lecture.
B. I have had *some training* but not enough to implement.
C. I have had *extensive training* in lecture and understand the concept well.

**Direct Instruction** *(When using direct instruction approaches, the teacher structures lessons in a straightforward sequential manner, discussion, worksheets, and drill.)*

### Level of Use

A. I do *not use/do not have time to use* direct instruction in my classroom.
B. I use direct instruction *very seldom* (e.g., once or twice during the course I teach).
C. I use direct instruction *seldom* (e.g., once or twice during each grading period).
D. I use direct instruction *often* (e.g., once a week).
E. I use direct instruction *very often* (e.g., every day).

### Level of Preference

A. I do not prefer direct instruction as a teaching practice for my subject.
B. Direct instruction is an appropriate practice that can be used occasionally in my subject area.
C. Direct instruction is a practice that is well suited to my course content.

### Level of Training

A. I have had *no training* in direct instruction.
B. I have had *some training* but not enough to implement.
C. I have had *extensive training* in direct instruction and understand the concept well.

**Simulation** *(A simulation is a representation of a manageable real event in which the learner is an active participant engaged in acquiring a new behavior or in applying previously acquired skills or knowledge)*

*(Continued)*

*(Continued)*

**Level of Use**

A.   I do *not use/do not have time to use* simulation in my classroom.
B.   I use simulation *very seldom* (e.g., once or twice during the course I teach).
C.   I use simulation *seldom* (e.g., once or twice during each grading period).
D.   I use simulation *often* (e.g., once a week).
E.   I use simulation *very often* (e.g., every day).

**Level of Preference**

A.   I do not prefer simulation as a teaching practice for my subject.
B.   Simulation is an appropriate practice that can be used occasionally in my subject area.
C.   Simulation is a practice that is well suited to my course content.

**Level of Training**

A.   I have had *no training* in simulation.
B.   I have had *some training* but not enough to implement.
C.   I have had *extensive training* in simulation and understand the concept well.

**Field Trips** *(When using field trips, teachers take students to a specific location where they may study or observe real things in direct interaction with specified concepts and/or skills to be learned.)*

**Level of Use**

A.   I *do not use/do not have time to use* field trips in my classroom.
B.   I use field trips *very seldom* (e.g., once or twice during the course I teach).
C.   I use field trips *seldom* (e.g., once or twice during each grading period).
D.   I use field trips *often* (e.g., once a week).
E.   I use field trips *very often* (e.g., every day).

**Level of Preference**

A.   I do not prefer field trips as a teaching practice for my subject.
B.   Field trips are an appropriate practice that can be used occasionally in my subject area.
C.   Field trips are a practice that are well suited to my course content.

**Level of Training**

A.   I have had *no training* in integrating field trips into instruction.
B.   I have had *some training* but not enough to implement.
C.   I have had *extensive training* in field trips and understand the practice well.

**Student peer coaching/peer tutoring** *(Peer coaching/peer tutoring involves students teaching other students either in cross age grouping or within their own class)*

**Level of Use**

A.   I *do not use/do not have time to use* peer coaching/peer tutoring in my classroom.
B.   I use peer coaching/peer tutoring *very seldom* (e.g., once or twice during the course I teach).
C.   I use peer coaching/peer tutoring *seldom* (e.g., once or twice during each grading period).
D.   I use peer coaching/peer tutoring *often* (e.g., once a week).
E.   I use peer coaching/peer tutoring *very often* (e.g., every day).

**Level of Preference**

A.   I do not prefer peer coaching/peer tutoring as a teaching practice for my subject.
B.   Peer coaching/peer tutoring is an appropriate practice that can be used occasionally in my subject area.
C.   Peer coaching/peer tutoring is a practice that is well suited to my course content.

### Level of Training

A.  I have had *no training* in peer coaching/peer tutoring.
B.  I have had *some training* but not enough to implement.
C.  I have had *extensive training* in peer coaching/peer tutoring and understand the practice well.

**Audiovisual Experiences** *(When providing audiovisual experiences, teachers use films, videos, tape recordings, and other media presentations to deliver the content of their instruction)*

### Level of Use

A.  I *do not use/do not have time to use* audiovisual resources in my classroom.
B.  I use audiovisual resources *very seldom* (e.g., once or twice during the course I teach).
C.  I use audiovisual resources *seldom* (e.g., once or twice during each grading period).
D.  I use audiovisual resources *often* (e.g., once a week).
E.  I use audiovisual resources *very often* (e.g., every day).

### Level of Preference

A.  I do not prefer audiovisual resources as a teaching practice for my subject.
B.  Audiovisual experiences are an appropriate practice that can be used occasionally in my subject area.
C.  Audiovisual resources are a practice that is well suited to my course content.

### Level of Training

A.  I have had *no training* in integrating audiovisual resources in instruction.
B.  I have had *some training* but not enough to implement.
C.  I have had *extensive training* in audiovisual resources and understand the practice well.

**Technology Assistance** *(Technology-assisted instruction involves the use of computers to assist in instruction of basic facts, skills, and concepts related to the subject as well as drill and practice, tutorial, gaming, simulation, discovery, problem solving, and other activities)*

### Level of Use

A.  I *do not use/do not have time to use* technology assistance in my classroom.
B.  I use technology assistance *very seldom* (e.g., once or twice during the course I teach).
C.  I use technology assistance *seldom* (e.g., once or twice during each grading period).
D.  I use technology assistance *often* (e.g., once a week).
E.  I use technology assistance *very often* (e.g., every day).

### Level of Preference

A.  I do not prefer technology assistance as a teaching practice for my subject.
B.  Technology assistance is an appropriate practice that can be used occasionally in my subject area.
C.  Technology assistance is a practice that is well suited to my course content.

### Level of Training

A.  I have had *no training* in computer/telecommunications.
B.  I have had *some training* but not enough to implement.
C.  I have had *extensive training* in technology assistance and understand the use of computers well.

**Small Groups/Structured Pairs** *(Students are organized into small groups to discuss/review a concept/ learning objective or to complete a teacher-directed assignment.)*

*(Continued)*

*(Continued)*

### Level of Use

A.   I *do not use/do not have time to use* small groups/structured pairs in my classroom.
B.   I use small groups/structured pairs *very seldom* (e.g., once or twice during the course I teach).
C.   I use small groups/structured pairs *seldom* (e.g., once or twice during each grading period).
D.   I use small groups/structured pairs *often* (e.g., once a week).
E.   I use small groups/structured pairs *very often* (e.g., every day).

### Level of Preference

A.   I do not prefer small groups/structured pairs as a teaching practice for my subject.
B.   Small groups/structured pairs is an appropriate practice that can be used occasionally in my subject area.
C.   Small groups/structured pairs is a practice that is well suited to my course content.

### Level of Training

A.   I have had *no training* in small groups/structured pairs.
B.   I have had *some training* but not enough to implement.
C.   I have had *extensive training* in small groups/structured pairs and understand the practice well.

**Projects** *(When using projects, teachers have students work on a task for an extended time period, alone or in small groups, usually to produce a tangible product.)*

### Level of Use

A.   I *do not use/do not have time to use* student projects in my classroom.
B.   I use student projects *very seldom* (e.g., once or twice during the course I teach).
C.   I use student projects *seldom* (e.g., once or twice during each grading period).
D.   I use student projects *often* (e.g., once a week).
E.   I use student projects *very often* (e.g., every day).

### Level of Preference

A.   I do not prefer student projects as a teaching practice for my subject.
B.   Using projects is an appropriate practice that can be used occasionally in my subject area.
C.   Using projects is a practice that is well suited to my course content.

### Level of Training

A.   I have had *no training* in student projects.
B.   I have had *some training* but not enough to implement.
C.   I have had *extensive training* in student projects and understand the use of projects well.

### II.     Staff Development Experiences

Please indicate whether you have participated in staff development (at least 4 hours) within the last five years on the following topics and the extent to which the staff development was helpful to you in your classroom.

**Helpfulness Scale**

|  | Did Not Participate | Not Helpful | Helpful | Very Helpful |
|---|---|---|---|---|
| Pacing guides | no | A | B | C |
| Curriculum alignment/audit | no | A | B | C |
| Discipline-specific planning within departments | no | A | B | C |
| Alternative assessments/evaluation methods | no | A | B | C |
| How to make effective use of class time | no | A | B | C |
| Dimensions of learning | no | A | B | C |
| Models of teaching | no | A | B | C |
| How to make effective use of class time | no | A | B | C |

Do you have adequate access to technology (e.g., computers, CD ROMs, etc.), to use in support of instruction?

_____ yes           _____ no

**III.    Teaching Experience/Workload**

How many years have you been teaching?            _____

How many classes do you currently teach this semester?            _____

How many course preparations do you have this year?            _____

How are you involved in instructional decision making in your school?

| Serve on school improvement team | yes | no |
|---|---|---|
| Serve as a department chair | yes | no |
| Serve on an instructional planning committee | yes | no |
| Serve on an instructional technology committee | yes | no |
| Serve on an Accreditation or Program Review Committee | yes | no |

---

Note: Special thanks to Elaine Jenkins, who assisted in the design of the original instrument under my direct supervision. This is a modified and improved version.

# NINETEEN

# A Guide to Traditional and Authentic Assesment for Classroom Use

It is clear that measuring student achievement constitutes a substantial portion of the practitioner's charge. The author believes that block scheduling contributes substantially to student achievement, but measuring students' progress is necessary no matter the schedule. How else will the institution determine if its curricular presentation and instructional practices are producing results? Although one may choose from many forms of assessment, all have the common end of evaluating programs and instruction for students. Politicians, parents, practitioners, and students have a considerable interest in measuring student performance. Basic knowledge of the various phases and types of assessment present in today's educational world is essential in understanding the assessment process and the need for multiple approaches. As teachers hear more about differentiated instruction and teaching the individual student, it is important to know that block scheduling allows opportunities for an array of personalized instruction. Queen (2009) highlights seven basic levels of personalizing instruction that go beyond the scope of this book. Following is a guide to both traditional and authentic assessment. It may be used to create checklists, slides, or other useful tools for student assessment.

When it comes to student assessment there tends to be an overuse of one or two procedures. It is important for teachers to realize that regardless of the scheduling format, the major purpose of assessment is to check to see how the student is mastering the content. Block scheduling allows the teacher more time to do more hands-on assessment such as presentations, and projects that can be done in class—not just pencil-and-paper tests.

# STUDENT ASSESMENT

# PART ONE

## Writing and Evaluating Test Items

### OVERVIEW

- Parts of a Test Item
- Categorizing Items
- Evaluating Test Items

### *Parts of Test Items—Stems*

#### The Stem
- The part of the question that gives the situation and delineates the task to be addressed.

#### Two Types of Stems
- Open stem
  An incomplete sentence is provided and the answer choices must finish the sentence.
- Closed stem
  A complete question is provided.

## *Parts of Test Items—Stems*

### General Rules for Stems

- Keep the stem concise to minimize reading time
- Include only relevant information
- The stem should be as complete as possible
- Use present tense whenever possible
- Students should know exactly what the queston is asking of them

### AVOID

- Stereotyping any age or gender group
- Using "politically incorrect" terms
- Using negative stems such as except, not, least, etc.

### DO

- Use a nonsexist writing style; if it is impossible, write the stem clearly and concisely without using the pronouns "his," "her," etc.
- Have an equal number of males and females in the stems
- Resist the use of clever names that may distract students
- If names are used, restrict them to first names or surnames

## *Parts of Test Items—Options*

### Options

- All of the answer choices for a question

### Two Types of Options

- Key
  The correct option.
- Distracters
  The incorrect options.

## *Parts of Test Items—Options*

### General Rules for Options

- There should be one single best option that students *with the appropriate knowledge* will recognize
- Distracters should not be easily recognizable as choices
- Distracters should be plausible to students *without the necessary knowledge* required to answer the question correctly
- Options should be about the same length, level of complexity, and detail
- If all options can't be the same length, make two long options and two short options
- Word the distracters clearly and concisely
- Distribute the position of the key randomly
- If applicable, use a logical basis for ordering options

### AVOID

- Using disparaging remarks in options so that the options are obviously wrong
- Making the key part of a pair of similar or contrasting options
- Using the words "never," "ever," and "always" as an option
- Using the terms "all of the above" or "none of the above"
- Using "multiple multiples" as options
  *Example:* A & B, C & B
- Making a distracter wrong for a minor reason causing an answer error under the stress of testing

### DO

- Make sure the key does not include one of the distracters
  *Example:* the distracter is "mix the chemicals" and the key is "mix the chemicals and turn on the Bunsen burner"
- Make sure the distracters do not include the key within their range
  *Example:* the distracter is "more than 5" and the key is "more than 10"
- If you find that the options begin with the same words or phrases, put this in the stem
  *Example:* Every option begins with the words "add the . . ."
- If any words from the stem appear in the key, make sure they appear in the distracters as well

### *Categorizing Items on Cognitive Levels*

#### Knowledge

- Remembering or recognizing appropriate terminology, facts, ideas, materials, trends, sequences, methodology, principles, and generalizations

The capital of Turkmenistan is:
  A. Ulaanbaatar
  B. Bishkek
  C. Astana
  D. Ashbagat*

### *Categorizing Items on Cognitive Levels*

#### Comprehension

- Understanding written communications, reports, tables, diagrams, directions, regulations, maps, etc.

The exploration to Lake Tanganyika began at
  A. Dodoma
  B. Arusha*
  C. Ujiji
  D. Tabora

### *Categorizing Items on Cognitive Levels*

#### Application

- Applying ideas, rules of procedure, methods, formulas, principals, and theories in situations

  In a walkathon to raise money for charity, Laura walked a certain distance at 5 mph, then jogged twice that distance at 8 mph. Her total time walking and jogging was 2 hours and 15 minutes. How many miles long was the walkathon?
  - A. 10 miles
  - B. 12 miles
  - C. 15 miles*
  - D. 17 miles

  *Formula:* rate × time = distance

### *Categorizing Items on Cognitive Levels*

#### Analysis/Synthesis

- Breaking down or putting together material or information in relation to is constituent parts and detecting the relationship of the parts and the way they are organized

  What was a major reason many former colonies in Africa experienced internal strife after achieving independence?
  - A. Colonial borders had separated culturally similar people and enclosed traditional enemies.*
  - B. The new nations wanted to form governments which were radically different.
  - C. The new governments wanted to nationalize the many industrial complexes.
  - D. There were too many diverse languages in the former colonies for effective communication.

## *Evaluating Test Items*

### Reliability

- The consistency of test scores
  Would a student score about the same on the test if he/she were to take it today and again next month?

- Improve the individual items through the process of item analysis
  Item analysis includes the following:
  - ☐ A review of the item's difficulty level
  - ☐ Discrimination data
  - ☐ The effectiveness of the distracters

## *Evaluating Test Items*

### Difficulty Level

- The *p*-value (or difficulty level) refers to the percentage of students who answered the question *correctly*.
  Therefore, a *p*-value of 0.95 means that 95% of the students answered it correctly

- Items that are too easy or too difficult take away from the test's reliability—they *don't discriminate* between those who know the material from those who do not

## *Evaluating Test Items*

### Determining Difficulty Level

- To determine the difficulty level, use the following formula:

$$\frac{\text{\# of students answering correctly}}{\text{total \# of students}}$$

- Look at any questions that have
  *p*-value of 0.30 or less
    *Check to make sure the key is correct first!
  *p*-value of 0.90 or more
    *Criterion-referenced questions should be above 0.90.

### *Evaluating Test Items*

#### Discrimination Index

Item discrimination indicates how well the item discriminates between the high-scoring and low-scoring students.

- Index of 0.00 means the item didn't discriminate at all between groups.
- Index of 0.20 to 0.29 indicates a reasonably good item.
- Index of 0.30 or higher is great!
- Negative discrimination occurs when the low group scores better on the item than the high group.

### *Evaluating Test Items*

#### Determining Discrimination Index

To determine the discrimination index, use the following formula:

$$\begin{array}{c}\text{\% of students high group*} \\ \text{answering correctly}\end{array} - \begin{array}{c}\text{\% students low group*} \\ \text{answering correctly}\end{array} = \begin{array}{c}\text{discrimination} \\ \text{index}\end{array}$$

*Use the top 27% and the bottom 27% of the scores on the test

*Example*:
10 of 14 high students got the item correct = 0.71
7 of 14 low students got the item correct = 0.50
0.71 – 0.50 = a discrimination index of 0.21

## *Evaluating Test Items*

### Effectiveness of Distracters

- Look at the distribution of answers among the distracters given in the item
- If a distracter has not been chosesn, it may not be effective and needs to be changed to something more plausible
- If student numbers taking the test are low, you may want to wait for another testing with the item to see if the distracter is chosen with the second group
  Remember to keep the first data!


## *Evaluating Test Items*

### Analyzing Item Data

- Review the Difficulty Index
  Look at items that have either very low or very high *p*-values
- Review the Discrimination Index
  Look at items that have low or negative values of discrimination
- Review the Effectiveness of Distracters
  Look at distracters that were not chosen by students
- Review the "history" of the item's data
  Data may change with teaching techniques, the "student grapevine," etc.

*Example*:

For a community project, an advanced biology student chose to teach groups about the prevention of various urinary and kidney diseases. When preparing material about the prevention of acute glomerulonephritis, the student will stress prevention through the proper treatment of
  A. Influenza
  B. High cholesterol
  C. Strep throat*
  D. Gonorrhea

### Item Data
  Data came from 2 testing times that were 1 year apart
  **Total # of students: 135**
  Difficulty index: 0.77 and 0.68
  Discrimination index: 0.33 and 0.36
  Effectiveness of distracters: All distracters chosen

# STUDENT ASSESMENT

## PART TWO

### Using Authentic Assesment for Student Evaluation

**The trouble with tests is . . .**
- "I'm just not good at taking tests."
- "You asked all the wrong questions."
- "I know a lot more than the test tells you."
- "Let me prove to you that I have learned."
- "Tests are dumb."

**What is authentic assesment?**
- Movement from paper and pencils tests
- Includes genuine, useful, and applicable, practice-based, transferable, and demonstrable items
- Includes skills, knowledge, and attitudes that can be carried beyond the classrom
- Goes beyond true/false examination

(For more information, see Merrell, 1998)

**Why do students need authentic assessment?**
- It helps to develop better brains!
  1967—Brain pioneer Marian Diamond of UCLA discovered that the brain can literally grow new connections with environmental stimulation:

  "When we enriched the environment, we got brains with a thicker cortex, more dendritic branching, more growth spines, and larger cell bodies."

  This indicates the brain cells communicate better with each other and have more support cells.
- This research suggests that the environment impacts the wiring of the brain as much as the person's actual experiences.

(For more information, see Jensen, 1998)

## *How to Maximize Brain Growth*

William Greenough, an expert on brain enrichment, emphasizes that two things are vital components of growing a better brain:

### Challenge

- Learning should include opportunities for problem solving and critical thinking.
- Provide new information and/or experiences in projects that are relevant to the students
- If there is too much or too little information or experience, students will get bored or give up.
- Vary times, materials, lessons, pedagogy.

### Feedback

- Feedback reduces uncertainty and increases coping abilities.
- Brain self-references: It decides what to do based on what has just been done.
- Feedback is most useful when it is immediate and specific, when it is learner controlled and when it is presented in several ways.

(For more information, see Jensen, 1998)

### Brain Enrichment

- Challenging problem solving: Problem solving not limited to one part of the brain.

  Can solve a problem on paper, with an analogy or metaphor, with a model, by discussion, with statistics, through artwork, or during a demonstration.

- Critical to expose students to a variety of approaches to solving a problem.

### Enrichment and Attention

- Students must be primed: They will learn better if they are told to look for new information or prompted to its location.

- Learning must be relevant, engaging, and chosen by the learner.

### Direct Instruction Learning Times

- Grades K–2: 5–7 minutes
- Grades 3–7: 8–12 minutes
- Grades 8–12: 12–15 minutes

After learning, the brain needs time for processing and rest; teachers must rotate activites.

(For more information, see Gardner, 1993; Jensen, 1998)

## How Do We Enrich Student Learning?

## Authentic Assesment

### Effective Implementation of Authentic Assesment (Rural School and Community Trust, 2001)

- Articulate the goals of instruction clearly.
  1. What should students know, understand, and be able to do? What important cognitive skills do you want students to develop?
     - ☐ Communicate effectively orally and in writing
     - ☐ Analyze issues using primary source and reference materials
     - ☐ Use the scientific method

  2. What social and affective skills do you want students to develop?
     - ☐ Work independently and also cooperatively with others
     - ☐ Be persistent in the face of the challenges
     - ☐ Have confidence in their abilities

  3. What metacognitive skills do I want my students to develop?
     - ☐ Discuss and evaluate their problem-solving strategies
     - ☐ Formulate efficient plans for completing independent projects
     - ☐ Reflect on the writing process they use, evaluate its effectiveness, and derive their own plans for how it can be improved

  4. What types of problems do you want them to solve?
     - ☐ Know how to do research
     - ☐ Predict consequences
     - ☐ Make healthy choices

  5. What concepts and principles do I want them to be able to apply?
     - ☐ Understand cause-and-effect relationships in history and everyday life
     - ☐ Criticize literary works based on plot, setting, motive, etc.
     - ☐ Understand and recognize the consequences of substance abuse

### Effective Implementation of Authentic Assesment

- Determine valid and appropriate evidence for meeting instructional goals.
  1. How will we know when students understand what we most want them to understand?
     *Standards for Student Work in Mathematics* (Newmann, Lopez, & Bryk, 1998)
     - ☐ Mathematical analysis: Students demonstrate thinking by going beyond simple recording and reproducing of algorithms.
     - ☐ Mathematical concepts: Students demonstrate understanding by representing concepts in different contexts or real-world application.
     - ☐ Written mathematical communication: Students demonstrate elaboration of their understanding in the form of diagrams or symbolic representations.
     - ☐ Habits of study and work: Students demonstrate skills by using time wisely, completing work on time, and showing initiative.

- Ensure that assessment tasks are complex, realistic, and generate multiple sources of data.
  1. Does the task require students to display their knowledge on multiple dimensions?
  2. Are the genres, contexts, and content typical of real-world work in this area?
  3. Does the task produce evidence that can be evaluated upon completion?

**Effective Implementation of Authentic Assesment**

- Construct clear, well-understood rubrics for assessing student products.

  What differentiates levels of student performance—from excellent to insufficient—on the various components required by the task?

Three types of rubrics

| Particular Trait Rubrics | Analytic Rubrics | Holistic Rubrics |
|---|---|---|
| Single out one or two criteria to evaluate in a complex performance and ignore other elements for purposes of assessment. | Track all the criteria or standards demonstrated by students in a performance and allow for individual ratings of each one. | Merge all the criteria into a comprehensive description of the performance. |
| They provide especially targeted information. | They require more than one score for each piece of student work, providing more detailed information about a student's performance. | The benefit is to assess the student's overall performance on a particular task; they also allow for comparing work over time. |

### Effective Implementation of Authentic Assesment

- Involve students in developing rubrics and evaluating their own work.

*Self-Evaluation Checklist for Expository Essay*

Initial each statement that you feel describes your work. Explain anything you cannot initial, giving reasons. Attach this to your paper.

_____ My paper has a definite purpose: it works.

_____ My title indicates my point or slant.

_____ I had a specific audience in mind as I wrote and revised.

_____ The details and word choices paint the right picture and give the right feel.

_____ I can explain why I placed every puncuation mark as I did.

_____ Each paragraph contains a clear idea and topic sentence.

_____ I checked each sentence to make sure it was complete.

_____ The transitions are smooth.

_____ The ending is effective in wrapping things up.

(For more information, see Perrone, 1992)

### Multiple Intelligence and Authentic Assessment

- Multiple intelligences and authentic assesment are natural partners.

- Several optional assessment formats may be implemented based on a student's dominant intelligence.

- Optional assessments blend cohesively with the many types of authentic assessment.

## Multiple Intelligences

### Verbal/Linguistic

- Debates
- Portfolios
- Quotation reactions
- Rough drafts/final drafts
- Vocabulary
- Word associations

### Logical/Mathematical

- Experiment logs
- Logic exercises
- Pattern games
- Rubrics
- "What if" exercises

### Visual/Spatial

- Flow charts/graphs
- Hands-on demonstration
- Photo albums
- Scrapbooks
- Murals/montages

### Body/Kinesthetic

- Case studies
- Charades/mimes
- Dramatizations
- Skill demonstration
- Physical exercize routines

### Musical/Rhythmic

- Checklists
- Creating raps/songs
- Musical performances
- Orchestrating music
- Dances

## Multiple Intelligences and Authentic Assessment

### Interpersonal

- Buzz sections
- Group jigsaw puzzles
- Project posters
- Scavenger hunts
- Think/pair/share

### Intrapersonal

- Autobiographical stories
- Feelings diaries/logs
- Individual conferences
- Reflections
- Self-study reports

### Naturalist

- Recognizes flora and fauna
- Makes consequential distinctions in the natural world
- Includes farmers, botanists, conservationists, biologists, environmentalists

### *Types of Authentic Assessment*

#### Graphic Organizers

- The mind spontaneously organizes information as it is learned
- Graphic organizers help to visually organize new information
- Represent similarities and differences
- Detect patterns and relationships
- Relate new information to previous learning
- Link interdisciplinary topics
- Display information, ideas, and concepts
- Types of graphic organizers
  Webbing
  Cause/Effect
  Story Map
  Venn Diagram
  Double Bubble

  (For more information, see Tombari & Borich, 1999)

### *Types of Authentic Assessment*

#### Self-Assessment

- Self-assessment allows students the opportunity to evaluate their performance or product.
- Evaluation leads to self-correction and improvement.
- Self-assessment provides student ownership and analysis of products.

#### Methods

- Video Reflection
- Student-Led Conferences
- Journals

## *Types of Authentic Assessment— Self-Assessment*

### Video Reflection

- Use of videotape to assess and improve performance in areas of chorus, band, physical education, or the arts
- Teacher or proficient student models the desired production
- Use rubric for presentation

Implementation of Video Reflection

*Application*: High school chorus
*Objective*: Students will sing a ballad in stratified vocal sections. Teacher will model a ballad demonstrating the criteria needed for the production

- ☐ Video is made of students singing in groups of mixed vocal sections
- ☐ Students use teacher-generated rubric to assess strengths and weaknesses upon review of the video

## *Types of Authentic Assessment— Self-Assessment*

### Student-Led Conferences

- Conference with parents led by students
- Teacher = Facilitator
- Several conferences conducted at once in classroom (teacher circulating in room)
- Discussion centered around student *portfolio* of work
- Collection of student work
- Shows academic progress over time

(For more information, see Bailey & Guskey, 2001)

## Types of Authentic Assessment— Self-Assessment

### Implementation of Conferences

| BEFORE | DURING | AFTER |
|---|---|---|
| Set learning objectives and work with students to create portfolio of work. | Circulate around to each family group and make individual student comments. | Schedule extra time with parents if follow-up needed. |
| Build in reflection/ edit time and role-play conferences with students | Facilitate when needed. | Read and process evaluations from parents and students. |
| Prepare a family-friendly environment. | Express gratitude for parental involvement. | Debrief process with students. |

## *Types of Authentic Assessment—*
## *Self-Assessment*

### Journals

- Use of non-structured writing to evaluate short stories and novels

- Permits personal reflection/writing

- Allows for synthesis of ideas and evaluations rather than rigid mechanical corrections

- Can be used as dialogue between student and teacher

Implementation of Journals

*Application*: Middle school Language Arts

*Objective*: Students will reflect in their journals using the following questions from Chapter 14 and 15 of *A Day No Pigs Would Die*:

1. If faced with the same dilemma as Rob, would you have had the courage to act as he did?
2. Do you think the ordeal with Pinky made Rob a stronger young man? How?
3. What do you perceive as Rob's new challenges as man of the house at 15?

### *Types of Self-Assessment*

#### Rubrics

- A guide for evaluating student work
- Use specific criteria to assess project mastery
- Allow for a variety of student skills to be assessed
- Hold learners to high levels of achievement
- Minimize scoring subjectivity and bias
- Can be generated by both teacher and student

#### Types of Rubrics

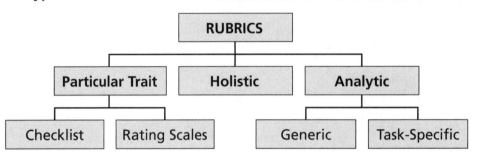

## *Types of Self-Assessment—Rubrics*

### Particular Trait Rubrics

Checklist:

- Discrete, observable behaviors
- Observer only watches to see if behavior occurred or not
- Extemely efficient
- Require simple judgments
- Used as diagnostic tools

Rating Scales:

- Assessing complex products
- Assigns numbers to certain levels or degrees of performance
- Continuum that indicates the frequency or quality of the behavior
- Requires more time than checklists

(For more information, see Tombari & Borich, 1999)

## *Types of Self-Assessment—Rubrics*

### Holisitic Rubrics

- Observer estimates the overall quality of the product, demonstration, or exhibit
- Assigns numerical value to that overall quality
- Gives an index of performance
- Requires only one judgment
- Cannot serve as diagnostic rubric since specific strengths and weaknesses are not noted

### *Types of Self-Assessment—Rubrics*

#### Analytic Rubrics

Generic:

- May be broadly applied to several assignments in varying disciplines
- Useful because of time saved and broad use possible

Task-Specific:

- Allows for analysis of specific learning outcomes
- Relevant to one content topic
- Can provide a framework for concepts to be learned and then assessed

### *Types of Self-Assessment—Rubrics*

#### Developing Analytic Rubrics

- Measure your goals

  Learning outcomes should match rating assesment

  - Will you expect evidence of knowledge acquisition?
    - ☐ Design a rating scale that reflects this
  - Do you wish to assess problem-solving strategies?
    - ☐ Rating scales should assess their use
  - Will you be observing the processes learners show as they complete the task?
    - ☐ A checklist may need to be constructed

(For more information, see Tombari & Borich, 1999)

## *Types of Self-Assessment—Rubrics*

### Developing Analytic Rubrics

- Select an appropriate scoring system
  - Particular trait rubrics
    - ☐ Checklists
    - ☐ Rating scales
  - Holistic rubrics
  - Analytic rubrics
    - ☐ Generic
    - ☐ Task-specific

(For more information, see Tombari & Borich, 1999)

## *Types of Self-Assessment—Rubrics*

### Developing Analytic Rubrics

- Indentify the criteria to be evaluated
  - Type of criteria (varies per type of rubric)
    - ☐ Conceptual understanding
    - ☐ Systematic approach to task?
    - ☐ Is the answer correct?
    - ☐ Is the work presented neatly?
  - A successful approach
    - ☐ Consider the task and imagine an excellent student's response to it!
  - Select the number and detail of criteria
    - ☐ All important aspects of performance should be found in the criteria
    - ☐ Each criteria should be specific, but not too detailed
  - Use subcriteria or elements when necessary and relevant

(For more information, see Danielson & Abrutyn, 1997)

### *Types of Self-Assessment—Rubrics*

#### Developing Analytic Rubrics

- Decide on the number of points for the rubric
  - Detail in distinctions
    - ☐ Larger numbers of points can provide specific feedback, but can be cumbersome
    - ☐ Limit rubrics to 4–6 points
  - Divide the line between acceptable and unacceptable performance
  - Provide general headings for different points

### *Types of Self-Assessment—Rubrics*

#### Developing Analytic Rubrics

- Writing the descriptions of performance levels should include:
  - The language used
    - ☐ Serve to further define the criteria
    - ☐ Use positive rather than negative wording
  - All subcriteria or elements defined
  - Distance between points
    - ☐ Distance between points on a scale should be equal

(For more information, see Danielson & Abrutyn, 1997)

### *Types of Authentic Assessment*

#### Portfolios

- What is a portfolio? A collection of student work over a period of time
- Provides a rich array of what students know and can do
- Provides for individual or group accountability
- Can single-subject or interdisciplinary

  (For more information, see Tombari & Borich, 1999)

### *Types of Authentic Assessment—Portfolios*

#### Benefits of Portfolio Use

- Show a learner's ability to think and problem solve
- Tell about a learner's persistence and effort
- Show a learner's skill in self-monitoring and ability to be self-reflective
- Can alter the nature of classroom instruction
- Means to communicate academic achievement to parents and other teachers
- Supplement regualr report card grades

  (For more information, see Tombari & Borich, 1999)

### *Types of Authentic Assessment—Portfolios*

#### What Makes a Portfolio a Portfolio?

- Developing a portfolio offers the student an opportunity to learn about learning.
- The portfolio is something that is done *by* the student, not *to* the student.
- The portfolio is separate and different from the student's cumulative folder.
- The portfolio must convey explicitly or implicitly the student's activities.
- The portfolio may serve a different purpose during the year from the purpose it serves at the end.
- A portfolio may have multiple purposes, but these may not conflict.
- The portfolio should contain information that illustrates growth.
- Finally, many of the skills and techniques that are involved in producing effective portfolios do not happen by themselves.

### *Types of Authentic Assessment—Portfolios*

#### Building a System for Portfolio Assessment

#### Step 1: Decide on the purpose

- Monitoring student progress
- Communicating what has been learned to parents
- Evaluating how well something was taught
- Showing off what has been accomplished
- Assigning a course grade

(For more information, see Tombari & Borich, 1999)

### *Types of Authentic Assessment—Portfolios*

#### Building a System for Portfolio Assessment

#### Step 2: Identify Cognitive Skills and Dispositions

- Knowledge organization
- Cognitive strategies
  - ☐ Analysis, interpretation, organizational revising
- Procedural skills
  - ☐ Editing, drawing, speaking
- Metacognition
  - ☐ Self-monitoring, self-reflection

### *Types of Authentic Assessment—Portfolios*

#### Building a System for Portfolio Assessment

#### Step 3: Decide who will plan the portfolio

- Teacher
- Parent
- Students
- Ideal situation involves planning from all three!

### *Types of Authentic Assessment—Portfolios*

#### Building a System for Portfolio Assessment

#### Step 4: Choose the products and number of samples

- Ownership
  - ☐ Involve parents and students in learning
- Portfolio's link with instruction
  - ☐ Connect portfolios and learning outcomes

### *Types of Authentic Assessment—Portfolios*

**Building a System for Portfolio Assessment**

**Step 5: Determine the scoring rubrics**

- Type of rubric: checklist, rating scale, holistic, analytic
- Rubric for each entry in the portfolio
- Scoring criteria for the portfolio as a whole product

### *Types of Authentic Assessment—Portfolios*

**Building a System for Portfolio Assessment**

**Step 6: Aggregate all portfolio ratings**

- Learners should receive a score for each draft and final product in the portfolio
- Decide how to aggregate scores
- Develop a procedure for combining all scores

### *Types of Authentic Assessment—Portfolios*

**Building a System for Portfolio Assessment**

**Step 7: Determine the logistics**

- What are the timelines?
- How are the products turned in and returned?
- Where are final products kept?
- Who has access to the portfolio?

### *Types of Authentic Assessment—Portfolios*

**Building a System for Portfolio Assessment**

**Step 8: Plan a final conference**

- Plan to meet with individual students
- Include parents if at all possible
- Discuss the learner's development and academic achievements

# References

Adams, D. C., & Salvaterra, M. E. (1997). Structural and teacher changes: Necessities for successful block schedule. *High School Journal, 81*(2), 98–105.

Adey, P., & Shayer, M. (1990). Accelerating the development of formal thinking in middle and high school students. *Journal of Research in Science Teaching, 27*(3), 267–285.

Adler, M. J. (1982). *The Paideia proposal: An educational manifesto.* New York: Macmillan.

Arnold, D. E. (2002). Block schedule and traditional schedule achievement: A comparison. *NASSP Bulletin, 86*(630), 42–53.

America 2000: An education strategy. (1991, December). *Congressional Digest, 70*(12), 294–296.

Asayesh, G. (1993). Ten years after *A Nation at Risk. The School Administrator, 50*(4), 8–14.

Babcock, B. (2000). *Learning from experience: A collection of service-learning projects linking academic standards to curriculum.* Madison: Wisconsin Department of Public Instruction. (ERIC Document Reproduction Services No.ED444920)

Bailey, J. M., & Guskey, T. R. (2001). *Implementing student-led conferences.* Thousand Oaks, CA: Corwin Press.

Barr, B. (1994). Research on problem solving. *Elementary School Journal, 5 (3),* 237–247.

Becker, W., & Englemann, S. (1971). *Teaching: A course in applied psychology.* Chicago: Science Research Associates.

Beckman, D., King, B., & Ryan, S. (1995). Block scheduling: A means to improve school climate. *NASSP Bulletin, 79*(571), 1–65.

Bell, T. H. (1993). Reflections one decade after *A Nation at Risk. Phi Delta Kappan, 74*(8), 592–597.

Bennett, W. (1988). *American education: Making it work.* Washington, DC: U.S. Department of Education.

Beyer, B. (1988). *Developing a thinking skills program.* Boston: Allyn & Bacon.

Blake, R. (1984). *Discovery versus expository instructional strategies and their implications for instruction of hearing-impaired post-secondary students.* New York: Author. (ERIC Document Reproduction Service No. ED248651)

Bloom, B. S. (Ed.). (1956). *Taxonomy of educational objectives: The classification of educational goals: Handbook I, cognitive domain.* New York: Longmans, Green.

Bohince, J. (1996). Blockbuster ideas: Activities for breaking up block periods. *Science Teacher, 63*(6), 20–24.

Boocock, S. S., & Schild, E. O. (1968). *Simulation games in learning.* Beverly Hills, CA: Sage.

Boyer, E. (1983). *High school: A report on secondary education in America.* New York: Harper & Row.

Boyer, M. R. (1993). Avoid the isolated road. *School Administrator, 50*(3), 20–21.

Brophy, J. (1996). Working with shy or withdrawn students. *ERIC Digest* (ERIC Identifier ED402070).

Brookhart, S., Moss, C., & Long, B. (2008, November). Formal assessment that empowers. *Educational Leadership 66*(3).

Bruner, J. S. (1966). *Toward a theory of instruction.* Cambridge, MA: Belknap Press of Harvard University.

Burke, D. L. (1997). Looping: Adding time, strengthening relationships. *ERIC Digest* (ERIC Identifier ED414098).

Butts, D., & Jones, H. (1966). Inquiry training and problem solving in elementary school children. *Journal of Research in Science Teaching, 4*(1), 12–24.

Canady, R. L., & Hopkins, H. J. (1997). Integrating the curriculum with parallel block scheduling. *Principal, 76*(4), 28–31.

Canady, R. L., & Rettig, M. D. (1995a). *Block scheduling: A catalyst for change in high schools.* Princeton, NJ: Eye on Education.

Canady, R. L., & Rettig, M. D. (1995b). The power of innovative scheduling. *Educational Leadership, 53*(3), 4–10.

Canady, R. L., & Rettig, M. D. (1996). Block scheduling: What is it? Why do it? How do we harness its potential to improve teaching and learning? In R. L. Canady & M. D. Rettig (Eds.), *Teaching on the block* (pp. 1–27). Larchmont, NY: Eye on Education.

Canady, R. L. & Rettig, M. D. (1997). *Teaching in the block: Strategies for engaging active learners.* Princeton, NJ: Eye on Education.

Carnegie Council on Adolescent Development. (1989). *Turning points: Preparing American youth for the 21st century.* New York: Carnegie Corporation.

Carnegie Task Force on Teaching as a Profession. (1986). *A nation prepared: Teachers for the 21st century.* New York: Author.

Carroll, J. M. (1990). The Copernican plan: Restructuring the American high school. *Phi Delta Kappan, 71,* 358–365.

Carroll, J. M. (1994). Organizing time to support learning. *School Administrator, 51*(3), 26–28, 30–33.

Cawelti, G. (1994). *High school restructuring: A national study.* Arlington, VA: Educational Research Service.

Chesler, M. A., & Fox, R. S. (1966). *Role-playing methods in the classroom.* Chicago: Science Research Associates.

Clark, C., & Peterson, P. (1986). Teachers' thought processes. In M. Wittrock (Ed.), *Handbook of research on teaching* (pp. 225–296). New York: Macmillan.

Coalition of Essential Schools. (1999). The cycle of inquiry and action: Essential learning communities [Special issue]. *HORACE, 15*(4).

Collins, K. (1969). The importance of a strong confrontation in an inquiry model of teaching. *School Science and Mathematics, 69*(7), 615–617.

Congressional Digest. (2008). No Child Left Behind revisited. *Congressional Digest, 87*(5), 129.

Cookson, P. W., Jr. (1995). Goals 2000: Framework for the new educational federalism. *Teachers College Record, 96*(3), 405.

Corley, E. (1997, October). *Teacher perceptions regarding block scheduling: Reactions to change.* Paper presented at the annual meeting of the Mid-Western Educational Research Association, Chicago.

Costa, A. (1985). *Developing minds: A resource book for teaching thinking.* Alexandria, VA: Association for Supervision and Curriculum Development.

Couch, R. (1993). Synectics and imagery: Developing creative thinking through images. In R. Braden, J. Clark Baca, & D. Beauchamp (Eds.), *Art, science, and visual literacy: Selected readings from the Annual Conference of the International Visual Literacy.* Blacksburg, VA: International Visual Literacy Association. (ERIC Document Reproduction Service No. ED363330)

Crosby, E. A. (1993). The at-risk decade. *Phi Delta Kappan, 74*(8), 598–604.

Dallman-Jones, A. (1994). *The expert educator.* Fond du Lac, WI: Three Blue Herons.

Danielson, C., & Abrutyn, L. (1997). *An introduction to using portfolios in the classroom.* Alexandria, VA: Association for Supervision and Curriculum Development.

Davidson, N. (1971). *The small group-discovery method of mathematics instruction as applied in calculus.* Madison: Wisconsin Research and Development Center for Cognitive Learning. (ERIC Document Reproduction Service No. ED162879)

Davis-Wiley, P., George, M., & Cozart, A. (1995, November). *Block scheduling in the secondary arena: Perceptions from inside.* Paper presented at the annual meeting of the Mid-South Educational Research Association, Biloxi.

Day, M. M., Ivanov, P., & Binkley, S. (1996). Tackling block scheduling: How to make the most of longer classes. *The Science Teacher, 63*(6), 25–27.

Dewey, J. (1910). *How we think.* Boston: Heath.

Dewey, J. (1938). *Experience and education.* New York: Macmillan.

Dexter, K. M., Tai, R. H., & Sadler, P. M. (2006). Traditional and block scheduling science preparation: A comparison of college science success for students who report different high school scheduling plans. *The High School Journal, 89,* 22–32.

DiBiase, W. J., & Queen, J. A. (1999). Middle school social studies on the block. *The Clearing House, 72*(6), 377–383.

Downs, R. B. (1975). *Heinrich Pestalozzi, father of modern pedagogy.* Boston: Twayne.

Doyle, D. P. (1991). America 2000. *Phi Delta Kappan, 73*(3), 184–192.

Dragositz, A. (1969). *Curriculum innovations and evaluation: Proceedings of the association for supervision and curriculum development pre-conference seminar.* Princeton, NJ: Princeton University Press.

Drew, N. (1987). *Learning the skills of peacemaking: An activity guide for elementary-age children on communicating, cooperating, resolving conflict.* Torrence, CA: Jalmar.

Duel, L. S. (1999). Block scheduling in large, urban high schools: Effects on academic achievement, student behavior, and staff perceptions. *The High School Journal, 83,* 14–25.

Dukes, D. D. (1978). *A study comparing measures of auditory discrimination to other measures relative to reading achievement.* Unpublished master's thesis, East Tennessee State University, Johnson City.

Dukes, R. L., & Seidner, C. J. (1978). *Learning with simulations and games.* Beverly Hills, CA: Sage.

Edwards, C. H., & Allred, W. E. (1993). More on A Nation at Risk: Have the recommendations been implemented? *The Clearing House, 67*(2), 42–48.

Edwards, C. M. (1995). Virginia's 4 × 4 high schools: High school, college, and more. *NASSP Bulletin, 79*(571), 23–41.

Edwards, C. M. (1995). The 4 × 4 plan. *Educational Leadership, 53*(3), 16–19.

Eggen, P. D., & Kauchak, D. P. (2001). *Strategies for teachers* (4th ed.). Boston: Allyn & Bacon.

Eisner, E. (1979). *The educational imagination: On the design and evaluation of school programs.* New York: Macmillan.

Elam, S. M., Lowell, C. R., & Gallup, A. M. (1992). The 24th annual Gallup/ Phi Delta Kappa poll of the public's attitudes toward the public schools. *Phi Delta Kappan, 74*(1), 41–53.

Elefant, E. (1980). Deaf children in an inquiry training program. *Volta Review, 82*(5), 271–279.

Engel, B. S. (1994). Portfolio assessment and the new paradigm: New instruments and new places. *Educational Forum, 59*(1), 22–27.

Ennis, R. H. (1993, Summer). Critical thinking assessment. *Theory Into Practice, 11,* 179–186.

Erikson, E. (1980). *Identity and the life cycle.* New York: Norton.

Evans, W., Tokarczyk, J., Rice, S., & McCray, A. (2000). Block scheduling: An evaluation of outcomes and impact. *The Clearing House, 75,* 319–323.

Farmer, R. F., Gould, M. W., Herring, R. L., Linn, F. J., & Theobold, M. A. (1995). *The middle school principal.* The Practicing Administrator's Leadership Series. Thousand Oaks, CA: Corwin Press.

Fields, E. (1977, January). *How to evaluate proposed curriculum changes.* Paper presented at the annual meeting of the National School Boards Association, Houston, TX.

Forsten, C., Grant, J., & Richardson, I. (2000). Multiage and looping: Borrowing from the past. *Principal, 78*(4), 15–16, 18.

Frasier, C. H. (1997, January). The development of an authentic assessment instrument: The scored discussion. *English Journal,* pp. 37–40.

Furness, P. (1976). *Role play in the elementary school: A handbook for teachers.* New York: Hart.

Gabel, D. L. (Ed.). (1994). *Handbook of research on science teaching and learning.* New York: Macmillan.

Gable, R. A., & Manning, M. L. (1997). In the midst of reform: The changing structure and practice of middle school education. *Clearing House, 7*(1), 58–62.

Gardner, H. (1993). *Multiple intelligences: The theory in practice.* New York: Basic Books.

George, P. S., & Alexander, W. M. (1993). *The exemplary middle school* (2nd ed.). Fort Worth, TX: Harcourt Brace.

Gerking, J. L. (1995). Building on block schedules. *The Science Teacher, 62,* 23–27.

Gesell, A. L. (1971). *The first five years of life: A guide to the study of the preschool child.* London: Yale University Clinic of Child Development.

Gillies, R. M., & Ashman, A. F. (2000). The effects of cooperative learning on students with learning difficulties in the lower elementary school. *Journal of Special Education, 34*(1), 19–27.

Glickman, C. D., Gordon, S. P., & Ross-Gordon, J. M. (2001). *Supervision and instructional leadership: A developmental approach* (5th ed.). Needham Heights, MA: Allyn & Bacon.

Glynn, S. M. (1994). *Teaching science with analogies.* Athens: University of Georgia, National Reading Research Center.

Goals 2000: Educate America Act (1994), P.L. No. 103–227.

Goldberg, M. & Renton, A. M. (1993). Heeding the call to arms in *A Nation at Risk. The School Administrator, 50*(4).

Goodlad, J. I. (1984). *A place called school: Prospects for the future.* New York: McGraw-Hill.

Goodlad, J. I. (1990). *Teachers for our nation's schools.* San Francisco: Jossey-Bass.

Gordon, W. J. (1961). *Synectics.* New York: Harper & Row.

Green, J. A. (1969). *The educational ideas of Pestalozzi.* New York: Greenwood Press.

Guetzkow, H. (1995). Recollections about the inter-nation simulation (INS) and some derivatives of global modeling. *Simulation & Gaming, 26,* 453–470.

Guidelines for appropriate curriculum content and assessment in programs serving children ages 3 through 8: A position statement of the National Association for the Education of Young Children and the National Association of Early Childhood Specialists in State Departments of Education. (1991). *Young Children, 46,* 21–38.

Gullo, D. (1992). *Developmentally appropriate teaching in early childhood: Curriculum, implementation, and evaluation.* Washington, DC: NEA Early Childhood Series.

Gunter, M. A., Estes, T. M., & Schwab, J. (1990). *Instruction: A models approach.* Boston: Allyn & Bacon.

Guskey, T. R., & Bailey, J. M. (2001). *Developing grading and reporting systems for student learning.* Thousand Oaks, CA: Corwin Press.

Gutek, G. L. (1986). *Education in the United States: An historical perspective.* Englewood Cliffs, NJ: Prentice-Hall.

Hackmann, D. G. (1995). Ten guidelines for implementing block scheduling. *Educational Leadership, 53*(3), 24–27.

Hansler, D. D. (1985). *Studies on the effectiveness of the cognition enhancement technique for teaching thinking skills* (Report No. CS-008-331). East Lansing, MI: National Center for Research on Teacher Learning. (ERIC Document Reproduction Service No. ED266432)

Hart, W. H. (2000). *A comparison of the use of instructional time in block scheduled and traditionally scheduled high school classrooms.* Doctoral dissertation, University of North Carolina at Charlotte.

Heitzman, A. J. (1983). Discipline and the use of punishment. *Education, 104,* 17–22.

Henderson, J. G., & Hawthorne, R. D. (2000). *Transformative curriculum leadership* (2nd ed.). Upper Saddle River, NJ: Prentice Hall.

Hermann, G. (1969). Learning by discovery: A critical review of studies. *Journal of Experimental Education, 38,* 59–71.

Hertz-Lazarowitz, R. (1990, April). *An integrative model of the classroom: The enhancement of cooperation in learning.* Paper presented at the annual meeting of the American Educational Research Association, Boston.

Hickman, D. G. (1995). Ten guidelines for implementing block scheduling. *Educational Leadership, 53*(3), 24–27.

Hodgkinson, H. (1993). American education: The good, the bad, and the task. *Phi Delta Kappan, 74*(8), 619–623.

The Homes Group. (1990). *Tomorrow's schools: Principles for the design of professional development schools.* East Lansing, MI: Author.

Hottenstein, D. S. (1998). *Intensive scheduling: Restructuring America's secondary schools through time management.* Thousand Oaks, CA: Corwin Press.

Huff, L. (1995, May). Flexible block scheduling: It works for us. *NASSP Bulletin, 79,* 19–22.

Huggins, P., Manion, D. W., & Shakarian, L. (1998). *Helping kids handle put-downs: Teaching assertion, use of humor and self-encouragement.* Longmont, CO: Sopris West.

Hunter, M. C. (1982). *Mastery teaching.* El Segundo, CA: TIP.

Hurley, J. C. (1997a). The 4 × 4 block scheduling model: What do teachers have to say about it? *NASSP Bulletin, 81*(593), 53–63.

Hurley, J. C. (1997b). The 4 × 4 block scheduling model: What do students have to say about it? *NASSP Bulletin, 81*(593), 64–72.

Institute for Educational Leadership. (2000). *Leadership for student learning: Reinventing the principalship.* Washington, DC: Author.

Ivany, G. (1969). The assessment of verbal inquiry in junior high school science. *Science Education, 53*(4), 287–293.

Jarrett, D. (1997). *Inquiry strategies for science and mathematics learning.* Portland, OR: Northwest Regional Educational Laboratory.

Jasparro, R. (1998, May). Applying systems thinking to curriculum evaluation. *NASSP Bulletin, 82,* 80–84.

Jenkins, E., Queen, A., & Algozzine, B. (2002). To block or not to block: That's not the question. *Journal of Educational Research, 95,* 196–202.

Jennings, J. F. (1995). School reform based on what is taught and learned. *Phi Delta Kappan, 76*(10), 765–769.

Jensen, J. (1998). *Improving student achievement: Schools as a learning organization, a collection of articles.* Portland, OR: Portland Public Schools.

Johnson, D. W., & Johnson, R. T. (1992). Implementing cooperative learning. *Contemporary Education, 63*(3), 173–180.

Johnson, D. W., & Johnson, R. T. (1994). *Learning together and alone: Cooperative, competitive, and individualistic learning.* Boston: Allyn & Bacon.

Johnson, D. W., Johnson, R. T., & Holubec, E. J. (1993). *Circles of learning: Cooperation in the classroom* (4th ed.). Edina, MN: Interaction Book.

Johnston, J. H., & Johnston, L. L. (1993). Planning for the human response in middle grade reorganization. *School Administrator, 50*(3), 22–43.

Jones, H. (1966). The development of a test of scientific inquiry, using the tab format, and an analysis of its relationship to selected student behaviors (Report No. SE-002-034). East Lansing, MI: National Center for Research on Teacher Learning. (ERIC Document Reproduction Service No. ED013212)

Jones, K. (1980). *Simulations: A handbook for teachers.* New York: Nichols.

Jones, K. (1987). *Simulations: A handbook for teachers* (2nd ed.). New York: Nichols.

Jones, K. (1988). *Interactive learning events: A guide for facilitators.* New York: Nichols.

Joyce, B. (1978). Toward a theory of information processing in teaching. *Educational Research Quarterly, 3*(4), 66–77.

Joyce, B., & Calhoun, E. (1996). *Creating learning experiences: The role of instructional theory and research.* Alexandria, VA: Association for Supervision and Curriculum Development.

Joyce, B., & Weil, M. (1983). *Models of teaching.* Englewood Cliffs, NJ: Prentice Hall.

Joyce, B., Weil, M., & Calhoun, E. (2008). *Models of teaching* (8th ed.). Boston: Allyn & Bacon.

Kagan, S. (1992). *Cooperative learning.* San Juan Capistrano, CA: Kagan Cooperative Learning.

Kaplan, D. A. (1993, September 20). Dumber than we thought. *Newsweek*, 44–45.

Kemmis, S. (1980). *Seven principles for program evaluation in curriculum development and innovation* (Report No. TM810286). Geelong, Australia: Deakin University. (ERIC Document Reproduction Service No. ED202869)

Kennta, B. (1993). Moving with cautious velocity. *School Administrator, 50*(3), 17–19.

Khazzaka, J. P. (1997–1998, December–January). Comparing the merits of a seven-period day to those of a four-period day. *High School Journal*, 89–97.

Klesius, J., & Searls, E. (1990). A comparison of two methods of direct instruction of preservice teachers. *Journal of Teacher Education, 41*(4), 34–45.

Knight, S. L., DeLeon, N. J., & Smith, R. G. (1999). Using multiple data sources to evaluate an alternative scheduling model. *The High School Journal, 83*(1), 1–13.

Kolstad, R., & McFadden, A. (1998). Multiage classrooms: An age-old educational strategy revisited. *Journal of Instructional Psychology, 25*(1), 14–18.

Ladousse, G. P. (1987). *Role play.* New York: Oxford University Press.

Lare, D., Jablonski, A. M., & Salvaterra, M. (2002). Block scheduling: Is it cost effective? *NASSP Bulletin, 86*(630), 54–71.

Lasley, T., & Matczynski, T. (1997). *Strategies for teaching in a diverse environment.* Belmont, CA: Wadsworth.

Leslie, C., & Halpert, J. E. (1996, December 9). One class fits all. *Newsweek*, p. 71.

Lewis, A., & Smith, D. (1993, Summer). Defining higher order thinking. *Theory Into Practice*, 40–48.

Lewis, A. C. (1991, June). America 2000: What kind of nation? *Phi Delta Kappan, 72*(10), 734–735.

Lilley, I. M. (1967). *Friedrich Froebel: A selection from his writings.* Cambridge, UK: Cambridge University Press.

Lunenburg, F. C., & Irby, B. J. (2000). *High expectations: An action plan for implementing Goals 2000.* Thousand Oaks, CA: Corwin Press.

Lyman, L., & Foyle, H. C. (1998). Facilitating collaboration in schools. *Teaching and Change, 5*(3–4), 312–339.

Maidment, R. (1973). Differentiated staffing. *NASSP Bulletin, 57*(369), 53–56.

Maidment, R., & Bronstein, R. H. (1973). *Simulation games: Design and implementation.* Columbus, OH: Merrill.

Maltese, A. V., Dexter, K. M., Tai, R. H., & Sadler, P. M. (2007). Breaking from tradition: Unfulfilled promises of block scheduling and science. *Science Educator, 16*, 1–7.

Marsh, C., & Willis, G. (1995). *Curriculum alternative approaches, ongoing issues.* Englewood Cliffs, NJ: Prentice Hall.

Matthews, J. L. (1997). Alternative schedules: Blocks to success? *NASSP Practitioner, 24*(1), 1–8.

McBurney, D. H. (1995, February). The problem method of teaching research methods. *Teaching Psychology*, 36–38.

McClure, P. (1998). *State policies to support middle school reform: A guide for policymakers.* New York: Carnegie Corporation, Council of Chief State Offices. (ERIC Document Reproduction Service No. ED441273)

McCormick, R., & James, M. (1983). *Curriculum evaluation in schools.* London: Croom Helm.

Merchant, G. J., & Paulson, S. B. (2001). Differential school functioning in a block schedule: A comparison of academic profiles. *The High School Journal, 84*(4), 12–20.

Merrell, H. J. (1998). Performance based tests improve student learning. *Kappa Delta Pi Record, 34*(4), 124–128.

Miller, B. (1997). Educating the "other" children. *American Demographics, 19*, 49–54.

Moore, G., Kirby, B., & Becton, L. K. (1997). Block scheduling impact on instruction, FFA, and SAE in agricultural education. *Journal of Agricultural Education, 38*(4), 1–10.

Morine, H., & Morine, G. (1973). *Discovery: A challenge to teachers.* Englewood Cliffs, NJ: Prentice Hall.

Nadler, R. (1998). Failing grade. *National Review, 50*(10), 38–40.

*Nation at risk, A.* (1983). Retrieved May 3, 2002, from www.ed.gov/pubs/NatAtRisk/index.html

National Committee on Excellence in Education. (1983). *A nation at risk: The imperatives for educational reform.* Washington, DC: U.S. Government Printing Office.

National School Board Association. (2008, August). As election nears, NCLB future subject of talk. *American School Board Journal*, 14.

Nelson, B., & Frayer, D. (1972). *Discovery learning versus expository learning: New insight into an old controversy.* Madison: Wisconsin Research and Development Center for Cognitive Learning. (ERIC Document Reproduction Service No. ED061532)

Neufeld, B. (1995). *Improving principals' practice: The influence of professional development on principals' work in middle school reform efforts supported by the Edna McConnell Clark Foundation.* Cambridge, MA: Education Matters. (ERIC Document Reproduction Service No. ED386521)

Newmann, F. M., Lopez, G., & Bryk, A. S. (1998). *The quality of intellectual work in Chicago schools: A baseline report.* Chicago: Consortium on Chicago School Research.

Ngeow, K. Y. (1998). *Enhancing student thinking through collaborative learning.* Bloomington: Indiana University, ERIC Clearinghouse on Reading, English, and Communication. (ERIC Document Reproduction Service No. ED42258698)

Noble, M. C. S., & Dawson, H. A. (1961). *Handbook on rural education: Factual data on rural education, its social and economic backgrounds.* Washington, DC: National Education Association of the United States, Department of Rural Education.

North Carolina Department of Public Instruction. (2000). *Standard course of study.* Raleigh, NC: Author.

Olson, L. (2000, January 19). New thinking on what makes a leader. *Education Week*, pp. 1, 4–15.

Olson, L. (2000, November 1). Principals try new styles as instructional leaders. *Education Week*, pp. 1, 15–19.

O'Neil, J. (1995). Finding time to learn. *Educational Leadership, 53*(3), 11–15.

Ornstein, A. C., & Hunkins, F. P. (1998). *Curriculum foundations, principles, and issues* (3rd ed.). Needham Heights, MA: Allyn & Bacon.

Ornstein, A. C., & Levine, D. U. (1989). *Foundations of American education* (4th ed.). Boston: Houghton Mifflin.

Oxford, S. I., & Letcher, J. H. (1995, December). *Block scheduling.* Paper presented at the annual research forum of the Department of Education. Wake Forest University, Winston-Salem, NC.

Parsons, J., & Smith, D. (1993). *Valuing students: Rethinking evaluation.* Alberta, Canada. (ERIC Document Reproduction Service No. PS021745)

Payne, D., & Jordan, M. M. (1996). The evaluation of a high school block schedule: Convergence of teacher and student data. *American Secondary Education, 25*(2), 16–19.

Perrone, V. (1992). Stop standardized testing in early grades. *Education Digest, 57*(5), 42–47.

Pendell, M. J. (2008). How far is too far? The spending clause, the Tenth Amendment, and the education state's battle against unfunded mandates. *Albany Law Review, 71*(2), 519–543.

Piaget, J. (1954). *The construction of reality in the child.* New York: Basic Books.

Piaget, J. (1969a). *The child's conception of time.* New York: Basic Books.

Piaget, J. (1969b). *The mechanisms of perception.* New York: Basic Books.

Piaget, J., & Inhelder, B. (1969). *The psychology of the child.* New York: Basic Books.

Picciotto, L. P. (1996). *Student-led parent conferences.* New York: Scholastic Professional Books.

Pike, K., & Salend, S. J. (1995, Fall). Authentic assessment strategies: Alternatives to norm-referenced testing. *Teaching Exceptional Children,* pp. 15–20.

Pisapia, J., & Westfall, A. L. (1997a). *Alternative high school scheduling: A view from the teacher's desk.* Richmond, VA: Metropolitan Educational Research Consortium. (ERIC Document Reproduction Services No. ED411335).

Pisapia, J., & Westfall, A. L. (1997b). *Alternative high school scheduling: Student achievement and behavior.* Richmond, VA: Metropolitan Educational Research Consortium. (ERIC Document Reproduction Services No. ED411337).

Pisapia, J., & Westfall, A. L. (1997c). *Alternative high school scheduling: A view from the student's desk.* Richmond, VA: Metropolitan Educational Research Consortium. (ERIC Document Reproduction Services No. ED411336).

Platten, M. (1991, March). *Teaching concepts and skills of thinking simultaneously.* Paper presented at the meeting of the annual conference of the National Art Education Association, Atlanta, GA.

Queen, J. A. (2000). Block scheduling revisited. *Phi Delta Kappan, 82*(3), 214–220, 221–222.

Queen, J. A. (2002). *Students' transitions from middle to high school: Improving achievement and creating a safer environment.* Larchmont, NY: Eye on Education.

Queen, J. A. (2009). *Beyond differentiated instructions: The seven levels of personalized instruction.* Charlotte, NC: Writer's Edge Press.

Queen, J. A. (2009). *Curriculum practice in 21st century schools.* Charlotte, NC: The Writer's Edge Press.

Queen, J. A. (2009). *The seven habits of successful teachers on the block schedule.* Manuscript submitted for publication.

Queen, J. A., & Algozzine, R. F. (2007). *Best practices for extended class periods.* Kings Mountain, NC: The Writer's Edge, Inc.

Queen, J. A., & Algozzine, R. F. (2009). *Seven steps to building student responsiblity: A secondary school discipline program.* Thousand Oaks, CA: Corwin Press.

Queen, J. A., Algozzine, R. F., & Eaddy, M. A. (1996). The success of 4 × 4 block scheduling in the social studies. *The Social Studies, 87,* 249–253.

Queen, J. A., Algozzine, R. F., & Eaddy, M. A. (1997, April). The road we traveled: Scheduling in the 4 × 4 block. *NASSP Bulletin, 81,* 88–99.

Queen, J. A., Algozzine, R. F., & Eaddy, M. A. (1998). Implementing 4 × 4 block scheduling: Pitfalls, promises, and provisos. *The High School Journal, 81*(2), 107–114.

Queen, J. A., Algozzine, R. F., & Isenhour, K. G. (1999, January). First-year teachers and 4 × 4 block scheduling. *NASSP Bulletin, 83,* 100–103.

Queen, J. A., Algozzine, R. F., & Watson, J. R. (2009). *Block scheduling today: The state of block scheduling.* Manuscript submitted for publication.

Queen, J. A., Black Welder, B. B., & Mallen, L. P. (1996). *Responsible classroom management for teachers and students.* Columbus, OH: Merrill Education/Prentice Hall.

Queen, J. A., Burrell, J. R., & McManus, S. (2000). *Planning for instruction: A year-long guide.* Upper Saddle River, NJ: Prentice Hall.

Queen, J. A., & Gaskey, K. A. (1997). Steps for improving school climate in block scheduling. *Phi Delta Kappan, 79*(2), 158–161.

Queen, J. A., & Isenhour, K. G. (1998a, November). Building a climate of acceptance for block scheduling. *NASSP Bulletin, 82,* 95–104.

Queen, J. A., & Isenhour, K. G. (1998b). *The 4 × 4 block schedule.* Larchmont, NY: Eye on Education.

Randall, V. (1999, March–April). Cooperative learning: Abused and overused? *Gifted Child Today Magazine,* pp. 14–16.

Reinhartz, J., & Beach, D. M. (1997). *Teaching and learning in the elementary school: Focus on curriculum.* Upper Saddle River, NJ: Merrill.

Rettig, M. D., & Canady, R. (2000). *Scheduling strategies for middle schools.* Larchmont, NY: Eye on Education.

Rettig, M. D., & Canady, R. L. (1996). All around the block: The benefits and challenges of a non-traditional school schedule. *School Administrator, 53*(8), 8–14.

Riley, R. W. (1993). A new direction for education. *Principal, 73*(1), 5–7.

Romano, L. G., & Georgiady, N. P. (1993). *Building an effective middle school.* New York: McGraw-Hill.

Rothstein, R. (2008). *Leaving no child behind.* The American Prospect, Inc. Retrieved December 17, 2007, from http://www.prospect.org/cs/articles?/

Rosenshine, B. (1971). *Teaching behaviors and student achievement.* London: National Foundation for Educational Research.

Rosenshine, B. (1978). *Academic engaged time, content covered and direct instruction.* Paper presented at the annual meeting of the American Educational Research Association (ERIC Document Reproduction Service No. ED152776).

Rosenshine, B. (1985). Direct instruction. In T. Husen & T. N. Postlethwaite (Eds.), *International encyclopedia of education* (Vol. 3, pp. 1395–1400). Oxford, UK: Pergamon Press.

Rosenshine, B. (1995). Advances in research on instruction. *Journal of Educational Research, 88*(5), 262–268.

Routman, R. (1988). *Transitions: From literature to literacy.* Portsmouth, NH: Heinemann.

Routman, R. (1994). *Invitations: Changing as teachers and learners, K–12.* Portsmouth, NH: Heinemann.

Rural School and Community Trust & Harvard Documentation and Assessment Program (Eds.). (2001). *Assessing student work.* Retrieved November 24, 2008, from http://www.ruraledu.org

Russell, J. F. (1997*).* Relationships between the implementation of middle-level program concepts and students' achievement. *Journal of Curriculum and Supervision, 12*(2), 169–185.

Saks, J. B. (1999). The middle school problem. *American School Board Journal, 186*(7), 32–33.

Salvaterra, M., Lare, D., Gall, J., & Adams, D. (1999). Block scheduling: Students' perception of readiness for college math, science, and foreign language. *American Secondary Education, 27*(4), 13–21.

Sanders, J. R. (1992). *Evaluating school programs: An educator's guide.* Newbury Park, CA: Corwin Press.

Schlenker, R. M. (1986). *Planning training sessions that start, go, and end somewhere.* (ERIC Document Reproduction Service No. 276837)

Schroth, G., & Dixon, J. (1996). The effects of block scheduling on student performance. *International Journal of School Reform, 5*(4), 472–476.

Scieszka, J. (1999). *The true story of the 3 little pigs/by A. Wolfe.* New York: Viking.

Seitsinger, A. M., & Felner, R. D. (2000, April). *Whom and how is service learning implemented in middle level: A study of opportunity-to-learn conditions and practices.* Paper presented at the annual meeting of the American Education Research Association, New Orleans, LA. (ERIC Document Reproduction Service No. ED441741)

Sewall, G. T. (1991). America 2000: An appraisal. *Phi Delta Kappan, 73*(3), 204–209.

Shaftel, F., & Shaftel, G. (1967). *Role-playing for social values: Decision-making in the social studies.* Englewood Cliffs, NJ: Prentice Hall.

Sharan, S., & Sharan, Y. (1992). *Expanding cooperative learning through group investigation.* New York: Teachers College Press.

Shore, R. (1995). How one high school improved school climate. *Educational Leadership, 52*(5), 76–78.

Shortt, T. L., & Thayer, Y. V. (1998–1999). Block scheduling can enhance school climate. *Educational Leadership, 56*(4), 76–81.

Siefert, E. H., & Beck, J. J. (1994). Relationships between task time and learning giants in secondary schools. *Journal of Educational Research, 7*, 5–10.

Sigmon, C. (2001). Modifying four-blocks at the upper grades. Charleston, WV: Carson: Dellosa.

Silver, H. F., Strong, R. W., & Hanson, J. R. (1988). *Teaching strategies library.* Alexandria, VA: Association for Supervision and Curriculum Development.

Sizer, T. R. (1989). *Taking school reform seriously. Preparing schools for the 1990s: An essay collection.* New York: Metropolitan Life Insurance Co.

Sizer, T. R. (1984). *Horace's compromise: The dilemma of the American high school.* Boston: Houghton Mifflin.

Skrobarcek, S. A., Chang, H. M., Thompson, C., Johnson, J., Atteberry, R., Westbrook, R., & Manus, A. (1997, May). Collaboration for instructional improvement: Analyzing the academic impact of a block scheduling plan. *NASSP Bulletin, 81*, 104–111.

Slavin, R. E. (1983). *Cooperative learning.* New York: Longman.

Slavin, R. E. (1987). *Cooperative learning: Student teams.* Washington, DC: National Education Association, NEA Professional Library.

Slavin, R. E. (1995). *Cooperative learning: Theory, research, and practice* (2nd ed.). Boston: Allyn & Bacon.

Slavin, R. E. (1996). Cooperative learning in middle and secondary schools. *Clearing House, 69*(4), 200–204.

Slavin, R. E., Sharan, S., Kagan, S., Hertz-Lazarowitz, R., Webb, C., & Schmuck, R. (Eds.). (1985). *Learning to cooperate: Cooperating to learn.* New York: Plenum.

Snyder, D. (1997, October). *Four-block scheduling: A case study of data analysis of one high school after two years.* Paper presented at the annual meeting of the Mid-West Educational Research Association, Chicago.

Stahl, R. J. (1994). The essential elements of cooperative learning in the classroom. *ERIC Digest* (ERIC Identifier ED370881).

Staunton, J. (1997). A study of teacher beliefs on the efficacy of block scheduling. *NASSP Bulletin, 81*(593), 73–80.

Staunton, J., & Adams, T. (1997). What do teachers in California say about block scheduling? *NASSP Bulletin, 81*(593), 81–84.

Stratemeyer, F. (1947). *Developing curriculum for modern living.* New York: Columbia University Press.

Strawn, C., Fox, R. & Duck L. (2008 July/August). Preventing teacher failure: Six keys to success in moving beyond the sink or swim mentality. *The Clearing House.* Retrieved November 24, 2008, from http://www.highbeam.com

Suchman, J. R. (1962). *Elementary school programs in scientific inquiry for gifted students* (Cooperative Research Project No. D-076). Urbana-Champaign: University of Illinois, Research Board of the University of Illinois.

Sudzina, M. R. (1993, February). *Dealing with diversity issues in the classroom: A case study approach.* Paper presented at the annual meeting of the Association of Teacher Educators, Los Angeles. (ERIC Document Reproduction Service No. ED354233)

Svinicki, M. (1998). A theoretical foundation for discovery learning. *Advances in Physiology Education, 20,* 4–7.

Thiagarajan, S., & Stolovitch, H. D. (1978). *Instructional simulation games.* Englewood Cliffs, NJ: Educational Technology Publications.

Tombari, M. L., & Borich, G. D. (1999). *Authentic assessment in the classroom: Applications and practice.* Upper Saddle River, NJ: Merrill.

Trump, J. L. (1959). *Images of the future.* Urbana, IL: National Association of Secondary Principals.

Tyler, R., Gagne, R., & Scriven, M. (1967). *Perspectives of curriculum evaluation.* Chicago: Rand McNally.

U.S. Department of Education. (2008). Retrieved November 24, 2008, from http://www.ed.gov./policy/elsec/guid/sec/letter/html

U.S. Department of Education. (1997). *Third international mathematics and science study.* Washington, DC: U.S. Government Printing Office.

U.S. Department of Education. (1994, November). *Community update.* Washington, DC: U.S. Government Printing Office.

U.S. Department of Education. (1993). *Adult literacy in America.* Washington, DC: U.S. Government Printing Office.

U.S. Department of Education. (1983). *A nation at risk: The imperatives of educational reform.* National Commission on Excellence in Education. Washington, DC: U.S. Government Printing Office.

Van Ments, M. (1999). *The effective use of role-play: Practical techniques for improving learning.* London: Kogan Page.

Veal, W. R. (1999). What could define block scheduling as a fad? *American Secondary Education, 27*(4), 3–12.

Viadero, D. (1995). Against all odds. *Teacher Magazine, 6*(8) 20–22.

Watts, G. D., & Castle, S. (1993). The time dilemma in school restructuring. *Phi Delta Kappan, 75*(4), 306–310.

Watson, J. R., Queen, J. A. & White, W. (2009). *Flexible scheduling for America's schools.* Thousand Oaks, CA: Corwin Press. (in press).

Weddington, D. (1973). *Needs assessment for continuous curriculum revision* (Report No. JC780486). (ERIC Document Reproduction Service No. ED158826)

Weil, M., & Joyce, B. (1978). *Information processing models of teaching: Expanding your teaching repertoire.* Englewood Cliffs, NJ: Prentice Hall.

Weil, M., Joyce, B., & Kluwin, B. (1978). *Personal models of teaching.* Englewood Cliffs, NJ: Prentice Hall.

Weller, D. R., & McLeskey, J. (2000). Block scheduling and inclusion in a high school: Teacher perceptions of the benefits and challenges. *Remedial and Special Education,* 21, 209–218.

Wiggins, G. (1993). Assessment: Authenticity, context, and validity. *Phi Delta Kappan, 75*(3), 200–208, 210–214.

Wilson, C. (1995, May). The 4 × 4 block system: A workable alternative. *NASSP Bulletin, 79,* 63–65.

Wilson, J. W., & Stokes, L. C. (1999a). A study of teacher perceptions of the effectiveness and critical factors in implementing and maintaining block scheduling. *The High School Journal, 83*(1), 35–44.

Wilson, J. W., & Stokes, L. C. (1999b). Teachers' perceptions of the advantages and measurable outcomes of block scheduling design. *The High School Journal, 83*(1), 44–54.

Wilson, J., & Stokes, L. C. (2000). Students' perceptions of the effectiveness of block versus traditional scheduling. *American Secondary Education, 28*(3), 3–12.

Woodham-Smith, P. (1969). The origin of kindergarten. In E. M. Lawrence (Ed.), *Froebel and English education: Perspectives on the founder of kindergarten* (pp. 15–33). New York: Schocken.

Woods, G. S. (1998). *A study of self-concept as it relates to academic achievement and gender in third grade students.* Unpublished doctoral dissertation, Rowan University, Glassboro, NJ.

Wronkovich, M. (1998). Block scheduling: Real reform or another flawed educational fad? *American Secondary Education.* 26 (4), 1–6.

Zais, R. S. (1976). *Curriculum: Principles and foundations.* New York: Crowell.

Zepeda, S. J., & Mayers, R. S. (2006). An analysis of research on block scheduling. *Review of Educational Research, 76,* 137–170.

# Internet Resources

American Federation of Teachers: www.aft.org

Association for Supervision and Curriculum Development: www.ascd.org

Education Week on the Web: www.edweek.org

Educational Resources Information Center (ERIC): www.eric.ed.gov

Eisenhower National Clearinghouse: www.enc.org

International Society for Technology in Education: www.iste.org

Latest Middle Schools News and Views: www.middleweb.com

National Association of Elementary School Principals: www.naesp.org

National Association of Secondary School Principals: www.nassp.org

North Carolina Department of Public Instruction: www.ncpublicschools.org

Phi Delta Kappan International: www.pdkintl.org

Regional Technology in Education Consortium (RTEC): http://rtec.org

Search for education sites at http://Searchedu.com

U.S. Department of Education: www.ed.gov

Violence Among Middle and High School Students: www.ncjrs.org/txtfiles/166363.txt

www.blockscheduling.com

www.writersedgepress.com

Contact Dr. Queen for on-site staff development
go to www.blockscheduling.com
or call Block Scheduling.com 704-734-0677 or cell phone at 704-779-5795

# Index

## CORWIN PRESS

The Corwin Press logo—a raven striding across an open book—represents the union of courage and learning. Corwin Press is committed to improving education for all learners by publishing books and other professional development resources for those serving the field of PreK–12 education. By providing practical, hands-on materials, Corwin Press continues to carry out the promise of its motto: **"Helping Educators Do Their Work Better."**